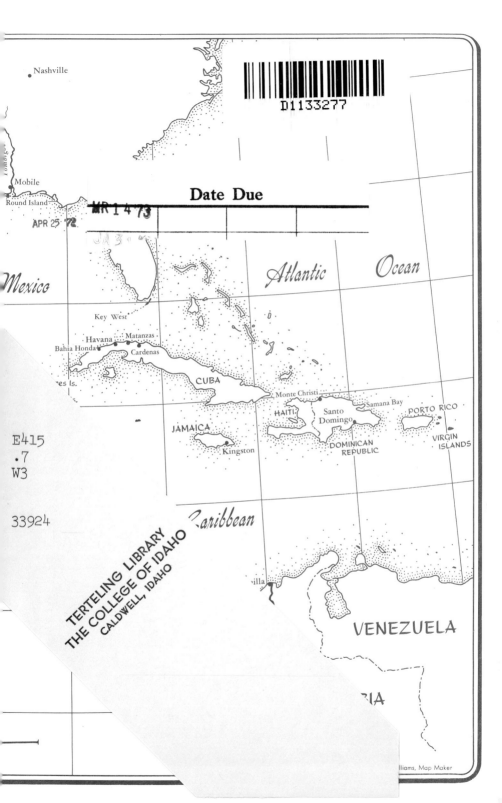

Nashville

D1133277

Mobile
Round Island
APR 25 '72

MR 1 4 '73

JA 3 ...

Date Due

Mexico

Atlantic Ocean

Key West

Havana Matanzas
Bahia Honda
Cardenas

es Is.

CUBA

Monte Christi
HAITI Santo
Domingo

Samana Bay

PORTO RICO

VIRGIN
ISLANDS

JAMAICA

Kingston

DOMINICAN
REPUBLIC

E415
.7
W3

33924

Caribbean

illa

VENEZUELA

IA

lliams, Map Maker

Destiny and Glory

Destiny and Glory

EDWARD S. WALLACE

Coward-McCann, Inc.   New York

© 1957 by Edward S. Wallace

Library of Congress Catalog
Card Number: 56-10029

Foreword

The political history of the 1850's has been so overdone that the resulting and unfortunate impression is that practically nothing else of importance happened in this country outside of the halls of Congress. But there were men of daring and action in this period; in fact, the filibusters were as reckless and colorful a lot of adventurers as this country has ever seen. That they were unsuccessful is a poor reason for hiding them in the wings and giving the entire stage to the politicians, and this story is an effort to rescue them, good and bad, for better or for worse, from an undeserved obscurity.

Nowadays the word *filibuster* has gained the general meaning of a politician who, according to Webster's Dictionary, "obstructs legislative action by extreme use of dilatory tactics, such as speaking merely to consume time." This, however, was not the original meaning of the word. It was derived from the Spanish *filibustero* which came from the Dutch *vrijbuiter* and meant an irregular military adventurer, a freebooter, particularly one who takes part in a hostile expedition to a country with which his own is at peace; and, perhaps it might be added, with the purpose of seizing and holding control of the invaded land. William the Conqueror and the Spanish *conquistadores* in the New World were filibusters, so were the Israelites following Moses into the Promised Land, and many, many others.

This book is about an epidemic (for it was infectious) of

5

filibustering, in the old sense, into Latin America which broke out with virulence in the United States between the Mexican and Civil Wars. There had been plots and actual forays before this period, almost all in the direction of Texas, such as Aaron Burr's conspiracy against Spain, the unsuccessful raid into Spanish Texas in 1800 led by Philip Nolan (Edward Everett gave his name by mistake to *The Man Without a Country* who was said to be his younger brother), and the Gutiérrez-Magee expedition to Texas of 1812, which ended in disaster. But these plots and excursions were premature, before the stage was really set. Then the winning of Texas independence and the overwhelming victory of the consequent Mexican War touched off a series of chain explosions of American filibustering expeditions. One attempt bred another until the Civil War extinguished these diversions of excitement and adventure in foreign lands. After the war there was one brief flareup when General Jo Shelby's Confederates rode into Mexico, but when that sputtered out the curtain came down on the American filibusters.

Two almost unknown expeditions have been included in this book: those into Yucatan and Ecuador; and the amazing and fascinating female filibuster, Jane McManus Cazneau (Cora Montgomery), has at last been given her due. William Walker necessarily takes the largest space and much effort was expended in looking for new material about him, particularly in trying to find the papers and a lost manuscript of General Charles Frederick Henningsen; but with no success, so that the Walker narrative is perforce based on known accounts. However, he is so surprisingly unknown that all this may be new to the average reader. The author hopes so, at least.

E. S. W.

Acknowledgments

The author is truly grateful to the following who have all been of practical help:

First of all, Mr. James T. Babb, Librarian, and the staff of the Yale University Library; in particular Mr. Archibald Hanna, Curator of the Collection of Western Americana; Miss Barbara D. Simison, peerless reference librarian; Miss Kathryn V. O'Connor, a nonpareil for guidance in its dark, Gothic mysteries; the Argus-eyed Mr. Edward George Kelly; and the elevator operators who efficiently overcome its unfunctional perpendicular handicaps. Then, also, Mr. George Kubler of the Yale School of Fine Arts for his help about Yucatan and the Mayas; and Mr. William Goetzmann of the Yale Graduate School.

Others to whom I owe thanks are: Mr. Winfield Shiras of Sarasota, Florida, who furnished me with much material about William Walker from his scholarly researches, through the years, in this country and Europe; Dr. Howard F. Cline, Director of the Hispanic Foundation of the Library of Congress, for his invaluable help on Yucatan; Mr. T. E. Hay of Locust Valley, New York, a veritable walking encyclopedia on obscure facts and people; Mr. Frederick L. Stagg of Boston for inside information about his great-grandfather General Juan José Flores of Ecuador; Mr. Stephen Riley of the Massachusetts Historical Society; the Louisiana Historical Society; Professor William N. Chambers of Washington

Acknowledgments

University, St. Louis; Colonel John M. Virden of Washington, D.C. (a real expert on the Confederate Army); and Mr. Thomas E. Hall of the Winchester Repeating Arms, New Haven. In Eagle Pass, Texas, to Mr. Ben E. Pingenot and Mrs. Dorothy O. Worrell for putting me on the track of the fabulous Jane McManus Cazneau, one of the earliest settlers of their home town; and to Mr. William E. Bard of Dallas, Texas, I am especially indebted for his kindness in giving me the benefit of his many years of research about the career of this fascinating and adventurous woman. Finally, I am deeply grateful for the generous sharing of detailed information about this same Jane Cazneau by Mrs. Jane Mayer and Dr. Enno Franzius of New York City who are writing a book about her dramatic career. And my sincere thanks go, as always, to that stellar typist and eagle-eyed correctionist, Miss Sherry Hawkins of Boston.

8

Contents

———— ◆◎◆ ————

Illustrations

Destiny and Glory

CHAPTER I

The Halls of Montezuma

IN APRIL, 1846, spontaneous hostilities on the Rio Grande began our war with Mexico. Some seventeen months later, just as dawn broke over the snowcapped volcanoes to the east of Mexico City on September 14, 1847, Major General John A. Quitman of Mississippi led his battle-scarred division cautiously through the streets of the city to the Grand Plaza, where the troops formed into line before the old viceroy's palace. It was a peculiar entry for a triumphant army. Quitman limped along with only one shoe at the head of the column, and behind him, carrying their arms at all angles, wearily plodded his men, including a detachment of U. S. Marines. All were in rags and covered with grime, crude bandages and the red stains of battle, for they had fought their way through one of the city gates the previous evening, and, before that on the same day, had victoriously stormed the famous Chapultepec Castle which guarded the southwestern approaches to the Mexican capital.

The sidewalks, balconies, windows, and housetops were

Parts of this chapter appeared in a somewhat different form in the fall issue, 1950, of *Military Affairs* under the title "The United States Army in Mexico City."

jammed with people who watched in silence the hated gringos filling the vacuum left by General Santa Anna's evacuation of the city during the night.

The American officers took their positions before their men in the plaza, and, as a tattered flag was hoisted on the pole of the palace, the bands played "The Star Spangled Banner" while the men presented arms and the officers saluted. This was the first time that our flag—and the only time that ours alone—has been raised over the capital of a conquered enemy country.

A few minutes later the sound of approaching cheering was heard and the commanding general, Winfield Scott, rode into the plaza escorted by a detachment of dragoons with drawn sabers. Scott cut a truly magnificent figure, even in his sixty-first year, being six feet four inches in height, wearing an immaculate blue dress uniform with gleaming gold epaulets and a cocked hat with flowing white plumes; mounted on a tall and heavy bay charger, he looked the acme of martial glamor, his resplendent aura symbolizing the glory of his dirt-covered army. Uncovering, he rode down the lines of his men and the bands played, in succession, "Hail Columbia," "Washington's March," "Yankee Doodle," and "Hail to the Chief"; the men presenting arms as he passed and then breaking into such cheering and hurrahing that it almost seemed as if another perennial earthquake was shaking the Halls of Montezuma which had once stood on this very spot.

The capture of Mexico City ended the official hostilities of the war, a conflict in which the American troops set a standard for courage and intelligent initiative against great odds which has never been surpassed in all our wars. A possible gauge of their achievements is that General Scott took about six months (almost half of which time was spent waiting in the city of Puebla for replacements) to fight his way into Mexico City from Vera Cruz with an army never exceeding ten thousand men, at least a half of whom were untrained volunteers. But, fifteen years later, from 1861 to 1863, an army of thirty thousand French regulars, including the famous Foreign Legion, took eighteen months to repeat this same march, during which time they suffered a decisive defeat at Puebla on May 5, 1862, today celebrated as one of the great national holidays of Mexico. And the evidence tends to show that the Mexicans were neither as well prepared nor as well armed during this later invasion.

The Americans occupied Mexico City for nine months, during the peace negotiations, until June 12, 1848. Years later, General Cadmus M. Wilcox, who had been a young lieutenant at the time, wrote:

> The Mexican capital, with its peerless climate and picturesque surroundings, its *alamedas, paseos,* theatres, bull fights, its dark-eyed señoritas and voluptuous señoras, had many alluring attractions, though it did not prove a Capua for the American soldiers; nor did they, like Hannibal's braves, exchange amid its Circean fascinations the role of sturdy warrior for that of listless sybarites.[1]

Flowery words but on the whole true, for the discipline was harsh by our present-day standards and there was little disorder or looting by the Americans; with one exception when a regiment of Texas Rangers, commanded by the fa-

[1] General Cadmus M. Wilcox, *History of the Mexican War,* Washington, 1892, p. 511.

mous Colonel Jack Hays, took the law into their own hands after one of their officers had been murdered in a tough district, and next morning some eighty bullet-riddled Mexican corpses were found in that section. "Old Fuss and Feathers," as the men called Scott, had his faults but he was a real disciplinarian, and in his precarious position so far from his base of supplies at Vera Cruz on the seacoast his hand fell heavy upon the malingerer or trouble maker; doubly so if he happened to be an officer.

The disciplinary punishments were severe. Infractions of a serious nature, such as drunkenness on guard, insubordination, and extreme disorderly conduct were punished by floggings or by "riding the wooden horse" from reveille to retreat, with a half hour out for meals, for periods up to sixty days. This was called being "bucked and gagged" by the men and consisted in being trussed on a sort of sawhorse and left in the broiling sun, a horribly painful procedure.

Mutiny and desertion, of course, were punished by death, and during this war a most curious mass example of the latter occurred—the only case known in which a body of United States soldiers, after deserting, subsequently formed a distinct corps in the enemy's army. These deserters were seduced by religious propaganda and promises of cash bonuses and land by the Mexicans, and formed two companies of infantry known as the "Battalion of St. Patrick" in the Mexican army, but were called the "Irish Deserters" by the Americans.

The attacking Americans captured some eighty-odd of these renegades, after desperate resistance, in the fighting just outside Mexico City. After a court-martial, about fifty were hanged at various intervals, mostly in the suburb of San Angel where stood until recently a wooden cross in their memory upon which was carved a gamecock, a pair of dice, and a skull and crossbones, symbolizing that these unfortunate men were brave and fought, gambled and lost.

General Scott took a literal interpretation of the Articles of War for the remaining men because they had deserted before the actual declaration of war, and he modified the death sentence to the following punishment:

> . . . to forfeit all pay and allowances; to receive fifty lashes on the bare back, well laid on; to have the letter D (for deserter) indelibly branded on the cheek with a red-hot iron; to be confined at hard labor, wearing about the neck an iron collar having prongs each six inches long (to prevent sleep), the whole weighing eight pounds, for six months; and at the expiration of that time to have the head shaved and to be drummed out of the service.[2]

There was considerable disorder for three days after the American entrance, for Santa Anna had opened all the jails upon evacuating the city and the released felons looted and sniped at the invaders; but these were soon ruthlessly eliminated. Another bad element, a constant source of trouble throughout the nine months' occupation, were the *leperos,* as the swarms of semicriminal professional beggars were called; and it was never safe (despite the vengeance of the Texans) for a lone soldier or even a small group to go unarmed at night. Assassinations of drunken soldiers were frequent until General Scott placed a strict curfew on all saloons and regulated the sale of liquor.

Scott soon issued a proclamation promising full religious

---

[2] *The American Star,* Mexico City, November 12, 1847.

freedom and civil rights to all law-abiding Mexicans, and the city quickly resumed its normal tone as the Americans turned to the pursuit of pleasure in their spare time. Everybody naturally went to a bullfight—usually only once—and often to the theater, the opera, and the circus. But the primary diversion of the immutable G.I.'s was the pursuit of the señoritas who quickly shed their initial fear of the northern barbarians and "surrendered unconditionally after trifling resistance"—much to the fury of their former Mexican admirers who dubbed each girl with the name of an American victory; thus a pretty, plump little brunette would be called "Cerro Gordo" (round hill), and a tall, lithesome blonde might become known as "Palo Alto" (tall stick).

Corporal Oswandel of the 1st Pennsylvania Volunteers, a particularly exuberant regiment, wrote that when the army first entered the city it was impossible to get a lady to go to any place of amusement but that this feeling changed almost overnight and that all was shortly in good order; his outfit was soon giving dances at its bivouac area in the suburb of San Angel, for which festivities various committees were appointed to buy food and liquor and to obtain the company of as many attractive señoritas as possible.[3]

In the city many dance halls soon opened and balls and masquerades flourished nightly with the sound of gay music, particularly the waltzes of Strauss, lasting until daybreak. These dance emporiums put out enticing notices of grand fandangos for officers only at $2 per ticket which admitted a gentleman and two ladies, or of balls at which real Ameri-

---

[3] J. Jacob Oswandel, *Notes of the Mexican War*, Philadelphia, 1883, pp. 464, 474. This diary contains amusing descriptions of the life and habits of the G.I.'s of the time.

can ladies were admitted free, or of sumptuous suppers served under police protection to preserve order. The most exclusive parties, however, were subscription affairs promoted by the younger officers which were held in a former convent near the Grand Plaza.

The G.I.'s, particularly the men of the volunteer regiments, resented the caste distinctions in the balls advertised for officers only, and on one such occasion over a half the men of Corporal Oswandel's regiment sneaked out of their camp, after taps, and attended a masquerade for officers only, dressed in native Mexican costumes borrowed from various friendly local bartenders. And so great was their indignation at the efforts of the newly arrived Brigadier General Caleb Cushing of Massachusetts (of China Treaty fame) to prevent such innocent diversions that they made the life of this politically appointed general a veritable bed of thorns.

Cushing had come up from Vera Cruz in November, 1847, after the fighting was over, and had been given command of the veteran New York, South Carolina, and Pennsylvania volunteers encamped at San Angel. Oswandel reported that at first the men considered him an inexperienced but rather good-hearted officer when he paid a native muleteer $12 out of his own pocket for oranges and bread which they had looted off some pack mules. The next day, however, the general clapped into the guardhouse some of the men who had equipped their tents with furniture from nearby deserted ranch houses by the time-honored means of "midnight requisitions," and the G.I.'s began to have their doubts, which were intensified when the general stopped one of the stages running into Mexico City and put off all except the officers; and that evening "when he rode past the quarters nearly all the men mocked and hooted at him." A week later, Oswandel wrote "some of our regiment and the New Yorkers have stolen Genl. Cushing's horse last night. . . . An ad out saying any one supplying information leading to return gets pass to city. Everyone that read this went away with a hearty laugh saying it was a pity that they didn't steal the general."

Another outburst of the men was directed at Senator Lewis Cass of Michigan, who probably never knew anything about it. On the evening of March 23, 1848, an announcement was read at retreat that Congress had deducted $1 per month from the $7 clothing allowance. As a private's (one grade only) pay was only $7 per month this deduction hurt. The bill to this effect was said to have been introduced by Cass and so great was the resentment that the men hanged him in effigy, Corporal Oswandel reporting: "Then a fire was built under him although some officers ordered it cut down, and a committee was appointed to present Mr. Cass with a leather medal and also nominate him for the next office as dogcatcher." Lewis Cass ran for President the following November on the Democratic ticket but was defeated by the Whig candidate, General Zachary Taylor, who had gained great popularity among the troops in the war. The normally Democratic states of New York and Pennsylvania went for Taylor by a narrow margin and won him the election; perhaps the returned volunteers of these states tipped the scales.

The soldiers sought souvenirs as eagerly as always and a

general order was issued early in October, 1847, directing
that "all pieces of ordnance of whatever calibre and all
colors, standards and guidons taken from the enemy and
now in possession of individuals will be immediately sent in
to . . . the ordnance office"—probably with the usual results. The only man made to disgorge was not a G.I. but a
general, the somewhat notorious Gideon Pillow of Tennessee, who was forced to return two Mexican howitzers taken
from Chapultepec Castle after its capture. The next spring
Phineas T. Barnum solicited "relics of war, military trophies
etc" and promised that "the names of all donors will be
affixed to articles presented and allowed free admittance
for 3 years to the museum." The all-time high in gruesome
souvenir hunting was probably attained by the Pennsylvania
volunteers as noted by Oswandel in his diary just before the
evacuation of Mexico City after the ratification of the peace
treaty of Guadalupe-Hidalgo in May, 1848. He wrote that
while on his way "into the city by way of the Tacubaya
Road, [he] saw several of our men digging up some of the
deserters hung last Sept. The ropes were still around their
necks. They are to cut their heads off, and then boil the
meat off and take their skulls to the U. S. as souvenirs."

Two newspapers for the soldiers were published in Mexico City during the occupation: the *North American,* a
staunch Democratic sheet, edited by Mayne Reid who afterwards became the well-known author of adventure stories
for the young; and the *American Star,* a strong Whig paper.
These rival newspapers were extremely partisan and often
went at each other hammer and tongs, especially during the
sitting of the Court of Inquiry looking into the bitter charges

preferred by Generals Winfield Scott and William Jenkins Worth against each other, which became probably the most acrimonious dispute in the annals of the United States Army —but that is a long and involved story by itself.

One of the editors of the *American Star*, Quartermaster Sergeant John H. Warland of the 9th Infantry, was an unusual character.[4] A graduate of Harvard College, class of 1827, he had previously been a reporter on newspapers in Boston and Lowell, and he made the *Star* a readable and amusing sheet; it is from this source that the best overall picture of the activities of the army during the occupation can be obtained.

Warland's regiment, the 9th Infantry, was a regular outfit which had been activated for the Mexican War and recruited solely in New England, where that war was highly unpopular and quite generally looked upon as a Southern plot to gain more land for the extension of the institution of slavery. The result was that the men and officers of the 9th got it from all sides: at home from their overwhelmingly anti-slavery neighbors, and in the army from the top brass who were usually Southerners and had it in for all New Englanders.

This regiment, despite an excellent war record under a gallant colonel, Truman B. Ransom of Vermont, who had been killed at the storming of Chapultepec, was banished from the delights of the Mexican capital to the humdrum

---

[4] Warland later gained a reputation as a writer of Whig campaign songs. In 1851 the notorious Benjamin F. Butler sued him for libel for an editorial in the *Lowell Courier* which called Butler an uncouth, drunken, political scoundrel, a demagog, and a Bornese Ape, and suggested that he should be hanged. Warland was found not guilty by the jury. He died in the Taunton (Mass.) Insane Asylum in 1872.

monotony of guarding the famous silver mine Real del Monte near the city of Pachuca, about seventy miles to the northeast. Worse than this banishment, however, was the arrival of three new top officers as replacements, Colonel Jones M. Withers and Lieutenant Colonel Jeremiah Clemens, both from Alabama, and Major William B. Taliaferro of Virginia, the colonel a West Pointer and all three evidently martinets. Life in the New England regiment became tense from then on.

But Sergeant Warland considered himself an exception to the orders sending the regiment out into the sticks, as he had been given verbal permission to edit the *Star* by General Scott. But in Warland's own words the three Southern officers "were full of bitterness toward the North, and objected to my having any editorial connection with the paper, or assuming any duties besides those growing out of my position as Quartermaster-Sergeant." [5] This bitterness was evidently not allayed by the sergeant's anti-Southern editorials and by a long poem he wrote (eighteen stanzas), featured on the front page, entitled "The Spirit of New England," a couple of sample stanzas of which went as follows:

> Break New England's lion spirit!
> Brand the braggart's name who spake it—
> While we our fathers' blood inherit,
> Though ye may rouse, ye cannot break it!
>
> Break New England's lion spirit!
> Ay—sooner think to break and tame

---

[5] Warland gave a complete file of the *American Star* to Harvard College which is now in the Houghton Library. With this he sent an explanatory letter about the sectional feeling in the 9th Infantry against their Southern officers from which come these quotations.

The wild gray eagle, if ye dare it,
And make him your ignoble game.

Perhaps the Alabama colonel had taken a course in poetry appreciation at West Point.

This poem, as Warland later wrote, "raised a strong feeling against me among the Southern officers of my regiment, and led, I presume, as much as anything to Col. Withers' action in my case," when "Col. Withers reduced me to the ranks and had me booked as a deserter," and in "the Southern officers of the regiment continually sending someone to *take* me to Pachuca at all hazards. But our New England officers preferred my continuing where I was, and always gave me a hint to be out of the way. . . ."

Fortunately for Sergeant Warland, General Scott finally intervened in his behalf and gave his status as editor official approval. Warland had strongly supported the general in the *Star* throughout all his controversies and this action only seemed like grateful if not poetic justice.

Toward the end of May 1848, after the peace treaty had been signed and the Americans were preparing to evacuate the Mexican capital, several articles and editorials appeared in the *Star* about the extremely serious conditions in the Mexican state of Yucatan where the revolting Mayan Indians were threatening to exterminate the white, Spanish-blood landholders. Yucatan was far larger then in area than it is today and as an isolated peninsula, thrusting out toward Cuba between the Caribbean sea and the Gulf of Mexico, it was cut off by impassable jungles and swamps from any communication by land with the rest of the country. The United States Navy controlled the Gulf of Mexico and Yuca-

tan had remained neutral during the war because of its isolation and internal troubles. But even before this, the state
had developed strong separatist tendencies and three times
previously it had tried to secede from Mexico and establish
itself as an independent republic. As the Indian rebellion,
beginning in 1847, gained dangerous headway, the white
Yucatecos sent the historian Justo Sierra O'Reilly[6] to Washington to ask annexation to the United States, and he
pleaded to President James K. Polk: "In the sacred name of
the living God, the affrighted people of Yucatan appeal to
the humanity of their happy and more fortunate neighbor,
the people of the United States, to save them from exter-
mination." Polk favored the proposed annexation to forestall
intervention by Spain or Great Britain, but Congress took
no action. The next step of the desperate white Yucatecos
was to try to enlist American mercenary soldiers to stem the
brutal tide of the bloodthirsty Indians.

The *American Star* carried a lead editorial on May 27,
1848 which read:

For Yucatan

A number of young men belonging to, and accompanying, the
American army in Mexico, have expressed a strong desire to go
to the assistance of the whites in Yucatan. Many have enrolled
their names, and a party of four or five hundred can easily be

---

[6] He was said to be the natural son of a priest of "distinguished family"
and of a wandering Irish lady named Maria Sierra O'Reilly. (*Enciclopedia
Yucatanense*, VII, Mexico City, 1944, p. 206.) There were many Irishmen
or their descendants in the Spanish colonial service. A captain general of
Cuba in the late 1790's was named O'Reilly and Justo Sierra's mother may
have been related to him. He gradually dropped the name O'Reilly. His
son, Justo Sierra, an even more prominent historian, has been called the
father of the modern Mexican intellectual trend. He refounded the National
University in Mexico City in 1910 after it had been closed for seventy-five
years.

made up. Those who wish to spend the summer in a delightful country, rather than return to their homes in the dull season, can find no better place in which to do so than in Yucatan, whilst at the same time they can assist the whites against the merciless Indians, and benefit themselves immeasurably.

A letter received from Mazatlan, on the Pacific, representing the coast there as unhealthy, and the uncertainty of vessels to California, has caused that expedition to be abandoned, and many who had enrolled themselves for that country have transferred their names to the Yucatan list. Information as to the full object of the expedition, the character of the country, etc. will be readily imparted . . . at the *Star* office.

The news of the discovery of gold in California was not yet known or the young men of the American army would probably have rushed there almost en masse. The Yucatan expedition appealed to many of these same young men, full of bull-meat and restlessness after months of inactivity in occupied Mexico. A few days later the *Star* carried the announcement that no soldier would be discharged until after his return to the United States but pointed out that it was as easy to sail to Yucatan from New Orleans as from any Mexican port.

News of the official ratification of the peace treaty of Guadalupe-Hidalgo was announced on the evening of May 27, and Oswandel wrote: "The camp went wild with joy and the bands of the regiments, supported by a singing and cheering mob of soldiers, serenaded the different *good* officers and a few prominent Mexicans." Three days later, his regiment marched out homeward bound. A delegation of the local bartenders came to bid them good-bye and brought a little pulque as a parting gift to some of their best customers; also to collect a few accounts which had been overlooked.

The barkeeps cheered the regiment heartily as they marched off, and a few walked along with the men for several miles.

On June 12, 1848, the Americans formally relinquished Mexico City in a ceremony held in the Grand Plaza. Before detachments of troops of both nations the American flag was lowered to a salute of thirty guns and the Mexican standard raised in its place. An American band broke into a rousing march and the last of the conquerors followed it out of the city and took the long trail to Vera Cruz. On the last day of July the final soldier embarked for home from that port.

In the succeeding years thousands of these young soldiers joined the gold rush to California or the filibustering expeditions into Latin American countries; and, later yet, many fought on both sides during the Civil War. The next seventeen years offered violent, scattered, and exciting adventures to the daring but it is with those who made the most reckless choice of all, the filibusters, that we are concerned.

Yet before embarking on the extraordinary exploits of the filibusters we should take a brief look at the temper and spirit of the 1850's, the age of "Manifest Destiny," when it was the flaming conviction of an exuberant faction that it was manifestly the eventual destiny of the United States to absorb huge chunks of its neighbors to north and south or even, as the extremists insisted, all the land in the Western Hemisphere. The final adjustment of the Oregon boundary, the decisive victory over Mexico, the discovery of gold in California, all started a rush into new lands and whetted the appetite for more. Most of the believers in "Manifest Destiny" belonged to the Democratic Party, for the Whigs, especially those in New England, were generally the conservative property holders who wanted no drastic change in the *status quo*. The majority of the active filibusters who tried to put this belief into effect by direct action were pro-slavery Southerners who, encouraged by the success in Texas, wanted more land to the south for their "peculiar institution," but there were some Northern Democrats, like Lewis Cass, and even New England Whigs, who wanted national expansion for its own sake.

During the Whig administration of Zachary Taylor, after the Mexican War, an honest effort was made to prevent filibustering expeditions (often without success because of local public sentiment), but when the Democrats came in again, in 1853, under Franklin Pierce, the lid practically came off and this continued, to a lesser extent, under his successor, James Buchanan. Not only did illegal filibustering flourish but the Pierce administration caught the current fever of expansionism to such a degree as to officially approach Russia about the purchase of Alaska, to broach the matter of annexation with the King of the Hawaiian Islands, to attempt the purchase of Cuba from Spain, and to make overtures toward the annexation of the Dominican Republic. None of these efforts, however, succeeded at the time and the only territorial gain was the land secured, along the Mexican border, by the Gadsden Purchase in 1853.

In short, the spirit of the decade was one of adventure and romance, an enthusiastic nationalism and conviction of America's imperial destiny, and an unshakable belief in our superiority to all the world. The American eagle really screamed defiance in those days and the filibusters were its epitome.

CHAPTER II

Into Yucatan

POOR Justo Sierra O'Reilly, supplicating help for Yucatan, spent a perfectly miserable winter in Washington in 1848. He shivered, as he kept a diary of his experiences,[1] at the penetrating cold, the "horrible frio" of the northern clime, so hard to bear for a thin-blooded native of warm and gentle Yucatan. His journal was, of course, written in Spanish, but he once lapsed into a few English lines to write:

> Forget me not!!
> Forget me not
> As I forget not thee!!

One can wonder whether the chilled and homesick emissary was jotting down these yearning words for his faraway señora, or if he had been taking English lessons in Washington from a warming American señorita.

He frequently visited the Senate chamber in his efforts to obtain official help for his beleaguered people, and mentioned meeting Daniel Webster, whom he considered its

---

[1] Justo Sierra O'Reilly, *Diario De Nuestro Viaje A Los Estados Unides,* (*La Pretendida Anexion De Yucatan*), edited by Hector Perez Martinez, Mexico, 1938.

most eloquent orator, and John C. Calhoun of South Carolina whom he described as *"mas feos* [very ugly] *y de ignoble fisonomia."* Calhoun opposed help to Yucatan and Justo Sierra was probably prejudiced. Among Sierra's supporters were Senators Sam Houston of Texas and John A. Dix of New York, and these he praised as good and able men. He called intermittently on President Polk and Secretary of State James Buchanan, and for a while it appeared that his quest might be successful. But it ended futilely when a report arrived in May that peace had been made in Yucatan (this afterwards proved false) and a bill to furnish help was consequently tabled and forgotten.

Justo Sierra protested this sidetracking of his mission, as he felt, quite rightly, that such a report was premature and unreliable. But to no avail. For, with the ratification of the peace treaty with Mexico that same month, the senators turned to sectional excitements and controversies about what to do with the huge area acquired from that country. Certainly there was enough of that without any further involvements and complications in Yucatan; besides, one of the terms of that treaty specifically barred any further aggrandizement by the United States from Mexican territory. And so the proposal to intervene officially in that peninsula died before a vote could be taken.

Down in New Orleans, the following summer, many of the returning, victorious American troops from Mexico passed through that port and a number of them, probably almost entirely Southerners, were discharged there. Some of these veterans then enlisted in a regiment of American volunteers which was being recruited in that city for service in Yucatan. The Northern and Western boys, however, had mostly had their fill of army life, of hot countries, and of the dust, dirt, and diseases of Mexico; they wanted above everything the cool shade of maples, oaks, and elms, the green grass beneath such trees, and the sound of clear, rushing brooks and streams, with an absence of crawling, creeping, and flying things. The more extreme Northerners even espoused the irreverent theory that Mexico had really won the war by forcing the United States to annex Texas.

New Orleans in the middle of the last century was all that has ever been said about it in song or fable—and then probably some. Here the Mississippi River steamboatmen, with the broken-down remnants of the old keelboat men and the waterfront roustabouts and stevedores, spent their wages. Here the crews of ships from all over the world landed to enjoy unchecked revelry, and here all the pleasure seekers of the Deep South gathered to spend the profits from their plantations of cotton, rice, and sugar. The rivermen were a turbulent lot, well described as "half horse, half alligator," as exemplified by the semi-legendary Mike Fink who quite easily could have licked his mythical rival Paul Bunyan with one hand tied behind him. Mixed in with this restless flotsam and jetsam of the great river were occasional wild Mountain Men down for a bender after long spells of trapping beaver in the far Rockies; and the Santa Fe boys enjoying the fleshpots of the metropolis of the South after a grueling round trip to the capital of New Mexico.

These men were floaters and restless wanderers, kept in adventurous circulation by the great river. They were wonderful material for the pioneering spearheads of colonization. It was they who had taken delight in scaring the British officials of the Hudson Bay Company out of a large part of the huge area called Oregon before the boundary settlement of 1846. In California their prototypes had started the Bear Flag Revolution and had helped the United States forces to win the Pacific Coast. It was this breed who had poured into Texas to cause such trouble for the Mexican officials before the revolution in 1836; and then had died at the Alamo, and later conquered at San Jacinto to achieve Texas independence. It was they who were indirectly responsible for the settlement of Utah because they had expelled the Mormons from Missouri and Illinois and thus caused the hegira of that persecuted sect to the Great Basin beyond the Rocky Mountains. They were a great factor in the Mexican War; to them it was a fight or a frolic, all leading to the sack of the Halls of Montezuma. They were the temper of the Mississippi River, the spirit of Manifest Destiny, usually linked with the extension of slavery in their zeal for the expansion of the United States. These were the men who flocked to the filibustering expeditions of the 1850's and later stormed to the early successes of the Confederacy. Like the Spanish conquistadores of the sixteenth century they burned themselves out. Had they succeeded in establishing another slave state besides Texas, or an independent country, in the Spanish-speaking lands to the south, the outcome of the War Between the States might have been far different. And they came very close to triumph in the grand effort in Nicaragua.

The success of the Texas revolution against Mexico had set a precedent and established one pattern for obtaining new lands for the United States in which the peculiar institution of slavery could be expanded; or rather re-established, for the countries to the south had abolished it after winning their independence from Spain. This technique was to infiltrate an area, such as Texas, as invited settlers, becoming citizens and giving lip service to the local laws. In Texas the incoming Americans nominally became Roman Catholics and foreswore slavery. The religious conversion, however, was but skin deep and the slaves they brought along were called indentured servants with no change whatsoever in their actual status. These settlers, after getting their roots down, had then revolted against Mexico in 1836, and, with the aid and assistance of their neighbors in the United States, had established the independent republic of Texas. Before a decade had passed they had gained annexation to the United States. This method had worked well in a sparsely settled region but it had to be changed for the more heavily populated regions below the Rio Grande.

The second way was for a group of Americans to enlist as a body in one of the factions of the constant revolutions in the new Spanish-speaking republics. One of the usual terms for enlistment was for every American volunteer to receive a sizable tract of land, contingent, of course, on the success of that particular faction. The implication was that these adventurers would then settle down as solid citizens to enjoy the fruits of victory. The catch was that they might also, as a cohesive and disciplined fighting force, take over the government itself and write their own tickets. And this is exactly what William Walker and his men later accomplished in Nicaragua.

Then, there was a third way as well—which can be called
the direct action method. This was to land, without subterfuge, on the coast of one of the southern republics and, after
establishing a beachhead, to proclaim a new government
with the bold invaders, or filibusters, as they were usually
called, holding all the key offices. This method, however,
lacked finesse, to say the least. It smacked of outright piracy
and outraged public opinion not only in the country attacked but in the United States and Europe. William Walker
tried this plan once in Lower California and Sonora, within
the Mexican republic, with disastrous results. Later, he more
suavely entered Nicaragua as the invited leader of a band
of American mercenaries on the side of the revolting Liberals, and, after some phenomenally successful infiltration
made himself, by sheer force of arms, the President of that
greatly distracted republic. That was the climax of all these
reckless expeditions and the grand filibuster which ended
all filibusters.

These, then, were the general type of men and these the
patterns for filibustering. The first expedition of this kind to
sally forth after the Mexican War was, quite naturally, the
one into Yucatan. There is no evidence that Justo Sierra had
any part in this particular foray. It seemed to be the result
of an agreement made directly with Governor Barbachano
of Yucatan by a group of Southern adventurers. Very probably the promoters of this regiment of American volunteers,
which embarked from New Orleans, had a vague objective
of the eventual annexation of Yucatan, despite the refusal
of the United States Senate to accept such a deal, served
up, as it were, on a silver platter. Also, considering the

leaders of this foray, it is a fair assumption that they set sail with a gleam in their eyes for siring a revival of slavery in that mysterious land.

Yucatan was a unique part of the republic of Mexico. Its northern and western coasts on the Gulf of Mexico were low, sandy, and semibarren. An outer key stretched along its north shore for some two hundred miles, with fairly frequent openings and a deep water anchorage within. Steep bluffs on its eastern coast faced the Caribbean sea, indented with bays and bordered by islands, such as Cozumel, where Cortez first landed on his expedition from Cuba for the conquest of Mexico. The peninsula was generally a sparsely settled low tableland of porous limestone with no rivers but with fairly frequent subterranean wells where the waters collected during the rainy season from May to October. Except for the cleared plantation areas near the northern and western coasts, it was a land covered by a jungle of brush, plants, and trees which had overwhelmed the ruins of what had once been the flourishing cities and the remarkably advanced civilization of the extraordinary Mayan race.

Not until several years after the conquest of the Aztecs and their capital (now Mexico City) high up on the interior plateau did the Spaniards turn to the subduing of Yucatan and when they did, they found the descendants of the ancient Mayas, whose civilization had already degenerated from its past grandeur, a tougher lot to conquer than the Aztecs. In 1527 the conquest of Yucatan was undertaken under the leadership of Francisco de Montejo, but it was never successfully extended over the whole peninsula and to this day the Mayas have preserved a sort of fugitive independence in the depths of the jungles to the south and along the east coast in what is now the territory of Quintana Roo.

The whites of Yucatan had injudiciously armed the Mayan peons on their plantations, and their untamed relations in the jungle, against the Mexican forces in their sporadic and shortsighted attempts to establish an independent republic, and this had eventually backfired. The Indians, having learned the use of firearms, quite naturally came to realize the power of their overwhelming numbers. The merchants in Belize in British Honduras to the south, whence traditionally came any help to trouble the Spaniards or their successors the Mexicans, furnished these downtrodden Mayas—who had always clung to some pride in their vanished glory—with weapons and supplies. And in 1847 these Indians rebelled. Within a year they threatened to wipe out bloodily all traces of the Spanish Christian civilization in the peninsula.

Just a few years before, an unusual American, John L. Stephens, had pulled Yucatan from obscurity and made it a place of considerable interest in the public mind during the early 1840's. A graduate of Columbia College (1822), he had practiced law in New York and gained some renown as a Tammany orator before making trips, for his health, to the Near East and Eastern Europe, which he recounted in two books which became best sellers of the late 1830's.[2]

---

[2] *Incidents of Travel in Egypt, Arabia Petraea, and the Holy Land*, 2 vols., New York, 1837. *Incidents of Travel in Greece, Turkey, Russia, and Poland*, 2 vols., New York, 1838.

In 1839 President Martin Van Buren appointed him as minister to Central America (or Guatemala as it was generally called)[3] and Stephens set out for his duties accompanied by an English artist, Frederick Catherwood, who had had some experience in archeology. Before this there had been some explorations and reports about the fabulous ruins of the ancient cities of the Mayas, almost by then covered and obliterated by the lush jungles of this area. Stephens never could find the government of Guatemala, which changed and moved so rapidly in the then current revolutions, but he and Catherwood spent their time wisely and well in exploring and picturing the ruins of the old Mayan cities of Copan, Uxmal, Palenque, and others. These reports drew wide attention and sparked the interest in the Mayan civilization which has mounted during the following century.

But it is doubtful that any of the American adventurers who enlisted in the volunteer regiment to fight against the rebellious Indians knew or cared anything for the archeological curiosities of the Yucatan peninsula. It is all very hazy today and only glimpses of what occurred can be gleaned from the New Orleans newspapers of the time and from some rather jumbled and inaccurate recollections of a quartet of octogenarian veterans of both sides of the fighting. The promoters of this regiment of volunteers seem to have been a small group of officers of the 13th Infantry, a regiment which had been authorized by Congress for the duration of the Mexican War only, and which was mustered out in the

---

[3] The five central American republics of today, Guatemala, San Salvador, Nicaragua, Honduras, and Costa Rica, were united for a time, after winning their independence, as the republic of Guatemala.

summer of 1848 in Mobile, Alabama. The leader appears to have been a former captain of the 13th named Joseph A. White from Georgia, who then became the colonel of these American volunteers. From the available names of his officers in the New Orleans newspapers it would seem that most of them had never held commissions in the United States Army, but they may well have served in the ranks or as non-coms during the just-ended Mexican War. The rank and file were probably a combination of ex-soldiers and the half-horse, half-alligator type who hung out around the New Orleans waterfront. All craved adventure and were lured by the promise of 320 acres of land in Yucatan to each man for his services.

Evidently Colonel White must have recruited about nine hundred men to serve in this American Volunteers Regiment and these seemed to have been transported to Sisal (now replaced by Progresso) on the north coast of Yucatan which then served as the port for the capital city of Merida. The next news of these volunteers from American sources is contained in a letter to the New Orleans *Daily Delta* of March 14, 1849, from one of the officers, Captain G. H. Tobin, dated January 18, 1849, and written from the old Spanish city of Valadolid (sic) deep in the heart of Yucatan. Extracts from this newsy missive are as follows:

MY DEAR DELTA:

Many happy returns of the season! Since shaking hands with you at New Orleans, we have all had plenty of hard marching and hard fighting, sometimes with short commons, and at others with plenty. Our march commenced on the day we arrived at Sisal, the seaport for Merida (the capital of the state) distant thirty-five miles. The road is excellent, and leads through many

beautifully situated villages and ranchos, now nearly destroyed
by the Indians. Merida is a very handsome city, and contains
25,000 inhabitants; it is said to have had a population of 60,000
some years ago. We remained there four days mustering in the
companies and commissioning the officers. My commission was
that of First Lieutenant. During our stay, a feast day occurred,
and we had a good opportunity of seeing the Yucateco belles.
They drove during the evening in their volantes, round and
round the Corso (their promenade), and made a graceful display
until after dusk. Many of them are as fair as the whitest Northern
ladies, and all elegantly and tastefully dressed. As to the
Peones, or serfs, the men are low-sized and athletic, and the
women, short, dumpy and very square-built, and look at a first
sight, rear view, like a feather-bed, or a whale's tongue. Our
route from Merida was through a large number of ruined
ranchos and towns to Taesucah [Teosuco], one hundred and
fifty miles, which we made at the rate of fifteen or eighteen
miles per night, resting during the heat of the day, wherever
water could be procured, and that was no easy matter. I have
not seen a stream yet, and wells are from six to twelve miles
apart, and one hundred and fifty [feet] deep, so that unless
we carry buckets and ropes, which we now do, they are of but
little if any service to us. At one small village, a curious animal,
called a Padre, got very drunk amongst the boys, and made a
foolish display of a valuable silver chalice, richly chased with
gold. In the morning the Padre awoke, missed his chalice, and
complained outrageously to Colonel White of the theft. The
Padre was a filthy little disgrace to his profession, and looked
like a man who wanted his bitters badly; and Colonel White
was obliged to turn him off, after an ineffectual attempt to dis-
cover the thief. The Padre then poured his bile on me in
Spanish and I was forced to threaten him with a broken cala-
bash, before he sheered off. This excited Captain M's anger;
and he swore "no matter how big a blackguard the Padre was,
his gown ought to protect him." He then accused me of having
stolen the chalice myself. I returned the compliment, and told
him I'd publish it. "Oh don't," said he, "for the Lord's sake;

what would Father Mullen or my wife say, if they heard it?
They'd think it was true." Some one composed a dogrel on it in
this wise:

> At home, M. is thought a saint,
> At sacrilege he'd surely faint;
> But, here, with vip'rous fiendish malice,
> He stole a drunken Padre's chalice.

The verse was chanted by every one until the poor Captain
became furious; but he was completely exonerated from the
charge on Christmas day, when we got into our first action with
the Indians, and the first man killed was the veritable thief.
[Probably the chalice was found among his belongings.]

We reached Taesucah, one hundred and eighty-eight miles
from Sisal, on the 23d December, rested the 24th, and started on
the 25th in search of the enemy; and, on my word, they were
not hard to find. I had thought, at first, this was a mere irruption
of savage Indians, but, I now discovered that it is in reality a
sort of servile war, and the Spartacus is a half-breed—a cross
between a British subject and a native of the soil; he is called
Prince Pat [Antonio Pat], and is said to be a man of talent,
education and wealth. Our road had been cut through a dense
chapparal, and was very tortuous. At almost every angle, Prince
Pat displayed his talents in the construction of barricades [here
called trancheros], and their sites were chosen with a skill that
would not be discreditable to the most accomplished engineer
from West Point.

At half a league's distance the firing began from behind the
trancheros; and the Yucatecos, led by their own officers, slipped
into the chapparal, on either side the road, and used as flankers;
and on a signal from their bugles, the Americans charged in
front, and in this way carried a dozen or fifteen barricades, led
on for the most part by Colonel White himself, though many of
us remonstrated with him, and requested to be allowed to take
his place. Captain Linton's company, which was in the advance,
was completely knocked up by the constant running from tranchero to tranchero, and Captain Freeland, who came next, was

also in the same fix. My little crowd passed Captain Freeland with a hole in his hat, and seven of his men dead or wounded near him. I thought we were ahead, and had only time to say "Bad luck to you, Captain Jack"; and received for answer, "The same to you, George." We then rushed on, and carried four more trancheros, and, in obedience to a recall from the bugles, returned to Taesucah, seven miles, carrying with us twenty-six killed or wounded Americans. Five were killed on the spot, four have since died, and the balance are more or less wounded. The Yucatecos lost fifteen or twenty men. They are excellent soldiers —far superior to the Mexicans of the North. . . .

Two days after we marched to a small town, and carried it after fighting through a league of barricades, and being fired on from almost every house. Our loss was ten or twelve. We rested there for the night, cooking hog meat, while the enemy was firing away at a "foolish distance." The town was burned by order, and we moved on to another at a short distance, had a few trifling skirmishes, and supped, and breakfasted next morning on hog meat, beef, veal, venison, goat flesh, chickens, peacocks and honey—a feast fit for the gods. But such feasts are, here, alas! "few and far between." I have been forced to take up my sabre belt three holes already.

We returned to Taesucah on the 29th, and, strange to say, without a shot. Here many of our officers tendered their resignations. All were promptly accepted by Colonel White, and the result is that I have received the captaincy of a dashing company through the kindness of the Colonel. The regiment was now nearly altogether, mustering between six and seven hundred men (many wounded) . . . and Colonel White was ordered to dispatch two hundred men, with eight hundred Yucatecos, to this ancient and beautiful, but now ruined city, Valadolid. Colonel White chose parts of four companies, and came on himself, leaving the balance of the regiment under the command of Lieutenant-Colonel Besaucon at Taesucah. The distance between the two cities is fourteen leagues, through an everlasting wilderness, with nothing to break the monotony, except the skirmishes and hanging of two prisoners taken.

Destiny and Glory

If you know the friends of Sergeant Francis Cunningham, of Captain Connelly's company (said to be well acquainted in New Orleans) tell them he was killed on December 25th, his body ripped open and his heart torn out. Donahue, of the same company, also was killed. I don't know the names of the rest.

Evidently there was a high proportion of Hibernian names among these soldiers of fortune; as always, the "Wild Geese" were ready to seek fortune at the cannon's mouth.

In the same issue of the *Daily Delta*, there was an account of the arrival from Yucatan, the day before, of two hundred and fifty men of the American Volunteers Regiment which that newspaper said had been disbanded in a manner disgraceful to the authorities of Yucatan. It claimed that:

The regiment left this city under a solemn promise from Governor Barbachano, that each private should be paid eight dollars a month, should receive a suit of clothes every three months, and at the expiration of the term of service, three hundred and twenty acres of land. The regiment was between three and four months in service. During that time, they had several severe engagements with the Indians, and . . . drove the enemy before them until they [the enemy] now have possession of no position of importance, except Bacalar [in southeastern Yucatan near British Honduras]. . . .

The regiment was besieged eight days in Tihosuco, and during that time was reduced to such an extremity that officers and privates had nothing to eat but cats and dogs. In several engagements, the loss in killed was from sixty to seventy, and from one hundred to one hundred and fifty were wounded. Although continually suffering hardships, owing to the salubrity of the climate but few of the men fell by disease. After all this, the only requital offered the men is the paltry sum of ten dollars each. Barbachano pleaded the poverty of the treasury, and

44

Colonel White feeling there was no prospect of the stipulations entered into with the regiment being fulfilled, at once requested that it should be disbanded which was acceded to.

The *Delta* went on to give a list of some of the Americans killed and wounded, and to say that a Captain R. J. Kelly was the only officer who stayed on in Yucatan; he had been authorized to raise a company from the disbanded volunteers and enough men remained to fill its ranks.

A somewhat different account of these volunteers can be gleaned from the pages of an extremely rare book written by a Yucateco and published in Merida in 1873.[4] The author seems to have had small use for the fighting tactics of these imported gringo mercenaries. He reports that these American auxiliaries (as he called them) landed in December 1848 at the port of Sisal from several small sailing vessels and marched immediately to the fighting front under the command of Colonel White. The end of the State's misfortunes seemed in sight—but, alas, what followed!

Colonel White and his men showed an impetuous desire to meet the Indian enemy and insisted upon advancing through the dense brush and jungle with no caution or respect for the foe, wrote Señor Baqueiro. They were dressed in thick and woolen clothes unsuitable for fighting in hot and humid Yucatan. They advanced in no intelligent order but scattered themselves along the foot and mule paths, loudly talking and joshing, and smoking pipes which sent up puffs of smoke marking their progress to the lurking

---

[4] Serapio Baqueiro, *Ensayo Historico Sobre Las Revoluciones de Yucatan desde El Año de 1840 Hasta 1864*, 2 vols., Merida, 1873. Vol. II contains scattered accounts of the American "Auxilaries."

enemy. They stopped at will to pick flowers and to admire some of the big trees. And they refused to take any advice from the worried Yucatecos who marched on their flanks. The inevitable result was an ambush by the waiting Indians, who had thrown up a line of carefully dug trenches and pits across the advance. The American "auxiliaries" at once tried to escape this trap by exuberant yells and a frontal charge against the entrenched enemy, a method which they had almost always successfully used against the Mexicans in the recent war. But these Mayans were different from the Mexicans they had previously met in combat and were not panic-stricken by the shrieking charges of the blond giants from the north. Instead they held their ground and poured a deadly fire into the onrushing gringos—with the result that the latter were almost completely destroyed.

This local historian went on to say that over a year later there was a report that Colonel White had gathered some five hundred American adventurers on an island in the Gulf of Mexico with the purpose of invading Yucatan to gain satisfaction for the broken promises of the authorities to the original volunteers. Part of this rumor was true. Colonel White had gathered a force on Round Island, below the mouth of the Pascagoula River in Mississippi. But these men were aimed at Cuba under the leadership of the unlucky Narciso Lopez. President Zachary Taylor took prompt action to enforce our neutrality laws and U. S. naval vessels dispersed these filibusters before they could act. This failure, however, did not prevent Lopez from leading two later expeditions into Cuba which finally ended in complete disaster.

There are a few other tales of the mishaps of these luckless Americans. Edward H. Thompson, an archeologist and
the United States Consul to Yucatan from 1885 to 1909,
made many discoveries among the Mayan ruins and once
owned a plantation around the ancient city of Chichen-
Itza which became a center for visiting archeologists and
other scientists. Thompson was the author of two romantic
novels, and of various articles about the Mayas, several of
which appeared in the rather recondite pages of the *Proceedings of the American Antiquarian Society*. One of these
articles, titled "A Page of American History,"[5] tells of in-
terviews which Thompson had with four octogenarian survivors of this fighting nearly sixty years before. Two of these
had been with the American Volunteers, and two with their
former enemies, the Mayan Indians.

Thompson was a bit shaky on his dates for he states that
in the year 1847 a "well-armed and perfectly uniformed
force of nine hundred and thirty-eight men disembarked at
the then port of Sisal, from sailing vessels hailing from
New Orleans, and were at once ordered to Merida, where
they went into barracks. . . ." This, of course, was a year
too early. He goes on to say he was told that of this original
number "only eleven lived to reach the United States" which
the contemporary reports in the New Orleans *Delta* show
to be untrue. However, Thompson culled some interesting
remembrances from these four old men, and there must have
been considerable truth amidst their natural mistakes.

One of the American survivors, according to Thompson,

[5] *Proceedings of the American Antiquarian Society*, New Series, Vol.
XVII, April 1905–April 1906, pp. 239-252.

was a native Pole named Edward Pinkus who had become
an American citizen and fought under General Winfield
Scott in the Mexican War. He claimed to have served as
adjutant under Colonel White in the Yucatan expedition
but remained in Merida, after his surviving comrades returned home, "wounded and sick nigh unto death." There
he married a native woman who had nursed him back to
life and health. He later fought under Benito Juarez against
the French invaders supporting the Emperor Maximilian.
He then established in Merida the finest tailoring establishment in Yucatan and lived to see his sons grow up to be
solid citizens of the state. He died in 1904. It was Pinkus
who stated that only eleven American survivors lived to
reach the United States again. He vaguely described some
of the jungle battles with "jaw-breaking" names,[6] saying
the Indians fought like devils to inflict heavy losses on the
Americans and that he himself was wounded three times.

The other American survivor, Michael Foster, was born
in Philadelphia in 1823. He frankly admitted that he had
been given the choice of going to jail or joining the Yucatan
expedition by the authorities in the States. Perhaps this
choice was typical of many of the volunteers. He also had
married a Yucateca after the fighting, and remained in his
wife's country. Thompson reported that the old fellow,
then in his eighty-second year, had almost forgotten his na-

---

[6] Some of the villages were Ohumboob, Oxkutzcab, Kancaboonot (the
inverted "c" was pronounced like a "dz"), Oitnup, Oonotchel, Yokoao;
Muxupip, Tzuhcacab, and Tzuctuk.

The revolting Indian leaders had such names as: Baltazar Ché, Pantaleon
Uh, Venancio Pec, Cecilio Chí, Florentino Chan, Benito Chim, and José
Isaac Pat.

tive tongue but spoke good Spanish and Mayan. He did not assert the same heavy American losses as had Pinkus but thought that nearly four hundred had been killed, which was probably a pretty fair estimate. He described the fatal ambush of the trancheros by saying, "The Indians there played us a trick; they made concealed pitfalls in the path and placed sharp pointed stakes at the bottom; then they appeared and dared us to come on; we rushed after them with hurrahs and many of our men fell into the pits; we lost many men that day but we killed a great many more of the Indians than they did of our men."

Thompson, in his archeological explorations, also ran across two aged, native Indians who had fought against the gringo invaders. The first of these was a solitary old fellow, living alone on his little *milpa* (cultivated patch) in the jungle, who remembered the strange white men who were so very brave and had caused so many Indian deaths. He recalled: "We had guns and powder from Belize but we had few balls and so often had to use small stones; also we made balls of red earth, well mixed with honey and hard dried in the sun. These balls made bad wounds and hard to heal. [The Mayan dum-dum bullet!] The stranger white men fought close together and for that reason it was easy to kill them. But they were brave men and laughed at death and before they died they killed many of our men."

The other Indian veteran, with the strange but engaging name of Leandro Poot, gave a vivid description of the invaders from the ncrth:

"When the strange white men came up against our people

we were perplexed and did not know what to do. Our quarrel was not with them and they spoke the language of Belize, and Belize was not against us [the rebellious Indians were supplied with arms from British Honduras], so we waited to see what was meant. Then some of our people who came over to us from the white man's side told us that these big stranger white men were friends of the white man of T'Ho [Merida] and had come to help him kill us. Then we fought them, but we had rather they had not come, for we only wanted to kill those that had lied to us and had done us great harm. . . . It was easy to kill the stranger white men, for they were big and fought in line, as if they were marching, while the white men from T'Ho and Sacci [city of Valladolid to the east of Merida] fought as we do, lying down and from behind trees and rocks.

"But these white men were very brave. . . . They laughed at death and went toward it with joy, as a young man runs to a handsome woman. . . . Some of the stranger white men were clothed in uniform . . . while others were naked to the waist, with a red cloth tied around their heads and their swords buckled about their waists. Their big bodies were pink and red in the sunlight and from their throats came their strange war cry, Hu-Ha! Hu-Ha! [evidently a hurrah]. They were brave men and shot keenly. Some of them were such good shooters that no man could hope to escape when once they pointed at him; no, whether he ran or walked or crawled, it made no difference unless he could hide behind a tree before the shot was fired. . . .

"So for a time we greatly feared these strange white men and only sought to keep out of their reach. Had they stayed behind their defences and only used their guns as they could use them, no one knows what might have happened, for our people were so scared of the big, pink-skinned men with their terrible cries and their death shots that they could not be made to stand up against them. But the stranger white men were too brave, for they threw their lives away, and when they found that we did not come up to them, they jumped over the wall that they had made and came to seek us. We hid behind the trees and rocks, wherever we could that they might not see us, and so, one by one, we killed them. They killed many of us, but we were many times their numbers and so they died. Brave men, very brave. Some died laughing and some with strange words in their own tongue, but none died cowardly. I do not think any escaped. I think they lay where they died, for in those days we had no time to eat or to sleep or to bury the dead."

There were a few aftermaths to these confusing reports. Justo Sierra O'Reilly, after his return to Yucatan from Washington, started a newspaper in Campeche called *El Fenix*.[7] Its early issues, in the autumn of 1848, mentioned the arrival of the American volunteers with enthusiasm which soon cooled after their repulse by the Indians and then swung to the other extreme and spoke of their excesses. After the main body of these volunteers had left, it praised the popular Captain R. J. Kelly, who remained with a hundred Americans to carry on the fight, and told of his sailing from Sisal on March 23, 1849 to take part in an attack on Bacalar, an isolated town held by the Mayan rebels, far to the south near British Honduras. Later, in the following

---

[7] A rather complete file is in the Library of Congress.

August, it reported that the gallant Kelly had been killed at the siege of that place, but gave no news of the fates of his followers. There is something rather poignant about the end of this adventurous young captain, leading his lonely band deep into the jungles of savage Yucatan; something so in contrast with the serious and constructive archeologists who later swarmed over the Mayan ruins.

Such are the fragmentary accounts of this strange and misty expedition which ended in disaster. It is almost completely unknown and the bones of the killed Americans have rotted into oblivion in the wilderness of Yucatan, a country so near in mileage but centuries distant in thought and customs. Possibly one or more of the frustrated survivors kept a journal of this expedition which may lie buried today in an attic trunk or in some local library in the Deep South. Unless one of these comes to light, there seems to be no firsthand account of these impetuous volunteers.

CHAPTER III

Cuba Libre

AFTER the collapse of the Yucatan venture, Cuba, the "Pearl of the Antilles," became the cynosure of all the hot-eyed Southern expansionists. There was also a modicum of like-minded Northerners who foresaw certain trade possibilities in that fair island, lying so strategically at the eastern side of the Gulf of Mexico. This acquisitive ardor, however, was something which had been simmering for a number of years, for Cuba was so obviously the key to both the Gulf of Mexico and the Caribbean sea that it seemed imperative for the United States to own it, or, at least, to see that it was controlled by a friendly power. This certainly meant not Great Britain, nor, to a lesser degree, France, and, as the least of evils, the continuance of Spanish rule. Not that Spain was a particularly friendly country (often quite the contrary) but she was weak and impotent and in no sense a threat. And there always existed the hope that Spain might some day be reasonable and sell Cuba to the United States for a fair price. But the Spaniards placed a sentimental value on that island, as one of the very few remnants of their once-glorious world empire, which was far beyond

any vulgar monetary price, and all American diplomatic
attempts to talk business along these lines had been haught-
ily rejected with Castilian pride. Any Spanish government
which would agree to such a humiliating deal would have
been overthrown within twenty-four hours by an infuriated
people, who would prefer the Pearl of the Antilles to sink
beneath the sea! And so it had stood for years.

The general opinion in the United States was that Cuba
was stewing in Spanish corruption and medieval backward-
ness and that the native Cubans, the Creoles, were ripe
for a revolution, following the pattern of the other former
Spanish colonies, and would welcome intervention and possibly annexation to the progressive and prosperous United
States. There was considerable wishful thinking in this opinion, founded as it was on what the Spaniards themselves
called the *leyenda negra*—the black legend. This so-called
legend was one of the most effective bits of war propaganda
which the English had started way back in the sixteenth century, in the days when England had fought for her life
against Spanish power. Even after the destruction of the
Spanish Armada in 1588 and the end of any real threat to
England, the black legend had rolled on with gathering mo-
mentum into the American colonies where it flourished. This
legend was that the Spaniards were generally corrupt, backward, and cruel to an extreme to all the natives of America
and, of course, to all Protestant heretics who fell into their
hands. Their government was said to be hopelessly reac-
tionary and opposed to all the free movements of modern
progress, commerce and industry and, naturally, death to

all democratic and liberal ideas. As a race they were reputed to have become degenerate and cowardly.

Nothing could have been further from the truth than these sweeping generalizations. The Spaniards had treated the American Indians far better than had the English and the Dutch—the latter two races simply exterminated them whereas the Spaniards went to infinite trouble to Christianize and civilize the Indians according to their standards. They had little race prejudice against the copper-skinned natives who were no darker than the Moors they had known in Spain for centuries. Often the lord of the castle had Moorish blood and a darker countenance than his feudal tenants. And so they had often intermarried and always freely interbred with the Indian women, for those Spanish conquerors were an exceedingly lusty lot. The results may have been debatable but certainly there had been no race exterminations. As for their reputed fanatical religious bigotry, true as this may have been in Spain proper, there were fewer people put to death by the notorious Inquisition in all the Spanish colonies than there were women executed as witches in the town of Salem, Massachusetts, alone.

But the black legend had been swallowed by the American people and particularly by the Southern expansionists. It fitted in so well with their rationalizations for extending their superior slave-holding civilization over the backward Hispanic countries. The only trouble was that while there was unquestionably friction between the native Creoles and the Spaniards, this was in effect a family fight—as bitter on occasions as those usually are—and probably only a minority of the Creoles wanted any outside interference by the gringos from the north. "Better the devil we know than the unknown devil."

In 1848 Narciso Lopez was the acknowledged leader of the Cuban malcontents and revolutionaries who hoped for an independent Cuban republic or even annexation to the United States as another slave state. He must have been an unusual man. A Creole himself, born in Venezuela, he had nevertheless taken the side of the Spaniards against his fellow countrymen led by Simon Bolivar and José Antonio Paez during the extremely cruel and bloody wars for independence in northern South America. Before the final victory of the revolutionists he had risen to the rank of colonel of cavalry in the loyalist forces and he accompanied the Spanish army when it withdrew to Cuba. There he married the daughter of a noble family and became Cuban in his interests and loyalties.

Going to Spain, he became a liberal in politics and championed the cause of Queen Maria Christina and her infant daughter Maria Isabel against Don Carlos, the late King's brother, in defiance of the traditional Salic law which excluded a female succession to the throne. These two women, incidentally, later did much to plunge Spain into even deeper depths of political and financial ruin. Lopez, as a cavalry leader, rose to the rank of field marshal in the Carlist Wars, which followed Christina's seizure of the throne, in which the conservatives rebelled against this illegal *coup d'état*. After a victory for the Queen's forces, Lopez returned to Cuba where he became Governor of

Trinidad, an important district in the center of the island. But in 1843 he was relieved of this lucrative job by Captain General Leopoldo O'Donnell (another high Spanish colonial official of Irish descent) and forced to enter business, in which mundane occupation he was unsuccessful because of inexperience and gambling losses.

From then on he plotted against Spain. He desired Cuban independence but not if it brought the abolition of Negro slavery as had happened in the Spanish colonies which had previously won their freedom from the mother country. It is impossible to say what Lopez's definite objectives were but he probably followed the pattern of the Cuban revolutionaries and hoped to achieve Cuban independence, possibly by the intervention of the United States, and to retain slavery as an institution. If the price for American help meant annexation he wanted the admittance of Cuba to the United States as a slave state.

Anyway, Lopez became the head of a revolutionary plot which was set to explode in 1848. There is evidence that the Cuban revolutionaries had approached General William Jenkins Worth, the best fighting general of the invading American forces in Mexico—a sort of prototype of General George S. Patton—and later they went to Robert E. Lee and Jefferson Davis in search of a leader who might attract volunteers from the returning American soldiers; but all three men, for various reasons, refused or were unable to lead an expedition into Cuba. And so the command devolved on Lopez, a magnetic personality, a courageous and inspiring leader of troops, but an innocent incompetent for the immense job in hand. In fact all the leaders of the filibustering expeditions seemed to lack the capacity for intelligent planning, sound tactics, and any faint idea of long-range strategy.

Lopez, however, must have been an attractive fellow who led with enthusiasm if not with caution and sanity, and certainly he was brave to a fault (another trait shared by all these wild filibuster leaders). The New Orleans *Bee* (June 8, 1850) thus described him:

> Gen. Lopez has an exceedingly prepossessing appearance. He is apparently about fifty years of age. His figure is compact and well set. His face which is dark olive, and of Spanish cast, is strikingly handsome, expressive of both intelligence and energy. His full dark eyes, firm, well-formed mouth, and erect head, crowned with iron grey hair, fix the attention and convince you that he is no ordinary man.

After the abortive rendezvous of the would-be filibusters under Colonel White on Round Island fizzled out because of the vigilance of the U. S. Navy, Narciso Lopez assumed the active leadership for further attempts into Cuba. Incidentally, Colonel White disappeared from the picture and it would be interesting to know why and what became of him. He probably followed the course of restless souls to California, for Frederika Bremer, the Swedish novelist who is called the Jane Austen of Sweden, wrote from Havana, Cuba, on February 17, 1851, that passengers on her ship were not allowed ashore because:

> News had reached the Spanish authorities of the island, that a certain Colonel White, one of the leaders in Lopez's robber-expedition against Cuba [factually he was not], was on board our steamer. . . . Some of the gentlemen were greatly displeased,

and wished anything but good to Colonel White, who, big and bony, with a red face and an Irish nose, and an untroubled and careless expression, now made his appearance on deck, walking up and down, smoking a cigar in the midst of the wrathful glances of the passengers. He merely intended, he said, to go to Chagres, on his way to California.[1]

Colonel White, she continued, then promised not to land, and the other passengers were allowed ashore. This must have been White of Yucatan and he seems to have disappeared into the setting sun of the Pacific.

In the spring of 1850 Lopez gave up all attempts to organize an expedition in New York City and moved out incognito into more friendly territory "to rest his hopes upon men of the bold West and chivalric South." It should be remembered that he faced extreme competition with the lure and excitement of the gold rush to California in recruiting young men for this dangerous mission, and one of his inducements was, "The gold is already dug and coined for which you will fight."

Stopping at Cincinnati, Lopez conferred with some veteran officers of the recent Mexican War to whom he promised high rank in Cuba and a bonus of $10,000 apiece. To privates he munificently offered the regular pay of the United States Army plus a bonus of $4,000, with a further offer of Cuban lands after one year's service. These were far more immediate rewards than any visionary and expensive trip to California and he succeeded in recruiting about 250 men in Ohio and Kentucky under the command of Colonel Theodore O'Hara, a veteran of the Mexican War

---

[1] *The Homes of the New World*, London, 1853, Vol. III, p. 60.

who is still more or less known as the author of the poem "The Bivouac of the Dead." [2] These men were outwardly enrolled as a company of California emigrants to appease the authorities who had squelched the rendezvous at Round Island as a violation of our neutrality laws. "Such a chance to carve out fame and fortune with the sword of Liberty, or at least to die gloriously 'mid the noble and the brave' had not been offered since the Age of Chivalry."

Evidently the California cloak did not fool many people. As they descended the Mississippi River their steamboat put into Vicksburg where a goodly number of the young adventurers walked up the levee to see the town. One bystander took a look and sang out "Cuba, by G-d! No such men as these go to California to dig. Did you ever see such a body of men! D-d if they ain't all gentlemen! What fire, intelligence and energy glows in every countenance!"

They arrived just above New Orleans about the middle of April 1850 and the officers had their hands full for a while in keeping these idle young men "within the bounds of prudence and propriety . . . in such close proximity to New Orleans." It seemed the expedition and its object "was the bar-room conversation all over the city"—but the authorities evidently turned a deaf ear to all this gossip. New Orleans was fanatically in favor of liberating Cuba and this feeling unquestionably had its effect on the elected local officials. But the Spanish Consul in New Orleans soon

---

[2] Written to commemorate the Americans who fell in the battle of Buena Vista, in February 1847, against the Mexicans under General Santa Anna, which until the Civil War was the bloodiest and fiercest engagement of the U. S. Army.

learned all there was to know about the expedition and kept his superiors in Havana well-posted on developments.

Finally the Kentucky Battalion,[3] two hundred and fifty strong, boarded a bark during the night of April 25th. Each man was furnished with a steerage ticket to Panama which was to be shown to any government official as proof that they were all bona fide emigrants for California and, of course, had never even dreamed of filibustering. On the pier, Narciso Lopez and two aides waved their adieus as long as they could discern the fading bark in the darkness. Lopez was to meet them later at a rendezvous unknown to all except the top brass. As Lieutenant Hardy, a later historian of the expedition, wrote: "A sadness crept over each breast as our bark ploughed her way towards the broad Gulf, and soon all sought relief from regrets and doubts in slumber."

About daylight the next morning a small fishing boat hailed the bark near the mouth of the Mississippi River. On board were two officers of the Kentucky Battalion and the editor of the New Orleans *Delta*, a newspaper which gave extreme support to liberating Cuba. Before the two vessels could contact, a U. S. Revenue cutter appeared which moved suspiciously, two or three times, around the bark, overloaded to the gunwales with men, but finally sailed away. It was lucky that the smack had not come alongside at the first meeting. It now did so and "ten boxes of splendid, recently-cleaned United States muskets were soon stowed away in the hold, and about ten thousand ball cartridges in

---

[3] Actually a good proportion of the men were from Ohio.

the captain's cabin." The editor of the *Delta*, a Mr. Sigur, considerately waited for all farewell letters to be written, and with enough of these to nearly sink the fishing smack he returned to New Orleans, smiling, as he waved godspeed, over "the ladies' names on many of the letters handed to him."

On the evening of the fifth day they sighted the north coast of Yucatan and one wonders if there were any veterans of the previous disastrous expedition into that dark and bloody peninsula among the men gazing from the ship's rail at the murky, low-lying shore. Hardy wrote: "Many of them wanted to land anywhere, they didn't care a d-n who inhabited the land—Mexicans, or Patagonians ten feet high—lizards, leopards or sea horses; they wanted to run and jump, and would fight for the privilege without supper, against barbarians, fishes or wild beasts!"

It took "the flat-bottomed, crab-sided old bark" another four days from there to work eastward to an island off the extreme northeast tip of Yucatan where it anchored in a pretty little bay. The Kentucky Battalion rushed ashore to regain its land legs and bathe in the refreshing waters of the Gulf. The men erected tents away from the few thatched native huts, "full of bugs and insects," and named their bivouac Camp Pelican. This island of Contoy was only seventy-five miles from Cuba and twelve miles north of Mujeres (Women) Island which had been the rendezvous agreed upon. But the old bark's slowness and the impatience of the men had decided the skipper to make land as soon as possible. Unfortunately there was no water on Contoy fit to drink and this made trouble.

Signal fires were lighted to guide the ship carrying Narciso Lopez and more filibusters under his command who were supposed to meet them at Mujeres Island. These fires instead attracted several Spanish fishing boats from Havana but they accepted in a friendly way the story that the men were on their way to California via Panama, which was indeed a perfectly plausible one. Then for four days a skeleton crew tried to sail the old bark on to Mujeres Island but adverse winds and a dead calm prevented this and it was forced to return to Contoy.

Discontent almost grew into mutiny upon the ship's return. Its cautious captain was thoroughly disgusted and apprehensive that word had reached the Spaniards of their position. Lieutenant Hardy, however, scornfully referred to this skipper as a typical Yankee and called him a "poor, niggardly, and treacherous old *slink*." The men had no clear understanding of the plans for the expedition, and were, "all hands from the Col. to the cooks, in a most unamiable mood." Colonel O'Hara then called the men together and promised that if Lopez and his reinforcements did not arrive within eight days he would lead them back to New Orleans. This restored the men's morale and with wild enthusiasm they gave "three cheers for Lopez, three for Cuba, and three for *annexation*," and "the shouting and hurrahing of the men drowned even 'old ocean's roar.'" The Spaniards anchored nearby "must have been somewhat astonished, and perhaps frightened, as they set sail before daylight for Havana."

Of course, these Spanish sailors went directly to the authorities—and this advance notice of an impending filibuster alerted all the naval and military forces in Cuba. It was typical of the almost incredible stupidity with which nearly all these filibustering expeditions were handled. The only things more inept than this total lack of any security precaution were the complete absence of any intelligence reports about the enemy and a total lack of any co-ordination with sympathizers on the island. The general idea seemed to be—land anywhere suddenly, charge straight ahead inland, run in circles, scream and shout loudly enough, and the natives would rise en masse to support you while the opposing soldiery would desert in droves to enlist under your banner. It hardly ever worked but most of the filibusters and certainly Lopez kept right on trying.

But the Americans "with good humor restored" on this desolate little island really seemed to enjoy themselves in the interim of waiting for their leader to arrive. The only untoward incident was early one morning when two of the cooks got into a fight and threw all the coffee pots simmering on the fires at each other. There was music and singing, and such popular airs as "Kitty and the Babies," "Grey Eagle," and "Santa Anna's Retreat" swelled out over the soft night air of the Caribbean. Drinking water and provisions were brought by friendly Yucatecos in their little canoes and these natives seemed to believe the Americans had come again to fight the Mayan rebels and "spoke in raptures of the 'great, tall Americanos' who had come to help them a few months before."

In the meantime, back in New Orleans, Colonel Chatham Robert Wheat, a Mexican War veteran, had raised a Louisiana battalion of volunteers part of which, the Kentucky chronicler Lieutenant Hardy disdainfully reported, were "worthless characters and blackguard rowdies . . . of New Orleans, who had applied for and been refused admission into the Kentucky Battalion." This outfit, to the number of a hundred and sixty men, set sail on a small brig about a week after the Kentuckians.

After them, Lopez and a so-called Mississippi Regiment embarked on the steamship *Creole*. Much had been expected of this latter unit which advance notices had claimed would consist of " 'five hundred men, the very flower of the Mississippi Volunteers in Mexico,' with batteries of artillery." The Mississippi Rifles, a collection of the young bloods of wealthy planter families, attended in the field by their slave body servants, had made an extraordinary record in the Mexican War under the command of Colonel Jefferson Davis, and if this same crowd enlisted under Narciso Lopez he could rightfully expect to lead a crack regiment. It was also rumored that the Governor of that state, John A. Quitman, would be in command of these volunteers. This was the same Quitman, a native of New York state but a Mississippian by adoption, who had led the entry of the advance party of American troops into Mexico City less than two years previously.

The Louisiana men on their brig whiled away the time by playing poker, using the printed bonds of the future Cuban republic as stakes. Soon afterwards, on a calm May morning, the two vessels met at an agreed point in the Gulf of Mexico and the men on the brig came aboard the steamer *Creole*. They found the Mississippi regiment disappointingly small as it contained only some 130 men instead of the anticipated five hundred, and very few of them bona fide Mississippians at that—and not a single piece of artillery. However, the best of feeling prevailed between the two sets of men. The magnetic Narciso Lopez circulated among the ranks, keeping the general morale good by his singularly attractive manner and by his bearing which "indicated great activity and power of endurance." He made several encouraging speeches to the assembled men and, all in all, kept their enthusiasm at a high level on the steamer.

On the morning of May 14, 1850, the *Creole* luckily sighted the ship and camp of the Kentucky Battalion at Contoy island and turned in to the anchorage. As it slowly approached "cheering commenced, the Kentuckians giving some of those famous Old Kentuck' yells, which used to terrify the Mexicans so awfully. The enthusiasm grew sublime, when, as the beautiful 'FREE FLAG OF CUBA' [about the same as the present one] was unfurled to the breeze, shout after shout by the United Army rent the air." A brief council of war was held and it was decided that the *Creole* should go on to Mujeres Island to fill her water tanks and return the next day to pick up the Kentuckians. Then on to Cuba as soon as possible.

A printed proclamation from Lopez to his followers was distributed to be read and digested during this wait. It was addressed to: SOLDIERS OF THE LIBERATING EXPEDITION OF CUBA! and appealed to the victors of the Mexican War, "the men of the field of Palo Alto and Churubusco," exhorting them "to strike from the beautiful limbs of the Queen of the Antilles the chains which have too long degraded her, in subjection to a foreign tyranny . . . to do for your Cuban brethren what a Lafayette, a Steuben, a Kosciusko, and a Pulaski are deathless in history for having aided to do for you; and eventually to add another glorious Star to the banner which already waves, to the admiration of the whole world, over 'The Land of the Free and the Home of the Brave.' " Certainly no subterfuge here about the annexation of Cuba to the United States.

It went on to say, "Your Cuban brethren have been compelled to wait and long for the hour when a first nucleus for their revolution shall be afforded them by a gallant band of sympathing [sic] friends . . ." and that "the patriotic people of Cuba will rally in joy and exultation to its support." It concluded on a golden note:

> And when the hour arrives for repose on the laurels which await your grasp, you will all, I trust, establish permanent and happy homes on the beautiful soil of the Island you go to free, and there long enjoy the gratitude which Cuba will never fail generously to bestow on those to whom she will owe the sacred and immeasurable debt of her LIBERTY.

It must have been a struggle to come down to earth after these precious words and turn to such mundane affairs as breaking camp, checking the arms and ammunition, and trying on the new-issued uniforms which consisted of "a red flannel shirt, a black cloth cap, with a Lone Star cockade, and 'any sort' of pants—the Captains generally wore white, the Lieutenants black, the men of various shades and stripes." The use of red shirts, which had been the badge of the European revolutionaries during the uprisings of 1848, was a novelty among Americans.

But all was not as harmonious as Lopez's Olympian proclamation. Thirteen men deserted from the *Creole* while it was taking on water at Mujeres Island;[4] and at Contoy nearly forty others decided they had had enough of filibustering, and of these about a dozen were of the proud Kentucky Battalion. Before these men were left behind, however, they were marched around the deck of the *Creole* for hours, with their hands tied behind them, amidst the hisses and groans of their former comrades, and then were forced to do the heavy, dirty work of transferring coal from the Kentuckians' ship to the *Creole*. Lieutenant Hardy wrote that the rest of the Kentuckians were glad "to get away from the filthy bark and her contemptible old Yankee captain."

All was finally in order, and the *Creole*, loaded almost to the gunwales with supplies, equipment, and 521 men (reduced from 570 by the desertions), sailed out into a rough sea "driving her course through the mountain billows that dashed across her boiler deck all that dreary night, toward that bright goal of the hopes and ambition of the 'Liberators'—THE ISLAND OF CUBA."

* 2 *

The old sidewheeler steamer *Creole* was so overloaded that it was difficult to keep her trimmed in the heavy seas

---

[4] They were soon picked up by a Mexican patrol boat and jailed for a while in Campeche. Some, after great hardships, managed to find ships to the United States. The others settled in Yucatan or enlisted to fight against the rebellious Mayas.

which she met that night, and the men were forbidden to move from their assigned quarters. She ran for two days north into the wind but rolled so that "her wheels would not half the time touch the water." Despite the physical discomforts a lieutenant was court-martialed and reduced to the ranks for insubordination, which was a salutary lesson to the undisciplined volunteers. This course away from Cuba (which lay east by north from Contoy) probably prevented several prowling Spanish men-of-war from capturing the *Creole*, for they knew by then of the expedition and were on the alert to intercept it. Whenever a strange ship hove into view the order was bellowed "Off with your red shirts!" or "Get below!" but several ships afterwards reported that they had noticed these colorful and conspicuous garments and the glint of arms from great distances. At times the *Creole* changed her course to avoid some large steamer which might be a Spanish cruiser. Narciso Lopez "paced the deck rapidly, spy-glass in hand, eagerly watching and examining the vessels, numbers of which were all the time in sight."

On the evening of the first day at sea the plans for the invasion were announced. The landing was to be at Cardenas, a small port on the north coast of Cuba, about ninety miles east of Havana. The railroad to Matanzas, a more important town thirty miles nearer to Havana, was to be seized and Matanzas itself to be captured, within twenty-four hours after the landing, and then made the center of recruiting of native sympathizers. Immediately after Matanzas was taken, a picked force of a hundred men was to rush on eastward to blow up an important bridge within nine miles of Havana, thus delaying any loyalist reinforcements from reaching the scene of action. Then five full regiments of native recruits were to be armed and mounted and with this nucleus of five thousand men Lopez expected soon afterwards to appear before Havana with an army of thirty thousand. A beautiful plan in theory except that it presupposed the Spanish high command to be slothful nitwits and that the Cuban natives would throw their caps over the moon for a spontaneous revolution sparked by gringo foreigners. Incidentally, Lopez did not speak English and all his orders, speeches, and exhortations had to be translated by an aide which, of course, added to the general confusion when later things did not go at all as planned.

At ten o'clock in the evening of May 18th, the *Creole* passed the lighthouse fifteen miles from Cardenas and, under a bright full moon, sailed shoreward past many ships and little islands. The ammunition had previously been unpacked and distributed and each soldier had been given sixty rounds of cartridges. Besides the rifles and muskets, two thirds of the men also carried bowie knives and revolvers. The Liberators (as they called themselves) stood tense and silent on the deck with the crack Kentucky Battalion in readiness to land first. The whispered report of the leadman in the bow or the officers' muttered orders, with now and then the muted clank of a saber, were all that broke the dead silence as the ship crept stealthily toward the harbor.

The moon had gone down by the time they neared a pier. "The city lay sleeping in beauty; sweet odors from its gardens already scented the air." Soon the *Creole* was snugly made fast, after the dauntless ship's captain had quietly swum to the wharf with a rope in his mouth. At this point some dozing watchmen on the pier awakened and fled in terror to spread the alarm.

The men poured off the ship, with the Kentuckians in the van, and formed into companies as soon as they reached the street. Lieutenant Colonel John T. Pickett, who had once attended West Point,[5] led two picked companies of the Kentuckians at the run through the town to capture the railroad station, a mile and a half beyond, and all the locomotives and rolling stock in the yards. A detachment of the Mississippians seized another station within the town and made prisoners of a guard of twelve armed men and all the railroad employees.

While these two detachments were securing the railroad facilities, Colonel O'Hara led the remaining four companies of Kentuckians from the pier toward the main plaza about which all government buildings and barracks were always located in a Spanish town. O'Hara found the streets blocked with teams and large wagons driven by Negroes and, in the confusion, lost his Cuban guide who had come with the expedition. He seized several Negro teamsters and probably was incredulous when they could not understand English as did the Negroes back in Old Kentucky; he may well have tried to make his terrified captives understand him by shouting at the top of his voice. At this point General Lopez fortunately appeared and pointed the way. The Spanish

---

[5] He entered the Military Academy with the class of 1845. Lieutenant Hardy wrote that he "was probably of two (sic) wild and erratic a disposition to remain long enough to graduate."

sentinels, however, had been alerted by the hullabaloo and began to challenge as the column approached the plaza; "*Halta! Qui vive! Qui vive!*" rang out. O'Hara answered "Friends and Lopez." At this answer in English the Spaniards quite naturally fired without further courtesies and the colonel received a disabling wound which forced him to retire to the *Creole*. The Kentuckians rushed past their fallen leader and into the plaza where firing began with the Spanish troops in the buildings.

General fighting then broke out, contrary to Lopez's hopes for a bloodless capture of the town, and for three hours the roar and crash of musketry and wild yells erupted through the darkness and clouds of powder smoke. Finally, the outnumbered and scattered detachments of Spanish troops gradually surrendered after they had suffered considerable casualties and one group had been literally burned out of the governor's palace on the plaza. The Americans, however, had paid a price of about equal losses, including Colonel Chatham Robert Wheat,[6] of the Louisiana regiment, who was severely wounded. During this thunderous battle a large number of the citizens escaped into the countryside to spread the alarm, for, all too soon, there were signs of intense activity and concentrations of loyal troops in the outskirts of the town.

By eight o'clock in the morning the Liberators had full possession of Cardenas and held as prisoners the highest civil and military officials. Guards were stationed at the

---

[6] He afterwards went to Nicaragua with William Walker, later became a major of the famous Louisiana Tigers in the Confederate Army, and was killed at Gaines Mill in June, 1862.

principal stores and everything was scrupulously paid for by the invaders. The strict discipline and prohibitions against looting, which many of the men had been used to under Generals Winfield Scott and Zachary Taylor in Mexico, had its effect and there were no disorders or excesses. Indeed, the Louisiana troops immediately put out the fire they had kindled in the governor's palace by using the local fire engines.

But the lull after the storm was demoralizing in other ways. The men were exhausted from the night's excitement and starving, as few of them had eaten anything but hard crackers for three days past, washed down by a very small allowance of water. All organization was lost as the men scattered about the town seeking food, drink, and rest. The reassured citizens met them with a frightened courtesy and proffered native rum which the filibusters drank in large quantities and this liquor, in their state of complete fatigue, had a stupefying effect and made the planned advances toward Matanzas impossible.

General Lopez then turned to the task of raising native recruits for the revolutionary cause. He walked about among the people, talking to them and distributing his proclamation. He managed to win over several of the captured Spanish soldiers who tore off their uniforms, trampled them under foot and shouted "Hurrah for Lopez and Liberty!" One of his Cuban aides paraded the streets behind a bugle and drum, beating for volunteers but, as Lieutenant Hardy reported, *"Not a single Cuban fell in."* They were not hostile and were even politely hospitable (an understandable attitude at the point of a gun) but as for enlisting under Lopez's banner, "No, señor. A thousand thanks, but it is impossible!"

This attitude was completely logical and showed the wishful thinking of Lopez and his American supporters, based on a lack of any good intelligence reports or any planned co-operation with the Cubans. The Spaniards had their own "black legends," in reverse, about the Anglo-Saxons, stemming from the old piratical raids of Francis Drake, Henry Morgan and many other English freebooters of the old days on the Spanish Main—and there were grim remembrances among the Creoles of their ancestors' firsthand sufferings from the outrages and excesses of these raiders. The outlandish gringo heretics, despite their restraint from atrocities and their leadership by a fellow Creole with several Cuban aides, were unwelcome and dangerous guests whom the citizens were anxious to get rid of as soon as possible. Besides, a growing rumor reported that a large body of Spanish troops was on the road from Matanzas and would arrive by midnight. Food and drink, certainly. And even a few old shotguns and forty or fifty fine horses for the use of the Liberators. But no enlistments! As Lieutenant Hardy reported it: ". . . all were greatly disappointed. Where were those 'hosts of friends' who were to have welcomed us? The Cubans scarcely dared to speak. They merely walked about, bowing and scraping to the red shirts. In truth, never were six hundred men in a more hopeless, lost, and desperate situation."

If the tale of Cuban friendship and co-operation had been greatly exaggerated, the rumor about the approaching Spanish troops certainly was not. By mid-afternoon a group of Spanish lancers had galloped about the outskirts of the town and reconnoitered the situation, which meant that all chances to surprise Matanzas were gone. To attack a superior and well-equipped advancing force with a brave but exhausted and partly drunken body of men without artillery promised small chance of success. To remain in Cardenas and allow Spanish war vessels to cut off all retreat and sources of supply while the Spanish army concentrated outside the town would mean annihilation. Something had to be done quickly and Lopez seized the only possibility, a hasty re-embarkation on the *Creole*, a quick run to the westward, and another landing, way beyond Havana, on the westernmost tip of Cuba at a point easier to obtain supplies and reinforcements from New Orleans, the hotbed of filibustering sympathies. He would then have the prestige of having already captured an important town and the satisfaction of having drawn all the Spanish troops in Cuba on a fool's errand to Cardenas. Besides, he knew and was well known in the west and with the captured arms and ammunition of Cardenas he could arm the natives and attack Havana on its weakest side.

But the immediate problem was to evacuate Cardenas— and quickly! Lopez ordered this at four in the afternoon and his surprised and scattered men began to reunite. A picked group of the Kentuckians remained in the plaza to cover the retreat as the men, supplies, and equipment were reloaded on the *Creole*. The Spaniards soon noticed the movement and an advance force, of horse and foot, entered the town to harass the retreating filibusters. A group of Spanish lancers, some hundred in number, after being checked in an effort to flank this rearguard by one of the parallel side streets to the waterfront, made a reckless, head-on, hell-for-leather charge at these covering Kentuckians; "whirling their lances, and quickly dodging from one side of their horses to the other, the Lancers came thundering on in gallant style." The Kentuckians held their ground and poured a murderous fire into these wild horsemen, and ". . . horses and riders began to bite the dust in bloody confusion. Before reaching the line, more than one-half lay stretched in death, the balance flying up cross streets in dismay. Again and again they returned with desperate fury, and senseless rashness, until the last squadron gallopped [sic] into the very midst of the Liberators, and but a single Lancer made his escape. Out of a hundred, seventy or eighty lay killed or wounded, their maddened horses dragging and trampling them to death."

The dazed but stalwart Kentuckians then moved in good order, carrying their comparatively few wounded, backward to the wharf where the *Creole* lay. There they erected a breastworks of sugar hogsheads, but the Spaniards had had enough of attack. An hour later, at nine o'clock, the last men embarked in the darkness; and the sidewheeler got under way amidst a farewell fusillade of Spanish shots from the shore. The steamer was a madhouse, the decks littered "with loaded muskets, rifles, pistols, sabres, and bowie-knives, thrown down by the exhausted men, who lay down to sleep in the very jaws of death." The men, however, had time for little more than a cat nap before the *Creole*, without a pilot, grounded with a crunching jar on a sand bar about five miles out. The tide was falling and a night of horror followed. Unless the ship was freed before daybreak they would be totally helpless before the Spanish warships which were converging on Cardenas, and not a man aboard would have the slightest chance of life. The heaviest provisions were thrown overboard, but the ship would not budge. Then the arms and ammunition went until the boxes projected above the water. Still the *Creole* would not move. As a last resort, nearly two hundred men were landed on a nearby islet, and this time the ship freed itself. The men were hurriedly taken aboard again, a brief stop was made to land the Spanish prisoners at the lighthouse, and the *Creole* stood out to sea just as the rising sun burned away the morning mists.

An excited discussion then arose as to what course to pursue. General Lopez wanted to follow his plan of landing again farther to the west. But the great majority of the American officers and men violently opposed this as madness because almost all the ammunition had gone overboard to lighten the ship. It was finally left to a vote of the men, who almost unanimously chose to make for the nearest American port. The plucky old general then begged to be put ashore with whatever men would follow him but when it was found that there was hardly enough fuel left, after the violent efforts to get off the sand bar, to make Key West, by common consent the *Creole* turned toward that port at full speed. That night the straining steamer came to anchor in the shallows about forty miles east of its destination.

The next morning a pilot was luckily found in a small coasting vessel, and the *Creole* again made full speed ahead toward Key West. Soon the smoke of a steamer was seen to the southwest and this proved to be the Spanish cruiser *Pizarro,* which took up the case as soon as the *Creole* was recognized. A race for the port developed, with the faster *Pizarro* steadily gaining; but the lighter-draft *Creole* was able to take several short cuts across shallows, and to keep ahead. The coal on the fleeing ship was exhausted but by burning red shirts, bacon meat, boxes, and barrels of resin the little sidewheeler just managed to reach a pier as the *Pizarro* turned into the harbor. The filibusters somehow got the wounded off and then jumped pell-mell ashore to safety as the frustrated Spanish warship, at battle quarters with guns run out, sheered off at the last minute from the fastened *Creole,* while its raging captain shouted violent protests at the port officials for allowing pirates to land in safety. But he made no effort to follow them on shore and that was the end of Narciso Lopez's first filibustering expedition into Cuba.

The men gradually dispersed by land or sea, but a sop was handed to the indignant Spanish captain when several Negro slaves who had stowed away at Cardenas were returned to him. Lieutenant Hardy wrote: ". . . seven niggers who had secreted themselves on board the *Creole* while at Cardenas and been brought away, were delivered into his august possession." The filibusters at least had respect for private property.

Lieutenant Hardy found passage on a brig bound for Tampa which was under the command of a New England skipper whom he disliked as much as the one with whom he had first embarked at New Orleans. He noted: "Capt. Barrett was a down East Yankee, and what was worse, a *Christian*. He was at that time a student for the Ministry in Yale College, and having been a sailor in early life, occasionally made voyages during vacation. Morning and evening he would have all on board assembled, when he would read the Scriptures, pray, and preach. But . . . the truth of a remark which the sailors often made of him . . . [was] notwithstanding his prayers, full of world-wide charity and solicitude for the welfare and salvation of the 'rest of mankind,' viz: 'that h-ll is full of such *Christians.*' He was likewise a poor excuse for a sailor, knew well enough how to make sail, but not to take it in."

Quite naturally, the Spanish government protested violently to the Department of State in Washington about this piratical foray into a friendly country and the futile attempts to prevent it in the United States. And looking back, a century later, it is hard to see how it could be called anything but piratical. A band of armed men, sailing from a supposedly friendly country, descended on an inoffensive coastal town and proceeded to shoot up the place in glorious style, burn and capture government buildings and property, kidnap the civil authorities, seize the town funds, and kill and wound over a hundred soldiers who were rightfully defending the port. European newspapers took up the attack as did the anti-slavery press in the North. Senator Daniel Webster of Massachusetts ably defended President Zachary Taylor from the criticisms of those Southerners who accused him of taking the side of despotism against liberal progress because of the dispersal of the first group of filibusters on Round Island by the U. S. Navy. But, all in all, it was a prolific source of embarrassment to the administration and action was taken to return indictments against the leaders of the Cardenas expedition.

It all came to nothing. Narciso Lopez was arrested at Savannah and released for lack of evidence. All the field grade officers (majors and above) of the expedition were indicted, as were J. L. Sigur, editor of the New Orleans *Delta* who had largely financed the *Creole*, a judge of the supreme court of Mississippi, a former U. S. senator from that state, and its governor, John A. Quitman (the barefoot general of Mexico City). Governor Quitman's indictment and arrest created the greatest excitement, for he threatened to call out the state militia to defend the threatened sovereignty of the State of Mississippi, but finally he resigned his office and submitted to arrest. It was impossible to obtain a conviction against any of these men from a jury and eventually they all went scot-free. The Spanish Captain General of Cuba made a few caustic remarks about the operations of justice in a democracy—and General Narciso Lopez returned to New Orleans to organize a new expedition.

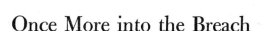

CHAPTER IV

Once More into the Breach

AFTER an unsuccessful attempt to ship arms for a new expedition from New York, Lopez and his supporters again centered their activities in the friendly atmosphere of New Orleans. A new captain general of great energy and activity arrived in Cuba and proceeded to squelch all liberal tendencies and put down the few abortive revolutionary plots with an iron hand. But reports of these futile uprisings were optimistically distorted by the wishful thinkers of New Orleans, and Lopez and his followers again gazed through rose-tinted spectacles at Cuba. Mass meetings were held throughout the Deep South, proclamations of Cuban independence were read to cheering crowds, and over $50,000 was raised for expenses. Men thronged to enlist and were of a higher type with more sincere motives than those of any earlier expedition, for our ancestors of a century ago were easily aroused by any true revolt against tyranny. At the same time, the enthusiasm for Cuban liberty was curiously mixed with a desire to preserve slavery in that island.

A new volunteer element was a group of Hungarian patriots who had fought under Louis Kossuth against Austria

81

and Russia. Narciso Lopez was much impressed by these colorful professional soldiers of fortune and gave them important positions on his staff, which added to the general gaiety while in New Orleans but later compounded confusion in the field because of their inability to speak English. This scrambling of Spanish, English, and Hungarian elements in his command was a bit baffling to the American rank and file and not too well received by them.

Again a steamer, the *Pampero*, was chartered and on Sunday, August 3, 1851, it sailed openly loaded with filibusters from a pier in New Orleans. A wildly enthusiastic crowd sped the parting adventurers with cheers as the ship pulled out into the Mississippi River. Farther down the stream a tug came alongside from which the arms and ammunition were transshipped. It was then found that the ship was overloaded and some of the men, largely against their will, were weeded out and put ashore. Two days later the *Pampero* was towed over the bar at the mouth of the great river, and headed for Key West, Florida.

The filibusters aboard numbered a little over four hundred and were of mixed nationalities. Lopez's staff was largely made up of Hungarian officers, men well seasoned in European warfare but completely inexperienced for the dense brush, chaparral, and forests of Cuba, and who knew but little English or Spanish. One of these, Major Louis Schlesinger, survived and wrote a vivid account of this disastrous expedition.[1] Also on the staff were a few Cubans and

---

[1] *Democratic Review:* "Personal Narrative of Louis Schlesinger of Adventures in Cuba and Ceuta." Issues of September, October, and November and December (one issue), 1852. These three issues covered his experiences with Lopez in Cuba. The name of the magazine was changed to the

Germans. The men were organized into one small company of Cubans and two battalions of Americans, one of which was commanded by Colonel William L. Crittenden, a young Kentuckian of excellent background, a nephew of the then Attorney-General of the United States, John J. Crittenden, who had formerly been a governor of Kentucky. Young Crittenden had graduated from West Point in 1845 and had served during the Mexican War as a second lieutenant of regular infantry.

The *Pampero* steamed uneventfully for two days across the Gulf of Mexico and put into Key West, where all aboard were relieved to find no U. S. naval vessels whose commanders might have had somber notions about enforcing the neutrality laws. Great was the rejoicing among the adventurers and the hospitable inhabitants who crowded aboard bringing champagne and other delicacies for the "liberators" of Cuba. Gloom was banished, healths were drunk, and joy reigned supreme. Rumors which had arrived that several towns in Cuba had rebelled stirred the impatience of all to get into action. Also, it was found that the ship did not have enough coal to proceed up the east coast of Florida to the St. John's River to take on artillery and more men gathered there as originally planned.

General Lopez then decided on a policy of "Audacity, always audacity!" and to strike immediately with a hot iron into western Cuba where he felt sure they would be unexpected by the Spaniards and well received by the native

United States Review for the January 1853 issue but it did not (nor did succeeding issues) continue the serial, as promised, about his experiences as a prisoner sentenced to hard labor in the quicksilver mines at Ceuta in Spanish Morocco. Schlesinger escaped and returned to the United States.

Creoles. He chose Bahia Honda, about fifty miles west of Havana, as an objective. There a beachhead could be established for later reinforcements, gathering in New Orleans and on the St. John's River, who could bring the artillery and heavy equipment. At worst, if they were attacked by overpowering forces, they could retire into the nearby rugged mountains and maintain themselves by the expert gunfire of the Americans until relieved.

And so, on the evening of August 10, 1851, the *Pampero* steamed out of Key West into the color and glory of the setting tropical sun amid cheers and huzzahs from the wildly enthusiastic crowd on shore. There was something symbolic in the silhouette of the departing steamer disappearing into the golden rays cast by the sinking sun on the water, for most of these men were to suffer incredible hardships and leave their bones to rot, unhallowed and unsung, in unmarked graves in Cuba.

At daybreak land was sighted at a point which could not have been more dangerous. The currents and a deviation of the compass (which Captain Lewis, former skipper of the *Creole*, blamed on the iron in the men's guns) had carried the *Pampero* off course and the point sighted was Morro Castle itself, the great Spanish fortress guarding Havana harbor. Recognition was mutual, for as the *Pampero* made a right-angle turn at top speed to the northwest, word was rushed to Captain General de la Concha, who alerted the government forces for immediate action and was able to dispatch these at once when definite news came later of the filibusters' landing. This unfortunate landfall was only the first of a long series of mishaps.

Once More into the Breach

In the early afternoon the *Pampero* turned again toward the island. It sighted a small, coasting schooner from which the weeping captain was forcibly taken to act as a pilot. Under his guidance the sidewheeler proceeded ever westward while the equipment and arms were issued to the men. Each received a musket and bayonet with a large supply of ammunition, and for a uniform every man was given a pair of gray pants and a blue shirt. Evidently the red shirts worn on the Cardenas expedition were considered unlucky.

After the distribution, General Lopez walked among the men "amusing them with his phrenological opinions of the different individuals." A century ago, the science of determining character by the conformation of the human skull— by feeling the bumps on one's head—was all the rage. As Captain Schlesinger wrote: "He [Lopez] was habitually observant of men in this point of view, and as the troops pressed upon him for his inspection of their heads he very freely gave his judgment, which was often received with much applause. To many he spoke in flattering terms, to others somewhat otherwise. It was rather a novel kind of military review, but everyone was anxious to pass under it."

Certainly if ever a bunch of men needed to have their heads examined, it was these recklessly courageous but wild and crazy filibusters who were to be so supremely misled into suffering and death.

About mid-afternoon the *Pampero* turned sharply in toward shore and entered the winding channel to a small harbor, the men tense and quiet, the only sound the rumbling and splashing of the paddle wheels. Suddenly the lookouts discerned two Spanish men-of-war at anchor in this sheltered port. Again the little steamer frantically wheeled around and at full steam ran from the surprised Spanish vessels. It soon outdistanced them as they pursued but they then sent news to Havana, so that the hue and cry became narrowed and channeled toward the west.

A bit farther down the coast, after dark, they headed in again and this time the mate of the *Pampero,* Mr. Fayssoux,[2] reconnoitered toward shore in a small boat which was spotted by the sentinels of a Spanish fort near Bahia Honda and hailed for identification. Fayssoux and his men silently and speedily rowed back to the *Pampero* which, with all lights out, was unseen, and then proceeded on westward again. This was the third time that day the steamer had headed directly into destruction and escaped, and General Lopez would have been sagacious to have heeded these warnings and turned about for home. But that stubborn leader was determined to land at all costs and his followers seemed to believe these narrow escapes were favorable omens. So on they went westward along the coast.

About ten o'clock that night a landing became imperative when the *Pampero* struck a coral reef near shore and stuck fast. Lopez immediately ordered a landing in the ship's boats. Some felt that the impressed pilot had purposely grounded them and wanted to shoot him. "The poor fellow was frightened half out of his wits" and especially so when "one of the men in the boat with him jokingly did fire his pistol over his head with pretended aim at him." But the

---

[2] A pint-sized fire-eater, a native of Missouri, he had served in the navy of the republic of Texas and on the *Creole* in the Cardenas expedition. Later he commanded William Walker's one-ship navy in Nicaragua with more skill and success than given to the land forces.

kindly General Lopez protected the hapless fellow for what was probably a natural accident and his life was spared. As they approached shore a fusillade of shots whistled harmlessly by the leading boat. A return fire dispersed the defenders, Creoles or Spaniards, who galloped off to spread the alarm. The men (about 450) and equipment were all ashore before dawn. General Lopez and his staff were the last to land, the General looking every inch the romantic revolutionary. Captain Schlesinger reported: "He was dressed in a white jacket and pantaloons, the former buttoning to the throat, with standing collar embroidered with a single star. He wore a red General's sash around his waist but no arms. Over his shoulder was slung a spy-glass in a leather case. . . . His countenance was all aglow with a subdued enthusiasm. In spite of his gray mustaches and beard, he looked almost a young man again. We were all struck with his noble aspect and fine bearing."

As he reached the shore he knelt and kissed the soil "of his 'beloved Cuba,' '*querida* Cuba.' These were his words of first salutation—alas! how soon were the same to be those of his last farewell." There were no crowds of enthusiastic Creoles, eager to enlist under the banner of freedom, to welcome the General and his men as they had been led to expect—and they never materialized. The greeting of shots as they rowed ashore, probably fired by natives, was typical of the hostility they encountered on all sides until the bitter end. But they were, at least, safely ashore and their morale soared for the time being.

In the meantime, the alert and energetic Captain General de la Concha in Havana was working shrewdly and swiftly to surround the landing party. His intelligence service in the States was far better than Lopez's in Cuba and he already knew that the invasion attempt would be made west of Havana before the filibusters had set a foot on shore. He had made his preparations accordingly and had stationed concentrations of troops in the threatened area which the local natives unquestionably knew about and which was probably the main reason for their lack of enthusiasm for the revolutionary cause. As soon as word of the true direction of the filibusters' ship was received, the man-of-war *Pizarro* (the same ship which had chased the *Creole* into Key West the year before) was loaded with troops and dispatched to land them near Lopez and cut off all chance of his receiving reinforcements or supplies by water. Concha then rushed orders to his garrisons in that area to converge and surround the unsuspecting invaders and this was effected almost as soon as Lopez reached shore. The Captain General was much pleased at developments. Lopez could not have walked into a better prepared trap.

But the filibusters were happily unaware of these sinister movements. In the morning, after a night of excitement and strenuous effort, Lopez decided to move his force inland about ten miles to a small village named Las Pozas which he could use as a base for operations. At the advice of his Hungarian chief of staff he then made the fatal blunder of dividing his men, and left the young Kentuckian and West Pointer, Colonel William L. Crittenden, with a force of 120 men to guard and to bring up later the supplies and equipment on the beachhead, while he led the remainder of his exhausted men on to this village. From then on everything went wrong as the lurking Spaniards moved in for the kill.

Lopez and his followers arrived at Las Pozas after a march in the overpowering summer's heat which left them completely fatigued and ravenous—for they had not slept nor eaten since the day before. They commandeered carts and oxen to send back to Crittenden for the large supply of reserve arms and ammunition; and then all turned to the finding of food and drink. Guards were stationed to protect property and these maintained discipline and complete order.

Next morning, around breakfast time, the Spaniards attacked. The filibusters formed at once and for two hours held off the enemy by the deadliness of their fire but refused to charge the enemy at a decisive time, by doing which, according to Captain Schlesinger, they might have won an overwhelming and decisive victory and changed the whole later unfortunate course of events. The whole battle lasted two hours under a broiling sun, and the final casualties to the three hundred-odd Americans were about twenty killed and twenty-five wounded while the Spaniards undoubtedly suffered heavier losses in a force of about four hundred men.

It was now obvious that an overwhelming number of Spaniards would soon close in on the little village and an immediate junction with Crittenden and the supplies was imperative. After that, Lopez planned to lead his combined forces into the mountains where they could organize and train and where he hopefully believed he would be reinforced by large numbers of Cuban volunteers. So, just after this battle, he sent about ninety men back along the road to the coast to find Crittenden and hasten him along.

This force soon ran into large numbers of Spaniards and all were forced back to rejoin Lopez's main command. The anxiety about Crittenden and the desperately needed supplies now became intense. Time was of the essence, for an immediate retreat to the mountains became less possible every minute; but without supplies, with what could they arm any native sympathizers who might join them? It was a nerve-racking wait under the burning sun and all could sense the ever-increasing build-up of the Spaniards in the surrounding silent brush and forest.

Finally, about midnight, a Captain Kelly and thirty-three of Crittenden's men arrived in camp. Their story was discouraging. Crittenden with his 120 men had started out that morning from the beachhead with the supplies loaded in two ox carts which moved at a snail's pace. They had come to within four miles of Lopez's camp when the Spaniards attacked them in force. Crittenden then made the same fatal mistake as had Lopez by dividing his small force, leaving Kelly and his men to guard the supplies while he led the remainder in a head-on charge against some of the attackers. The result was that the rest of the surrounding enemy at once fell on Kelly and he was separated from Crittenden. Kelly soon saw that a defense of the supplies by his small command was entirely hopeless and, his scouts reporting no trace of Crittenden's men who had disappeared, yelling at the charge, into the brush, he decided quite sensibly to join Lopez directly, which he succeeded in doing, guided by a native Negro, by advancing through the brush and thickets.

After Kelly's arrival all hope of seeing Crittenden again was abandoned. The supplies had been lost and there was no further sense in delay. The diminished band of liberators started at once toward the mountains. They had collected much clothing and ammunition which the repulsed Spaniards had left on the battlefield and these later sustained them. It was impossible to move their wounded and they were left behind with several Spanish wounded whom they had mercifully cared for after the battle in the hope that the enemy would reciprocate. It was a vain hope. The next day the advance guard of the Spaniards shot or bayoneted them to the last man except for two officers who farsightedly had committed suicide before the enemy's arrival. One of these was General Pragay, a Hungarian who had acted as Lopez's chief of staff.

Lopez and his men, exhausted from the daytime battle, staggered along a steep rough road for twelve miles until they halted to slaughter a cow for breakfast and to roast the fresh meat on their bayonets, which took the temper out of the steel and rendered many of them useless. They stumbled on that night by moonlight and in some way made an almost complete circle so that by morning, instead of arriving safely in the mountains to the south, they found themselves within three miles of their original landing place on the coast where there was a large force of Spanish soldiers. Their only chance then was a forced march and, leaving behind all the food, the weary and discouraged men straggled along all that day over the roughest sort of paths toward the interior mountains. Many men were lost and killed by their pursuers during that day of horror. The rough ground and the thorns and thickets tore the shoes of the survivors to bits and all were practically barefoot when they halted for the night.

From then on things went from very bad to much worse with, however, a few respites which only raised false hopes —and hope was all that sustained them. They wandered around in the back country almost constantly on the move, with no apparent purpose other than avoiding their pursuers, and with their strength daily diminishing as exhausted men fell to the ground or deserted in despair—usually to be killed immediately by the hostile natives. Somewhere along the way two Cubans joined the band—and these were the only recruits of the thousands Lopez had counted on; why these two should have enlisted under such a forlorn banner is unexplainable. The men's morale was further lowered when word came that the missing Crittenden and his men had been captured and all publicly executed in Havana. Occasionally they reached a plantation where the owner received them hospitably and furnished food and fuel, but always they moved on after a night's rest for fear their position would reach the Spaniards.

Finally, the inevitable second clash with the Spaniards occurred at the great coffee plantation of Frias which belonged to Lopez's wife and where the harried leader had hoped to find rest for his men. The Spaniards made a cavalry charge against the filibusters, strongly entrenched in a mango grove, and were bloodily repulsed by the deadly fire of the American sharpshooters, losing their commanding officer who was second only to Captain General de la Concha in rank. A great cheer arose for General Lopez as the enemy withdrew from the field, but the victorious filibusters did not linger on the spot and wearily turned again toward the heights.

Many of the surviving filibusters had thrown away their muskets, ammunition, and even some of their clothing during the exhausting marches of the previous days and now, when they reached the steeper paths of the mountains, others continued foolishly to lighten their burdens in this way despite their officers' frantic commands and pleas, for as Louis Schlesinger well noted, they might just as well have thrown themselves away as their arms. The night after the second battle a natural enemy greatly accelerated their ultimate destruction when a drenching, driving rainstorm soaked and impaired the remaining muskets (of which there were only about seventy-five left) and the ammunition. This left more than a half of the men helpless and simply an impediment to the others. But on they moved.

About this time the filibusters seemed to have developed doubts about Lopez's optimistic prediction that *mañana* they would join a strong band of Cuban insurgents or that the Spanish troops would desert in large numbers to their cause. Lopez was undoubtedly sincere but an extreme wishful thinker and his intelligence reports had been execrably unreliable. But he was an excellent officer, always bearing the worst hardships, and continually encouraging his followers by pats on the back and cheerful words which, unfortunately, were spoken in Spanish as he still knew but few words of English. In fact, the whole command was a sort of miniature but mobile Tower of Babel with Lopez and his staff conversing in Spanish, Magyar, German, and English. The men all knew that he was taking a bigger risk than any of them, since he was an outlaw condemned to death in Cuba and had absolutely no hope for mercy in case of capture. But they stuck to him, hoping against hope that some of his never-failing optimism would be fulfilled—and indeed, if Lopez could have landed in a more favorable spot and won important early successes, his belief in the natives' support might well have been justified, at least to some degree.

The continuous retreat went on and on along the mountain paths, the rain now falling most of the time and making the day's march a torture. As Louis Schlesinger wrote: "Our position was now a dreadful one indeed. . . . The rain seemed a concentration of forty days of deluge into two. . . . No pen could do justice to our sufferings through the terrible days that now ensued, and their more awful nights, in this savage mountain region. The cold during the nights was intense. The only slight degree of comfort from it we could get was standing huddled closely together, like sheep in a storm. The General had no other clothing than white linen. . . . We wandered about by day, but still found nothing edible in the savage and untrodden wastes of that dreadful mountain; not even fruits or palms. Exhausted by hunger, cold, wet, want of sleep, and for most of us loss of hope, stiff in every limb, and for the most part with bare, bleeding and swollen feet, there was our condition. . . ."

All order was lost, the remaining men, about 140 in number, struggling ahead as they pleased, most of them in rags, barefoot and without arms. About as many stragglers or deserters, who had struck out for themselves, wandered alone or in small groups aimlessly through the forests and brush. Lopez, at last seeing the hopelessness of it all, showed his real fineness of character by offering to surrender himself to the Spaniards in the hope of obtaining clemency for his followers. But his men had enough self-respect left to refuse this offer.

Finally, on August 23rd, less than two weeks after the landing, the end came. A body of Spanish cavalry suddenly charged upon the rear of the straggling column and scattered the filibusters in small groups in all directions, ruthlessly killing all those who were too slow to reach the protecting forests near the road or so ingenuous as to remain and beg for mercy. On the following day the Spaniards captured more of the dispersed filibusters hiding in the woods, and executed them to the last man. But the day after that orders reached the Spanish troops in the field to give quarter to all who might voluntarily give themselves up, and the filibusters surrendered in driblets as word of this clemency reached them, although a few wandered about in the mountains for as long as twenty days more, living on roots and plants. There was good reason for this act of mercy by Captain General de la Concha, for the execution of Colonel William Crittenden and his fifty men and the killing of all the wounded and overtaken stragglers of Lopez's command had been enough to surfeit the Spanish authorities, and certainly the lesson to future filibusters had gained tremendous publicity. There was no point in carrying these severe punishments any further and provoking extreme criticism from the outside world.

But Narciso Lopez, of course, was not included in this offer of mercy. Being a renegade Spanish officer he had already been posted as a traitor, and besides, because of his unusual charm of manner and ability to arouse confidence and enthusiasm, he was far too dangerous a man to spare. He was caught, about a week later, by the tracking blood-hounds of a party of Creoles who were all generously re-warded by the government. The local authorities treated Lopez and his men well enough and shipped them to Havana by water. There, on September 2nd, Narciso Lopez was publicly executed outside the city jail before an immense crowd of twenty thousand people. As a pronounced traitor he was denied the death of a soldier by shooting and was executed as a criminal by the Spanish method of the garrote. A large number of troops, horse and foot, surrounded a scaffold upon which the condemned general climbed escorted by priests and officials. After the last rites he spoke a few words to the crowd, then seated himself in the chair before an upright post from which projected a horizontal iron collar which could be tightened by a large iron screw from the rear. The Negro executioner adjusted the iron collar around his neck, gave a few quick twists to the iron turnscrew pressing against the back of his neck, and quickly strangled the gallant general. There were no demonstrations or disorders from the crowd, which was in marked contrast to its riotous behavior at the mass executions of Crittenden and his men a little over two weeks before.

Of the followers of Lopez who surrendered after the proclamation of clemency a few were freed at the request of influential friends in Cuba and the rest, about 160 in number, were shipped to the penal colony at Ceuta in Spanish Morocco under long sentences of hard labor in the quicksilver mines. Fortunately, Queen Isabella of Spain, probably at the request of President Millard Fillmore (the vice president who had succeeded President Zachary Taylor at the latter's death in July, 1850), granted the Americans among them a pardon soon after their arrival and these lucky men returned safely to the United States. Not so good was the fate of the Hungarians. The government of Austria-Hungary had no sympathy with these officers who had served in the movement for Hungarian independence in 1848 and made no efforts in their behalf. Some died under the hardships, some were eventually freed, and a few, including Captain Louis Schlesinger, escaped.

To complete this depressing account of failure we must now return to Colonel William Crittenden and his fifty men whom we left after their separation from Captain Kelly's detachment, which later joined Lopez. Crittenden's detachment had disappeared while charging a force of attacking Spaniards. They had run headlong into an ambush of sorts but had finally managed to cut their way through the surrounding Spaniards and for two nights had hidden miserably without food in the dense woods and brush. Finding all ways to Lopez blocked by strong forces of the enemy, they had eventually reached the coast where they put to sea in four small stolen boats with the hope of reaching Florida or Yucatan. When well at sea a Spanish man-of-war overhauled them and they surrendered as prisoners of war. This, of course, was while Lopez and his men were still at large and a threat to the authorities of Cuba.

As soon as Captain General de la Concha learned these conditions of surrender to the Spanish Navy (which had the traditional friction with the Army, as in all countries) against his recent and clear order of no quarter to any filibusters (or pirates, as he perhaps justly called them), he took immediate steps to nullify this agreement. He was chagrined that the Navy had not shot them out of hand and thus avoided all red tape and the excitement of an execution in Havana, and he at once ordered that all the prisoners were to be shot without a trial the morning after their arrival in Havana.

The sentence was carried out, on August 16th, before thousands of citizens of Havana, for word had traveled quickly through the city during the night. Colonel Crittenden, the leader, was shot first and alone. He was reported in the American newspapers (which probably romanticized this sad ending) as refusing to kneel or to be blindfolded and as saying in a clear voice, "A Kentuckian kneels to none except his God, and always dies facing his enemy!"

After Crittenden's execution the other Americans were brought forward in lots of six at a time, blindfolded, and forced to kneel with their backs to the firing squad which stood three or four yards behind them. Officers stood by the soldiers to deliver the *coup de grâce*, a shot in the head with a revolver to those not immediately killed. Some of the American newspapers reported that instead of this merciful shot, those who showed any life after each volley had their brains beaten out by the butts of muskets. It was also reported that the bodies of the executed filibusters were given over "to a bloodthirsty mob, composed of the lowest and vilest rabble, both white and black, of the city of Havana, who spat upon them, kicked them, and dragged them about by the heels. Many of the bodies were mutilated in the most horrible and shocking manner; the ears, noses, and other members being cut off and carried away by the brutal and frenzied mob, and exhibited in the streets and public houses of the city." [3]

Captain General de la Concha was a merciless man in his dealings with what he considered pirates but, good soldier that he was, it seems exceedingly doubtful if he would have allowed the mob to get out of hand to the extent described in the frenzied American press.

The only light touch in the whole ghastly, sickening, brutal business was an apocryphal story about one of these men.[4] The night before this mass execution the prisoners were given permission to write farewell letters to their families and friends. One poor devil could think of nobody in the whole world who would care if he lived or died. He was ashamed to be the only man in the crowd not writing a letter and determined to choose a friend; and realizing that the Spaniards would read all the letters, he decided he might as well pick a good one. So he wrote to Daniel Webster, the Secretary of State of the United States, and if the Spanish Governor wanted to execute an intimate friend of that august personage he would have to bear the consequences. His letter read:

Dan, my dear old boy, how little you thought when we parted at the close of that last agreeable visit of a week, which I paid you the other day, that within a month I should be 'cribbed, cabined, and confined' in the infernal hole of a dungeon from which I indite this. I wish you would send the Spanish minister

---

[3] Anderson C. Quisenberry, *Lopez's Expeditions to Cuba, 1850 and 1851.* Louisville, Ky., 1906, p. 94.

[4] Lawrence Oliphant, *Patriots and Filibusters.* Edinburgh and London, 1860, pp. 176-178.

a case of that very old Madeira of yours, which he professes to prefer to the wines of his own country, and tell him the silly scrape I have got myself into, if indeed it be not too late, for they talk of sending me 'to the bourne' tomorrow. However, one never can believe a word these rascals say, so I write this in the hope that they are lying as usual—and am, my dear old schoolmate, your affectionate friend.

According to the story, this joker was told to stand aside the next morning when his comrades were led to their deaths and was later shipped to Ceuta with Lopez's men whence he eventually returned safe and sound to the States.[5]

Never again until the Spanish-American War in 1898 did an organized group of Americans set aggressive foot on Cuban soil. After Lopez the Southern pro-slavery expansionists turned to diplomacy in their efforts to bring Cuba into the closed corporation of slave-holding states by purchase, and their efforts along this line were as energetic as they had previously been in the direct action of filibustering.

One would think that the unsuccessful results in Yucatan and Cuba would have cooled the ardor for filibustering in all other places as well, but the virus or germs of the disease seemed to have been wafted west and before long it broke out again with renewed virulence in California.

---

[5] Quisenberry doubts this story but says rumor had it that he was David Q. Rousseau, a bricklayer of Kentucky, who enlisted with Lopez at the age of twenty-four and afterwards served during the Civil War as a lieutenant in the Fifth Kentucky Infantry (Union) and in the Fifth Infantry U.S.A. However, there is no officer of this name listed in Heitmann's *Register of the United States Army*.

CHAPTER V

Filibusters for Flores and
Sorties into Sonora

EVEN in the same year (1851) in which Narciso Lopez was making his last and fateful foray into Cuba, the incurable contagion of filibustering had reached California. A band of about 250 men, described as "the flower of California's fighting men," was reported to have set sail from San Francisco on the steamer *Lightfoot,* financed and equipped by General Juan José Flores who was trying to regain the presidency and power in the little South American mountain republic of Ecuador. This group was said to have sailed south to Panama where it joined an expeditionary force of Spanish-American military adventurers and political adherents of Flores which was assembling there.[1]

The able and colorful Juan José Flores well deserves a few words of mention. Like Simon Bolivar a native of Venezuela, he had been one of Bolivar's top generals during the Wars of Liberation against Spain; in fact, next to Antonio

---

[1] Major Horace Bell, *Reminiscences of a Ranger.* Santa Barbara, California, 1927, p. 204 ff. This account was inaccurate although it was used by William O. Scroggs in his *Filibusters and Financiers.* New York, 1916, pp. 18-19. Its errors are shown following.

101

José de Sucre, he was probably the Liberator's favorite officer. After independence, General Flores had defended the original Republic of Colombia (then composed of the present countries of Panama, Venezuela, Colombia, and Ecuador) against a Peruvian invasion and, after defeating the aggressor, in conjunction with General Sucre, at the battle of Tarqui, he had been thanked "ten million times" by President Bolivar in a letter in his own hand. And it was to Flores that the disillusioned Bolivar wrote his anguished letter just before his death in 1830, which contained the much-quoted sentence, "He who serves a revolution plows the sea."

This letter rates a digression. The rest of it is not well known and it is just as gloomy as Bolivar's opinion about revolutions. In it he made six dire predictions about the futures of Democracy and America. Besides the one given above, which was No. 2, the others were: 1) America is for us ungovernable; 3) The only thing one can do in America is to emigrate; 4) This country will fall infallibly into the hands of frenzied mobs and later on pass into the power of petty tyrants of all colors and races; 5) After we have been devoured by every kind of crime and extinguished by ferocity, the Europeans will not deign to conquer us; and 6) If it were possible for a part of the world to return to primitive chaos—that would be the last period of America.[2] As may be guessed, none of these prophecies is inscribed on any of the countless monuments to the great liberator.

---

[2] This letter was written from Barranquilla, November 9, 1830 (Bolivar died the next month), and is now in the estate of the late Vicomtesse de la Villesbrune of Nice, France, a granddaughter of General Flores and a cousin of Mr. Frederick Stagg of Boston who showed the writer a photostat of the original.

Now all these pessimistic prognoses may seem to have nothing to do with a tale of American filibusters. But these predictions were exactly the beliefs upon which the theory of "Manifest Destiny" was based. The Latin American republics were supposed to be fast sinking into Bolivar's foretold anarchy, and apparently could only be rescued from this pit of despair by annexation, by one means or another, to the United States whose manifest destiny it was to lead these hapless countries out of the morass of misgovernment and on to the firm path of progress and prosperity.

But to return to General Flores, Colombia had been divided into three republics just before Bolivar's end, and Flores became the first President of its southernmost portion and is called the "Father of Ecuador." He remained as a conservative president, on and off, on a sort of rotation basis with the liberal Vicente Rocafuerte[3] until 1845 when a revolution sent him into exile where he remained, always attempting a comeback, until 1860 when he finally suc-

---

[3] The history books generally state that this rotation of office was dignifiedly agreed upon. Mr. Frederick Stagg (a great-grandson of General Flores) says, however, that Flores picked his successor in the following somewhat original manner. Rocafuerte, who came from a good Guayaquil family, had led an unsuccessful revolution against President Flores near the end of the latter's first term and had fled to the island of Puna in the estuary of the Guayas River. One of Flores' officers, a Colonel Gonzalez, captured him there and forcibly rolled him up in a mattress, tied around with a rope. Gonzalez then carried the outraged Rocafuerte in this bundle to Flores' headquarters in Guayaquil where he dumped it on the floor before the general and his staff and cut the rope. The benumbed and furious captive staggered to his feet and hysterically cursed his captors for this indignity but they were too weak from laughter over his ridiculous appearance to pay any attention. Finally, General Flores recovered himself enough to offer his bedraggled prisoner a drink and, after reasonable calm had been gained, he informed the mortified Rocafuerte that he had chosen him as his successor to the presidency of Ecuador. The writer much prefers this version which is bizarre enough to be completely true at that time and place.

ceeded in placing a conservative successor in the presidency of Ecuador.

The American leader of these California volunteers for Flores, according to this particular account, was an Alabamian named Aleck Bell, who had previously been a steamboat captain on the Tombigbee River in his home state, and who was said to have been "the handsomest man on the coast, near six feet high, as lithe as a Delaware and as graceful as a statue." He had left Alabama in a hurry after a little labor trouble with the crew of his steamboat. The men had struck for regular wages, which the financially harassed skipper had not been paying them, whereupon Aleck in some way persuaded them to go into the hold, battened down the hatches and went about his business on the river with a new crew. When the boat reached Mobile, several days later, the strikers were nearly dead from starvation. The local authorities failed to see the humor of this method of strike-breaking and Captain Bell took off for Texas, where he joined General Zachary Taylor's army and served through the Mexican War. After the peace, he gold-rushed to California with the other forty-niners, but, like the vast majority of those adventurous souls, failed to find his fortune in the setting sun. It was easy to recruit a force for filibustering from the disappointed and dead-broke backwash from the gold diggings and Aleck Bell gathered a hand-picked force to serve under General Flores.

According to Bell's story, the united expedition left Panama in a flotilla of two steam transports, convoyed by a small gunboat, which Flores was said to have purchased from the Peruvian government which had accorded him belligerent rights. They sailed up the Guayas River, silenced the defending shore batteries, and captured the city of Guayaquil. Thence, with his army greatly augmented by local volunteers, the general led his followers up the long, uphill road toward Quito, the capital, in the heart of the Andes mountains. On the march the American volunteers formed a distinct corps which camped separately each night away from the main army. Then:

One night there seemed to be a very unusual movement in camp. We could hear bodies of troops moving, men working in different directions, the rumble of artillery, for which we could in no way account until morning, when we found ourselves corralled by the whole army, with barricades and entrenchments in front of them, all facing inward toward us, horse, foot, and artillery. We were then informed that we, being more ornamental than useful, were to be disarmed, marched back to Guayaquil and shipped out of the country. Our military ardor had been very much damped by the tropical mists of the country, but this was too much; but still we bore it, because there was no way of getting around the thing. We were disarmed, marched under guard to Guayaquil and given a free passage to Panama, where we arrived destitute, disgusted and utterly surfeited with military expeditions.

Evidently the Ecuadorians had heard of the potential threats which an American corps could be to a Latin-American republic and they must have decided that, blood being thicker than water, it was better for both factions to effect a reconciliation and expel this dangerous foreign element in the early stages of the disease. The Americans, incidentally, were left to shift for themselves in Panama. Some later straggled back to California, including Aleck Bell who died in San Francisco in 1859.

Another and more credible account of this abortive filibuster can be found in the diplomatic correspondence of the
various Special Agents and Chargés d'Affaires of the United
States to Ecuador from 1845 on.[4] According to these letters
the American steamer *Quickstep* (instead of *Lightfoot*—
there must have been a near-translation in Spanish) arrived
at the island of Puna, just below the city of Guayaquil, in
the estuary of the Guayas River, in late May or early June
1852 (not 1851 as given in Aleck Bell's account). This
steamer was reported to have brought a group of forty
Americans from California to join a force which General
Flores was assembling on that island preparatory to attacking Guayaquil and which the United States Chargé d'Affaires, Courtland Cushing, reported to Secretary of State
Daniel Webster, on July 1st, was "plundering farms and vessels belonging to Ecuadorian citizens."

Mr. Cushing of Indiana resided in Guayaquil and he again
wrote Mr. Webster on August 1st, in high indignation, that
General Flores' fleet of six vessels had taken advantage of
the observance of our national holiday of July 4th by sneak-
ing up the river after dark amidst the fireworks and fire-
crackers being set off at a party at the chargés house, "when
many of the principal officers, lulled by the festivities of the
day, had no apprehensions of an attack" and proceeded "in
the most clandestine and assassin-like manner to attack the
City." During this bombardment, the outraged Mr. Courtland Cushing continued, "two 18-pound balls passed

---

[4] See William R. Manning, *Diplomatic Correspondence of the United
States: Inter-American Affairs, 1831-1860.* Vol. VI. Washington, 1935, p.
250 ff. Also *El Ecuador de 1825 a 1875, Por P.M.* Santiago, Chile, 1885, pp.
216-219.

through several rooms of my house one of them after killing my nearest neighbor Mr. Reina on his balcony, passed through my bedroom and parlor and lodged in an adjoining room." The next day the Flores fleet returned to the attack but finally sailed down the river where the general led his men ashore and eventually retreated southward to Peru. Later, in October, the Consul General of Ecuador informed our Department of State that certain American citizens had been with Flores in this unsuccessful attack and had returned to the United States to recruit more filibusters for another invasion under his command. This, however, was the end of any filibustering activities by Americans in Ecuador.

Aleck Bell's account was undoubtedly garbled in the telling for certainly Flores did not capture Guayaquil in either 1851 or 1852. The surrounding and subsequent deportation of the American volunteers by both sides of the contending Ecuadorians could possibly have taken place on the retreat to Peru but not on the way to the inland capital of Quito. But the chances are that Bell actually was a member of these filibusters, for Flores and his tale simply became twisted by word-of-mouth retelling.

★ 2 ★

The next filibustering expedition was a completely Gallic affair which, strangely enough, stemmed from California and not from France. The Apache Indians, those "tigers of the human species," had ravished the northwestern Mexican states for years, ever since the independence of that country from Spain in 1821. These terrible raiders had increased their depredations during the distractions of the war with the United States so that northern Sonora had become a veritable wasteland with ruined churches and haciendas, semi-deserted towns, and abandoned mines marking what had once been a thriving countryside under Spanish rule. Probably at no other time or in no other area in the Americas have the Indians ever wreaked such complete destruction and desolation. The authorities of Sonora finally resorted to desperate measures, such as offering high bounties for Apache scalps, but this backfired when unscrupulous American scalp hunters began cashing in on random Mexican scalps which bore similar coarse, black hair. The next plan was to induce foreign adventurers to garrison the frontier by offering them generous concessions to reopen the abandoned but extremely rich mines in this dangerous area. There was one definite restriction on this plan. No concessions were to be made to American gringos for the smarts and humiliations of the recent war, and the consequent loss of over a half the area of the Mexican republic to the victors was a very, very sore point indeed. And the lesson of nursing a nest of vipers (from the Mexican point of view), posing as loyal settlers in Texas, had been well learned. So, no Americans were desired under any circumstances but other foreigners, especially if Catholics, were, at the time, wanted to stem the horrible Apache raids which the Mexicans themselves seemed utterly unable to do.

Up in California, at this period, about every tenth man was a Frenchman and this Gallic element was a peculiar and important one. They mostly stuck to the towns and settlements where they ran restaurants and hotels and were very clannish, although they ranged in social status in their native land from the humblest peasant to the nobleman. Many were political exiles from the revolutions of 1848 and a large proportion had received excellent military training at home. They resisted assimilation and had no desire to become citizens, while the British, Germans and Scandinavians were quickly Americanized. The result was that they had little influence with the authorities and were often imposed upon in the mining camps and in the frontier towns. This naturally made them cliquish and discontented and many of them were ripe for recruiting for an adventurous project led by an ambitious countryman.

And such a leader appeared in San Francisco, in the autumn of 1851, in the person of the Marquis Charles de Pindray, a gay but penniless cavalier, who was described as "handsome, eloquent, full of courage and energy, with the strength of a giant and a skill at handling weapons which gained him a great reputation in France as a duellist, and had brought him all too many victims." These manly qualities naturally gave him an advantage in affairs of gallantry with the opposite sex in which the young nobleman was by no means remiss.

This ebullient young marquis had reached a colonizing agreement with the authorities of Sonora and in a short time he recruited a company of his fellow countrymen and raised enough funds to transport them by water to the port of Guaymas, Sonora, on the Gulf of California, where they arrived the day after Christmas, 1851. The Mexicans received them with demonstrations of the greatest joy, cheering, firing off salutes of musketry, and with music and dancing, for these were fellow Latins and Catholics, so different from the hulking, truculent, gringo heretics who had despoiled the mother country. Their stay in Guaymas became a continual round of banquets, fandangos, and general merrymaking which was possibly a poor preparation for the hardships ahead. The authorities provided the group with mounts, pack mules, ammunition and provisions, and promised to pay the men for their services.

From this hospitable city, de Pindray finally led his one hundred and fifty French followers and a number of Mexican volunteers to the interior town of Arispe. Their ultimate objective was the rich but abandoned mines of Arizona to the north but these they never reached. On their way they were met by John Russell Bartlett, of Providence, Rhode Island, the American commissioner in charge of the survey of the new boundary with Mexico as fixed by the peace treaty of 1848. Bartlett was a Yankee intellectual and humanist who later wrote well of his experiences but was utterly unsuited for anything as practical as a surveying job. His *Personal Narrative* for January 2, 1852 reads: "Soon after leaving [Hermosillo] we met a party of one hundred and fifty Frenchmen, who were emigrating from California. . . . They were a rather hard-looking and determined set of men with long beards and sunburnt faces. Each one carried a musket or rifle, besides which many had pistols." [5]

After being wined and dined at the town of Arispe the Frenchmen set out again, this time into the harsh and Apache-infested desert country to the north. Somewhere

---

[5] *Personal Narrative of Explorations and Incidents.* . . . 2 Vols. New York, 1854. 1, 472.

along the line in this adverse land friction developed between de Pindray and his followers and a mutual animosity arose between the French and the Mexicans. The leader became ill and in May, 1852, the expedition halted in a small hamlet where one morning the young marquis was found dead with a bullet hole in his head. Whether it was a suicide brought on by his illness and disappointment or whether he was murdered by a disgruntled follower was never determined. His followers turned back to the Mexican settlements but on their retreat they met a new French expedition bound for the mines, under the leadership of another nobleman, Count Gaston Raousset-Boulbon, and, joining together, the combined French forces proceeded on to some extraordinary adventures.

The count was a small man but his boyhood nickname of "Little Wolf" well described him. He had run through a fortune in France, had then served with the French forces in Algeria, and later, after unsuccessfully editing an extreme liberal newspaper in Paris, had arrived friendless and penniless in San Francisco. He, too, was attracted by the tales of the abandoned rich mines in Sonora. De Pindray was said to have invited him to join his expedition but the count evidently preferred to go it alone. He, however, took the precaution of first going to Mexico City where, with the help of the French Minister, he received encouragement from the Mexican government and private financial backing, with the understanding that this new syndicate was to share equally with de Pindray and his followers in the lands and mines they developed. It was assumed that this latter crowd had already arrived at the mines and commenced work.

111

Returning to San Francisco, he gained the support of the French Consul and quite easily enlisted 150 of his fellow countrymen. With these he landed at Guaymas at the end of May 1852, where he received as noisy and hearty a welcome as had de Pindray the previous autumn.

But alas for these Gallic adventurers, a new group, composed of native Mexicans, many of them high officials, now entered the field, and most potently included was Captain-General Blanco of Sonora, who commanded the military forces of the state and whose word was consequently law. Blanco proceeded to hamstring the Frenchmen with legal prohibitions and red tape from which there seemed no immediate escape. This enforced delay and the unhealthy summer climate of Guaymas, plus the natural dissipations of the idle men, had its ill effects on the well-being and morale of the group. Finally, they received permission to start north but only over a route which made no sense at all in its difficulty and indirectness. By this time the French adventurers were fed up with Mexican chicanery and they bolted for the northern mines by the shortest way. The furious Captain-General sent couriers after these disobedient colonizers, ordering them to obey all sorts of nuisance orders, but as these were received the eighty survivors of de Pindray's ill-fated venture arrived in camp as a reinforcement to the harassed Frenchmen; and by unanimous approval, with cheers and hurrahs, a complete defiance was dispatched to the overbearing Mexican general.

General Blanco then proclaimed the Frenchmen armed enemies of the government and the latter, deciding that they might now just as well go the whole hog, issued the usual *pronunciamento,* proclaiming independence, and raised the banner for an independent republic of Sonora in September 1852.

Then with swiftness and audacity the French count led his followers to attack Hermosillo (now the capital of Sonora). This was an incredible act. The city had twelve thousand inhabitants, and General Blanco commanded twelve hundred soldiers there, with artillery, behind adobe walls. The French numbered only 243 men and by every rule of warfare and common sense they should have been easily trounced and annihilated. But George Jacques Danton's dictum of *"De l'audace, et encore de l'audace, et toujours de l'audace"* carried the day and the spirit of that fiery orator must have smiled down on his fellow countrymen in this desperate assault in a strange and distant land. They captured the town, took it easily, and just missed seizing the bombastic General Blanco.

The trouble was that after this fantastic victory, the French filibusters had a tiger by the tail. Raousset and many of his officers and men were ill, possibly the natural reaction to the fleshpots of Guaymas mixed with the emotional strains of worry and the excitement of this phenomenal victory, and they also had a number of wounded. There was no chance of reinforcements arriving and the Frenchmen became heartily sick of the whole business and only wanted to retire in safety and with honor. So they offered to evacuate Hermosillo under a safe conduct back to Guaymas on the coast and to release all their Mexican prisoners in return for decent care for their own wounded whom they would have to leave behind. The Mexican authorities accepted these terms and twelve days after storming Hermosillo the French adventurers left the city and took the road to Guaymas. From that port most of them sailed, in December, 1852, back to California.

San Francisco gave Raousset a great ovation upon his return, for the Californians liked men of action and daring. Certainly he had achieved the greatest success of any filibuster up till that time. One would think he might have rested on his laurels and used his prestige to better his fortunes along conventional lines in California. But the bug of filibustering bit deep and the disease seemed incurable; suffering and hardship only seemed to increase the fever. And Raousset openly declared his resolve to return to Sonora with a suitable following at the first opportunity.

The next year, 1853, in Mexico, saw the perennial Antonio Lopez de Santa Anna (of the Alamo and Texas notoriety) back in the presidential chair and Raousset went to Mexico City in June to see him. The result was a contract in which the French count agreed to bring five hundred Frenchmen into northern Sonora to serve as a frontier guard against the Apaches with a stipulated regular pay for these volunteers. Later that year, in December, however, the Mexican President agreed to sell a large portion of this devastated frontier area to the United States, in what is known as the Gadsden Purchase, and took for himself a large *mordida*—a bite— of the sum paid to the Mexican republic. This sale, naturally, obviated the necessity of a garrison in that particular section. Whether Santa Anna realized in June the imminence of this real-estate deal is unknown, but anyway he canceled the contract with Raousset almost immediately after it was signed and, in its place, suggested that the count should become a naturalized Mexican and join his army. Raousset indignantly spurned this offer and both men flew into a rage which must have been a sight worth seeing, both being of fiery temperament. But the President held all the cards and the result was that the Frenchman fled for his life and Santa Anna proclaimed him an outlaw.

But the count returned safely to San Francisco where he found an American named William Walker busily preparing another filibustering expedition into Mexico. Raousset seemed not at all jealous of this new group and, though refusing to join the Americans, he apparently gave them the advice and counsel of an old-timer experienced at that sort of thing. Walker eventually became the giant of the filibustering profession, as we shall soon see; but his first venture, starting late that same year (1853) into Lower California, was as disastrous a failure as any of his predecessors' had been. Raousset, after all kinds of further negotiations with the Mexican government and interferences from the United States authorities, finally landed secretly in Guaymas with only eight followers in June 1854, where he joined a small number of Frenchmen who had preceded him there. This small group attempted to repeat their phenomenal victory at Hermosillo by attacking the Mexican garrison at Guaymas, but this was pressing their luck too hard and the prepared Mexicans withered a frontal attack by the filibusters with a devastating fire of shot and shell from behind adobe walls. Raousset then headed a last-ditch charge of desperation with twenty berserk followers but this was easily blown to pieces. The intrepid count literally had his hat and clothing cut to shreds by bullets and bayonets but miraculously was unharmed. Probably he would have been fortunate to die in the heat of battle for, soon afterwards, abandoned and betrayed by his followers and the French Vice Consul in Guaymas, he met death by a firing squad in the early morning of August 12, 1854. And thus the French attempts at filibustering also ended in the same old tragic pattern.

There was one more filibustering raid into Sonora which fits into this chapter geographically if not chronologically into the book as a whole. Its leader was an American, Henry A. Crabb, who had achieved fair success in California politics, having been elected to both branches of the legislature, but who had been an unsuccessful candidate for the United States Senate. Crabb was a native of Nashville, Tennessee, where he had been a schoolmate of William Walker's, and he continued this early friendship in California, where he was to some extent responsible for Walker's choice of Nicaragua as an objective of the greatest of all filibusters. Crabb had practiced law in Vicksburg, Mississippi, that citadel of Southern extremists, and had killed the editor of the local paper in a street gun fight. He was acquitted of a murder charge and soon thereafter joined a company of forty-niners to California; finally he settled in Stockton where he resumed the practice of law and entered politics. He married the daughter of a Manila (Philippine Islands) Spaniard, named Ainza, who had moved to Sonora with considerable wealth but had consequently been nearly ruined by the chronic disorders and confiscations of property in that almost anarchic Mexican state. The Ainza family had then migrated to California as refugees but despite their new

116

poverty they still had powerful connections in Sonora.

Crabb's wife's relations turned his attention to Sonora and their lost holdings in that state and in 1856 he, his wife and several members of her family joined a colonization company, largely made up of former Sonorans, which crossed the border into the ravaged Mexican state. They found the usual revolution going on and the "outs," led by an Ignacio Pesquiera who later set a new low in perfidy, begged Crabb to recruit a band of American volunteers for their cause, saying that they desired annexation to the United States and that these recruits would be a deciding factor to this end. Also, they very probably made all kinds of promises of future rewards to Crabb and his potential American followers. But soon afterwards the two warring factions made their peace and the Pesquiera crowd sought to cover up their traitorous invitation by loudly denouncing as *filibusteros* the very men they had invited to fight for their cause. But Crabb, excited by the prospects of much wealth and prestige which would undoubtedly be his if he could secure annexation of Sonora, and consequent comparative law and order in which to develop his rewards, hurried back to California to raise a body of filibusters which he organized early in 1857 under the outwardly innocuous name of the "Arizona Colonization Company."

These self-styled colonists went from San Francisco by sea to the port of San Pedro, near Los Angeles, where they equipped themselves with wagons, animals and supplies, and then took the difficult trail to Fort Yuma, facing the confluence of the Gila and Colorado Rivers. There the men were organized on a military basis and commenced a daily

routine of drill and guard duty. Most of the officers were
California politicians, of more or less prominence, but the
chief of artillery (of which they had none) was Thomas D.
Johns, originally from Pennsylvania, who had once been a
cadet at West Point and a lieutenant of regular infantry
during the Mexican War. Despite this new discipline many
of them got drunk and openly boasted that Sonora would
soon be theirs.

Word of all this soon trickled southward over the border
and caused the greatest excitement, for besides the two previous French forays into that state William Walker had
landed in Lower California in 1853 and proclaimed the independent republic of Sonora. That Walker's pretensions on
this, his first filibuster and a sort of practice run for his following very serious invasion of Nicaragua, verged on a
comic-opera affair and that he was soon driven out (with a
casualty percentage to his followers which could not have
been amusing to those involved) did not lessen the anxiety
of the Sonorans. Everything seemed to point to the eventual
annexation of the state to the United States and exaggerated
accounts of the maltreatment of their fellow countrymen in
Texas and California and the disallowance of many of the
old Spanish and Mexican land titles by the gringo courts did
not enthuse the Sonoran property owners toward annexation. Also, the loss of over half the area of the original Mexican republic to their northern neighbor by conquest and
the all-too-often arrogant and lawless behavior of transient
gringos had not endeared the United States to the average
Mexican. So they were alarmed and apprehensive at the
incursion of any new armed and organized band from the

north. And, of course, the now reconciled Pesquiera faction were worried lest their previous disloyal machinations with Crabb should come to light.

Crabb must have realized this obvious hostility and tried to placate it by a letter to the prefect of the Sonoran town of Altar whom he wrote from the village of Sonoita, just over the boundary, where he arrived with his men from Fort Yuma toward the end of March 1857. His words in this missive, however, seem more bombastic than conciliatory and, in effect, it appeared a veiled threat. He wrote that he had entered Sonora with a hundred followers—with nine hundred more to follow—"with positive invitations from some of the most influential citizens" with the purpose "of finding most happy firesides with and among you." His intention was to offend no one and he had made "only pacific proposals." It was true they were well armed but this was usual for all people traveling through Apache land. But, Crabb continued, he was surprised to find the officials were "collecting a force to exterminate me and my companions," and had "given orders to poison the wells, and that you are ready to employ the vilest and most cowardly weapons." In a crescendo of indignation Crabb then hurled the warning that "if blood is to flow, with all its horrors, on your head be it, and not on mine," and concluded by stating that he and his followers would go wherever they wanted to and would "act according to the dictates of natural law and self-preservation."

This defiance did not please the higher-ups in the Sonoran hierarchy and it must have especially concerned Crabb's former friend Ignacio Pesquiera, at whose invitation he had promoted the whole expedition, and who was now trying to keep his skirts clean. That perfidious schemer had become the "Substitute Governor of the State and Commander in Chief of the forces on the frontier" and he now let out a counterblast which reached such heights of Latin-American rodomontade that it is worth quoting in large part. It went:

FREE SONORIANS: TO ARMS ALL OF YOU

The hour has arrived which a short time since was announced to you, in order that you might prepare yourself for the bloody contest in which you are now about to enter.

You have just listened to the most explicit declaration of war which, in that arrogant letter, is made against us by the leader of the invaders. What reply does he merit? That we march to meet him.

Let us fly, then, to chastise, with all the fury which can scarcely be restrained in hearts full of hatred of oppression, the savage filibuster who has dared, in an evil hour, to tread on the national territory, and to provoke—madman!—our anger.

No pity, no generous sentiments for that rabble!

Let them die the death of wild beasts, who, trampling under foot the law of nations, and despising the civil law and all social institutions, are bold enough to invoke as their only guide the natural law, and to ask as their only help the force of brutes!

Long live Mexico! Death to the filibusters!

The oncoming Americans continued blithely on their way southward, probably ignorant of this fiery proclamation. It would have paid them, as a matter of military common sense, to have marched cautiously and in some kind of order. Instead of that they were straggling all over the road when they were ambushed in the morning of April 1st (appropriate in a macabre way) just outside the town of Caborca near Point Lobos on the Gulf of California. Young Johns's

120

flunking out of West Point is perhaps understandable. The Americans closed their ranks and rushed on into the town plaza exchanging shots with the concealed enemy. There, instead of seizing the church, always the best building for defense, they rushed into a row of adobe houses directly opposite, having suffered twenty-one killed and wounded during this running fight. Some hours later, realizing their inferior position, Crabb led a group of his men in an assault on the church, which the Mexicans had occupied, and attempted to blow open its doors with a keg of gunpowder. This attack was repulsed; several of the Americans were killed and some, including Crabb, were wounded. After that they were tightly besieged until April 6th when the besiegers set the roof of one of their sheltering houses on fire with a burning arrow shot by an Indian. The besieged Americans tried to blow off the burning thatch by exploding a keg of gunpowder in the room below but this only destroyed more of the house than the roof and gagged the exhausted defenders with suffocating fumes. This was the last straw and the disheartened Crabb asked for terms of surrender.

This was a fatal mistake and against the better judgment of his more experienced men. In the months just preceding, William Walker and his right-hand officer, Charles Frederick Henningsen, had often been in even more desperate straits in Nicaragua and had fought themselves out by audacity. But Crabb seemed to rely more on his heart than his head. The commander of the besieging Mexicans, standing in the belfry of the church, carried on a shouted midnight parley with a Spanish-American brother-in-law of Crabb's and promised the Americans a fair trial. When asked how the

wounded would be treated the Mexican replied that he had
a good physician who would care for them.

Crabb blindly accepted these terms. The Americans, leaving their arms, walked, one by one, across the road to the
church where they were bound with ropes and taken to the
local barracks. Two hours later a sergeant read an order to
them in Spanish which decreed their deaths at sunrise by a
firing squad. This was carried out in the early dawn near
the cemetery. They were shot in groups of five to ten and
their executioners became so unnerved at this callous butch-
ery that at first they wounded more of the condemned than
they killed, and the writhings of these dying men on the
ground made their aim progressively worse. The Americans
then were forced to stand at a closer distance with their
backs toward their executioners, and the shaking and nause-
ated firing squad finally completed its ghastly work. Crabb
was reserved for a solitary execution at the last. He was tied
with his face to a post and his hands above his head. A
hundred shots were said to have been poured into him as
his limp body hung by his bound hands. His head was then
cut off, placed in a jar filled with vinegar, and exhibited as
a trophy of victory over *los filibusteros Americanos* to the
exulting natives.

The only American spared was a fourteen-year-old boy
named Charles Edward Evans whom the Mexican commander took into his house as a servant until the American
Vice Consul at Mazatlan finally gained his release; and it
was from this boy that the details of this sickening affair
were learned. Young Evans swore that his older comrades
surrendered on the Mexican promise of a fair and impartial

trial and good care for their wounded. He declared that after the mass execution, their naked bodies were left unburied; the Mexicans boasted that "their hogs would fatten on the carcases of the Yankees"; and "the stink arising from the dead bodies was nauseating in town; and that the presence of the hogs was unbearable from their contact with carrion; and that he was shown the gold taken from the teeth of some of the Americans, and that he was also taken to see the head of Mr. Crabb, which was lifted from an earthen jar filled with vinegar."

The victorious Mexicans next captured and executed in the same manner a small party of sixteen more Americans which was following Crabb on the road to Caborca; and then finished the business by shooting four additional men who had been left behind ill in a ranch house just over the boundary line in the United States, near the Mexican village of Sonoita.

However, another small party of twenty-six men, coming to join Crabb, mostly escaped with their lives by refusing to trust any Mexican promises of mercy. Captain Granville H. Oury, later a delegate from Arizona to the first Confederate Congress in 1861, led this group which reached the outskirts of Caborca just before Crabb's surrender. The Mexicans made them the same offers of mercy but these men knew better than to listen and, turning around, they fought their way back to the boundary line with the loss of only four men. This, of course, is exactly what Crabb should have attempted.

The Mexicans justified this devilish Caborca massacre by saying the Americans had surrendered unconditionally, but even if this were true it would not justify the omission of some kind of a trial. It was simply an outrageous case of unrestrained lynch law, very probably instigated by the Pesquiera faction to cover up their earlier treasonable plottings with Crabb. They knew that dead men tell no tales. John Forsyth, the United States Minister to Mexico, made strong protests to the Mexican government and called for an investigation, but the mañana spirit and internal disorders in that republic caused the whole affair to become bogged down in the interminable red tape and delays of Latin-American diplomacy and nothing was ever done about it.

It should be said, in fairness, that the Mexicans had shown great forbearance with previous filibusters, at least with the French forays, and possibly the time had come for drastic action to stop these raids which were at best a nuisance and at worst might have become a real danger to Mexican sovereignty. But, of course, the French never were a real threat, whereas the gringos were always a danger as they had so often proved, and their past successes had goaded the Mexicans to a point of hysteria which burst forth in this dreadful mass slaughter. And remnants of this feeling still exist, for in 1926 a plaque was placed on the front of the Caborca church dedicated with "humble homage of gratitude" to "the defenders of their country who defeated the North-American filibusters"; and commemorative services are held in that town at every anniversary of this victory.

CHAPTER VI

Pierre Soulé in a Spanish China Shop

To BACKTRACK and digress from the direct-action fili-busters to the diplomatic efforts made to buy Cuba from Spain, shortly after Narciso Lopez's debacle, we run head on into an extraordinary character, Pierre Soulé of Louisi-ana, U. S. Minister to Spain, who certainly did not win friends or influence the right people in Madrid, but who, judging from the accounts of his contemporaries, was para-doxically enough a man of unusual personal charm and mag-netism. When earlier serving as a United States Senator from Louisiana, he was described as the most brilliant ora-tor of that forensic body (this, of course, was after the hey-day of Henry Clay, Daniel Webster, and John C. Calhoun) and as a man of delicate features, with eyes and hair of a dark, rich color, and with a grace of manner and expression which typified a type of masculine beauty peculiar to the South. Fredrika Bremer, the famous Swedish novelist and traveler, wrote "that flowery, beautiful Louisiana could not have sent to Congress a more worthy representative. . . ."

This masculine siren, however, was not a native son of fair Louisiana but a Frenchman who had come to the United

States in his twenty-fifth year. He had soon blended into the Creole atmosphere of New Orleans and then had steadily risen through his abilities as a lawyer, financier and orator (and, also, possibly because of his marriage to a local Creole belle of an influential family) until he became the acknowledged successor to John C. Calhoun in the Senate as the leader of the extreme states rights faction.

Soulé's early French background is interesting because of the later complications which it seemed to have caused. He was born in the French Pyrenees in 1801, the son of a brilliant Napoleonic officer, and was earmarked by his parents for the Church; but the boy rebelled in his teens and turned to the law and to republican views in his politics. He joined various liberal organizations and wrote for republican publications which were strongly opposed to the reigning Bourbons, with the result that he was arrested and sentenced to prison in 1825. Escaping, he finally reached the United States by way of England and Haiti and, landing in Baltimore, he worked his way inland to stay for a while with Andrew Jackson at his Hermitage near Nashville, Tennessee; shortly afterwards he acted as a gardener for the Dominican monks at their monastery in Bardstown, Kentucky, to repay them for their kindness to him while ill. Thence he went to New Orleans and his subsequent rise to success and fame.

Soulé gradually became one of the leading lights of a radical faction in the Democratic Party called "Young Democrats" who were extreme pro-slavery men and advocates of its expansion under the philosophy of Manifest Destiny. The more conservative members of the party were referred to by this group as "Old Fogies" and the Young Democrats were as aggressive as their youthful title implied. The acquisition of Cuba as another slave state for the Union was the immediate objective of these determined and dedicated young men and quite naturally they had supported Narciso Lopez's filibusters into Cuba by deed and word on every possible occasion, with Pierre Soulé doing a manful part on the floor of the U. S. Senate. After Lopez's complete failure, Pierre Soulé seized every opportunity publicly to demand the acquisition of Cuba, by purchase if possible but by force if absolutely necessary. The Whig administrations of Zachary Taylor and his succeeding vice president, Millard Fillmore, paid little attention to these insistent proposals, but they disturbed the Spanish government as they were conscientiously reported to Madrid by Señor Calderón de la Barca, its Minister in Washington—and, to put it very mildly indeed, Pierre Soulé was most certainly not considered a friend of Spain.

Then the wheel turned and the incredible happened. The Democrats won the Presidential election of 1852 and the successful candidate, Franklin Pierce of New Hampshire (a Southerner in sympathy if not in geography), found himself in the White House with a heavy political debt to Pierre Soulé for his active support during the election campaign. There was talk of rewarding the brilliant Louisianan by a cabinet appointment and when this was found impossible because of other commitments, he was considered as our minister to Russia; but the Imperial Government at St. Petersburg made it very plain that it wanted no man there with such extreme republican views. France was out of the question because of Soulé's former subversive activities

127

which grated on the new emperor, Napoleon III, as much as it had on his Bourbon predecessors. Great Britain had been promised to the more influential James Buchanan and so the only important post left was that as minister to Spain. It was an absolutely mad choice and the fiery Soulé proceeded to aggravate a very bad situation indeed.

To begin with, on the night before he sailed, a farewell send-off was given to him by the exiled Cuban revolutionaries living in New York and hundreds of their sympathizers. These people assembled in Fulton Street and marched up Broadway behind the music of Dodsworth's Band to the New York Hotel where Mr. Soulé and his family were staying. The United States flag and the flag of the independent republic of Cuba (the same as carried by Narciso Lopez) were borne aloft at the head of the procession, but the striking features were illuminated transparencies which bore such delicate sentiments as "Cuba must and shall be Free," and one in particular which, turning to verse, read:

> The Antilles Flower
> The true key of the Gulf
> Must be plucked from the Crown
> Of the Old Spanish Wolf.

As the ruler of Spain was young Queen Isabella II, a corpulent woman with eczema who was very sensitive about her appearance, the last line must have been singularly offensive to her when the reports of the Spanish agents in New York arrived. As a matter of fact, she took it very well indeed, as she did all of the later extraordinary gyrations of Mr. Soulé in Madrid.

When the parade reached the Soulés' hotel, the pride of

Louisiana came out on a balcony and made a fiery speech about the wrongs of Cuba and closed with a peroration in which he declared that America controlled the fate of the Old World and should act accordingly. The band played "Hail Columbia" and "Yankee Doodle" and midst wild cheers and hurrahs the Soulés retired, the demonstrators marched back down Broadway, and the Spanish agents went home to write their reports. It was an absolutely wild send-off for the delicate mission of Mr. Soulé, whose prime purpose was to obtain Cuba from Spain by purchase in a tactful and diplomatic manner.

With Soulé were his charming Creole wife, née Armantine Mercier of New Orleans, and his son Nelvil, who soon proved to be a hot-headed chip off the old block. The family landed in France and spent some time shopping and sightseeing in Paris where father especially enjoyed himself, for he was still on the French books as a fugitive from justice but, of course, now enjoyed diplomatic immunity from the political sins of his youth. The French secret service glowered at him and trailed him about the city but Mr. Soulé was unperturbed and enjoyed himself immensely with a marked air of independence. Finally the Soulés reached Madrid in October 1853, about six months after the official appointment.

The Spanish court was the most conservative and hidebound court in all Europe—and also probably the most corrupt. Ferdinand VII had come back to the throne after the defeat of Napoleon and the ousting of the French emperor's brother Joseph, who had ruled for a while by the grace of French bayonets. Incidentally, it was during all the confusion of the Napoleonic Wars and their aftermath that the Spanish colonies in the Americas had won their independence. Ferdinand died in 1833 and left his crown to his three-year-old daughter Isabella, with her mother, María Christina, as regent. This was contrary to the old Salic law forbidding a female succession and the Conservatives rebelled to place Carlos, the King's younger brother, on the throne. Then came the bloody Carlist Wars and almost-anarchy, but somehow young Isabella won out and became full ruler at the age of thirteen in 1843. The Queen Mother had mostly distinguished herself during these tense years by a series of scandalous amours, culminating in a marriage to a young soldier of her guard, and by her reckless financial profligacy. It proved to be a case of "like mother—like daughter" and Isabella despite her obesity and eczema soon started on a long line of lovers which finally ended with a terrific affair, years later, with the sulphurous General Daniel Edgar Sickles,[1] the one-legged United States Minister to Spain, after our Civil War.

To absorb the onslaught of the fire-eating Pierre Soulé the Spanish government had recalled its Minister to the United States, Don Angel Calderón de la Barca, and promoted him to be Minister of Foreign Affairs on the rather sensible theory that he had had considerable experience with Americans and would be able to handle this aggressive exponent of get-Cuba-at-any-price. De la Barca was an able man but his main support was his wife, an ineffably winning and clever woman whose *Life In Mexico* is one of the most entertaining books of travel ever written and a classic of

[1] Dan Sickles had crossed the Atlantic with the Soulés on his way to become secretary of the legation in London under James Buchanan.

its kind.[2] Madame (why not Señora nobody seems to know) Calderón de la Barca was a Scots girl who had taught school in the United States before meeting her Spanish husband. When Spain finally recognized the once jewel of her colonial empire as the new republic of Mexico, Calderón de la Barca was sent as the first Ambassador of the mother country and it was during his stay there that his wife wrote of her experiences in that land.

To everyone's astonishment and relief Pierre Soulé behaved with great discretion and tact after his arrival—at least just long enough to instill a false confidence in the diplomatic circles of Madrid. Then the hot-headed Louisianan sent a letter to the Queen in which he declared that Russia and the United States were the only nations in the world of any real importance; "everything else was rotten (*pourri*) and that all other nations must, for their safety, seek an alliance with one or other of these Leviathans." [Soulé seems an unwitting prophet.]

After this rather brash prediction of the future glory of the two great frontier countries of the world, Soulé's son Nelvil stepped up the excitement considerably by making a scene at a grand ball given by the French Ambassador, the Marquis de Turgot. It seems that young Soulé overheard the Duke of Alba, one of the grandees of Spain, whose wife was a sister of the French Empress Eugénie, remark to certain bystanders that his mother, Mrs. Pierre Soulé, a ravishing Creole beauty who "was positively *la reine du bal*," bore a resemblance, in her evening gown, to Marie of

---

[2] Mme. Calderón de la Barca, *Life In Mexico* (New York, 1931). This modern edition was sponsored by the Junior League of Mexico City.

Burgundy, the dissolute wife of Louis X. The two Soulés
bitterly resented this snide remark and converging on the
Duke, the father gave His Spanish Grace a push which
nearly floored him and certainly upset his dignity. Nelvil,
the son, followed this up with a challenge to a duel which
was fought soon afterwards with heavy, long Spanish
swords. This duel lasted for half an hour until both con-
testants were exhausted but fortunately nobody was hurt;
and it would seem that the honor of the Soulé family had
been upheld, particularly as young Nelvil had been forced
to fight with the choice of weapons of the challenged duke.
As duels in America were almost always fought with pistols,
fencing being a comparatively neglected art, young Nelvil
Soulé may be said to have acquitted himself with considerable credit in holding his own in this encounter.

If the matter had been allowed to rest there all would
probably have been well, but Pierre Soulé for some reason
was not satisfied with the result and proceeded to make
trouble and complications by challenging his host of that
fateful evening, none less than the French Ambassador,
the Marquis de Turgot himself. As the French influence
at the Spanish court was paramount at that particular time,
it was certainly not a master stroke of diplomacy. There
were undoubtedly many hidden reasons for this astonishing
challenge. De Turgot was from a noble family of the old
Bourbon aristocracy whereas Soulé came from simple stock
and had been exiled from France by the last of the Bourbons. Very probably de Turgot had showed a prejudice
against Soulé from the start by a series of petty slurs and
slights, each in itself too insignificant to be formally noticed

but in their aggregate galling to an extreme. Soulé had been unpopular before his arrival because of his stand on Cuba, and de Turgot must have continually added to this prejudice, with the other diplomats taking their cues from him as the most influential member and *doyen* of the diplomatic corps in Madrid. Probably the affair at de Turgot's house was the final straw that broke his patience. Anyway, this time a duel was fought with pistols and Pierre Soulé placed a well-aimed shot in the French Ambassador's knee (which was his reported intention before the duel) which took the representative of the Emperor Napoleon III out of circulation for a long time and, in fact, crippled him for life.

After this startling affair the Soulés were sent to Coventry in Madrid society but this ostracism did not faze the indefatigable Pierre. He continued to call on the Queen and her mother, who did not share the prevailing Francophile sentiments of their court. And he spent many evenings tête-à-tête with the Queen Mother, Christina, and was reported to have worked out a deal for the purchase of Cuba in which the United States would pay a bankrupt Spain 120 million dollars for the island with a guarantee to preserve all Spanish rights, with certain privileges to Spanish shipping, and very special privileges to Christina's huge properties there. He must have stood equally well with Queen Isabella, for one day he crashed into her reception room leading a visiting American gentleman who was not in the prescribed formal dress for the occasion straight past the outraged court functionaries, who protested that nobody in all history had ever been received in such plebeian garb, and presented his fellow countryman to the Queen who, the visitor reported, was all affability to the mercurial Soulé.

She wore [reported this American] a black dress very décolletée, and the charms which it concealed were evidently of ponderous proportions. Upon her hands, which are very large, and which looked swollen, she wore lace mitts, not gloves, leaving the fingers bare. Her whole skin was red, and had the appearance of being affected by some cutaneous disorder. . . . I certainly did not fall in love with her Majesty at first sight.[3]

This American visitor also wrote that he found Soulé confident of accomplishing the purchase of Cuba while indignantly denying any intention of bribing the Spanish Cortes to obtain a favorable vote. Soulé told him, however, that if he had a fund of $500,000 he would like to lend it to certain members of that legislative body who were in financial distress. But his plan to alleviate the hardships of the Spanish legislators was not approved in Washington and the lack of this early lend-lease for impoverished Iberian politicians may have been a major factor in his ultimate failure.

About this time, Madame Calderón de la Barca wrote a semi-anonymous book, *The Attaché in Madrid*, which was published in New York in 1856. The author was purported to be a young German diplomat and the book to have been translated from the German. She was, of course, skating on thin ice, since her husband was the Minister of Foreign Affairs. In this delightful book she described the life of Madrid and, under her cloak of anonymity, rather archly wrote of her elderly husband at a reception: "I also saw

---

[3] Maunsell B. Field, *Memories of Many Men and of Some Women*. New York, 1874, p. 76.

Calderón de la Barca, who seems the oldest member of the cabinet; has white hair and whiskers, and a peculiarly good face."

Her comments on Pierre Soulé were that he was "a red-hot democrat, whose late speeches in his own country, in favor of the annexation of Cuba, have naturally excited a vast amount of prejudice against him, in this. It seems to us a strange nomination on the part of the President of the United States." But her personal impression of him seems very fair. She wrote:

He has a very remarkable countenance; dark, deep-set eyes; his hair cut after the fashion of the ancient French republicans. He is very polished in his manner, and speaks well—slowly, in rounded flowing periods. As the French say, *il s'écoute en parlant*. He seems very desirous to make himself agreeable, but is, perhaps, somewhat too confident of his own powers.

Another feminine reaction to Soulé was that of the Hon. Mrs. Edward Twisleton, born Ellen Dwight of Boston, a niece of Mrs. George Ticknor, who had married an Englishman and visited Madrid with her husband during a tour of the Continent. She was a gifted, attractive woman of wealth, position and intellect, and one night she sat next to Pierre Soulé at dinner. This happened to be the first time the Soulés had been invited out after the notorious duel with the French Ambassador and Ellen Twisleton was "much struck by the fine head and splendid, flashing eyes of the gentleman. . . ." She continued: "We had an immense deal of conversation; he seems to be not only a democrat, but a demagogue, evidently a high-tempered and very excitable man. . . ." She thought there was some excuse for

135

young Nelvil Soulé's duel with the Duke of Alba because of the youth's extreme sensitiveness about his mother's appearance; but none whatsoever for his father's with the French Ambassador, and decided "it was a piece of bad temper on Soulé's part, for which the unfortunate host pays by being lamed for life. . . ." [4] And she concluded that Soulé's ostracism was on the whole well deserved.

But alas for all Pierre Soulé's hopes and castles in Spain! Circumstances broke against him. Just at this crucial time the authorities of Havana seized an American steamer, the *Black Warrior,* for certain technical violations of the customs regulations of that port. The steamer had been touching at Havana for a long time, always ignoring, with the tacit consent of the sensible port authorities, an irritating and senseless rule about the declaration of cargoes in transit. This minor violation harmed nobody and facilitated the ship's clearance. However, a new and eager Governor General decided to do the usual new-broom sweeping and, discovering the technical evasions of the port rules by the *Black Warrior,* he high-handedly seized the ship. One thing led to another and before long the two countries were on the verge of war over this incident. Seeing that the hopes of a friendly real-estate deal had evaporated in the heat of this dispute, Soulé then tried to use mailed-fist and big-stick methods and to frighten the Spaniards into making the sale of Cuba as a way to a peaceful solution. While both governments were blasting each other with threats and bellicose dispatches, Soulé added considerably to the general

---

[4] *Letters of the Hon. Mrs. Edward Twisleton Written to her Family.* Edited by Ellen Twisleton Vaughan of Boston. London, 1928, p. 174.

tension by publicly consorting with members of the subversive Spanish republican movement and other people in the bad graces of the government, probably on the theory that this would frighten the poverty-stricken monarchy into making a deal before it was supplanted by these republicans with American encouragement and aid.

The climax to it all came when he met with James Mason, our Minister to France (afterwards the Confederate agent to Great Britain) and James Buchanan, the Minister to Great Britain, to publicly issue with them the famous Ostend Manifesto in October 1854. This was the high note of the school of Manifest Destiny and Southern imperialism. It declared in effect that the United States should buy Cuba at once and that by this sale "the interests of Spain would also be greatly and essentially promoted" because the purchase money could put that near-bankrupt country on its financial feet and effect many internal improvements. Then it went on to say that "if Spain, dead to the voice of her own interests, and actuated by stubborn pride and a false sense of honor, should refuse to sell Cuba to the United States . . . then, by every law, human and divine, we shall be justified in wresting it from Spain if we possess the power."

Certainly no more untactful statement was ever issued by responsible diplomats and the repercussions were enormous. The United States Department of State repudiated it completely, the Spanish Cortes overwhelmingly voted against even considering the question of Cuba's sale, and Pierre Soulé, recognizing at last the hopelessness of his mission, resigned his ministership in December 1854 and returned home. But despite the adverse and cumulative criticisms since, the Ostend Manifesto was forthright and American. If it had received the proper amount of backing from Washington it just possibly might have worked. Certainly the purchase of Cuba would have spared both countries the later Spanish-American War, and Spain would have had the money without the headaches and the humiliations of her eventual defeat. Its effect on the United States would have been to strengthen the South, and Cuba might just possibly have been the factor to tip the scales for a Confederate victory in the impending Civil War.

Pierre Soulé returned to resume his law practice in New Orleans. He became a supporter of William Walker in Nicaragua and visited him there during his short period of glory; later he successfully defended him in the United States courts against charges of violating our neutrality. He was against secession but went with the Confederacy and opposed the military rule of Benjamin (Beast) Butler in New Orleans. For this he was arrested and sent to New York and Boston, but fled to Nassau and Havana (some irony there), ran the federal blockade and tendered his services to President Jefferson Davis in Richmond; but the latter was rather hostile and only made him an honorary brigadier general without any chance at active service. After the peace Soulé joined ex-Senator William M. Gwin in an unrealized project to settle Confederate veterans in the Mexican state of Sonora and died a few years later in 1870.

One other attempt was later made to buy Cuba from Spain. This came after the Civil War, after the slavery issue had been settled once and for all, and it was made during the Republican administration of President Ulysses S. Grant so that the desire to obtain the island was solely for its economic and strategic advantages. The United States minister who again tackled this delicate problem was the fiery Daniel Edgar Sickles.

Dan Sickles was a native New Yorker who, while a Democratic congressman in Washington, had shot and killed Philip Barton Key, son of the writer of "The Star Spangled Banner," in 1859 for having an illicit affair with his young wife, the daughter of an Italian music teacher. He was acquitted, after a sensational front-page trial, on the plea, used for the first time, of aberration of mind. Afterwards he became reconciled to his straying wife but she soon died. At the outbreak of the Civil War Dan Sickles organized the New York Excelsior Brigade and led it, as colonel, in the Peninsula Campaign. Later, as a major general, he was credited with stopping Stonewall Jackson's victorious advance at Chancellorsville. At Gettysburg, in command of the III Corps, he defended the two Round Tops against Longstreet's onslaughts but lost half of his men and his own right leg in the bloody, swirling fighting. In 1869 he was appointed Minister to Spain with instructions to reopen negotiations for the purchase of Cuba, for which the Grant administration was said to be willing to pay as high as $250,-000,000. In this he failed, as had Pierre Soulé.

Queen Isabella had been driven into exile by a revolution when Sickles arrived in Madrid and was living over the French border in Biarritz with her latest lover, an Italian opera tenor (her flagrant amours even exceeded those of her mother). Spain was bankrupt and in chaos, with a military junta attempting to rule the country and find a suitable king to replace the erring Isabella. Dan Sickles had met her years before, when he was secretary to James Buchanan at the legation in London, while on a trip to Madrid when Pierre Soulé was Minister, and a spark had been ignited between these two kindred souls. He now went to call on her and this smoldering mutual attraction quickly broke into flames. He found her fat but generous and good natured and a pleasant anodyne to the depressing memory of his own marriage, and she saw in the hardened, one-legged fire-eater a masculinity lacking in the Italian singer, who was quickly sent packing while Dan Sickles moved in. They openly lived together in Paris, which was not exactly a propitious place from which to conduct the delicate negotiations for buying Cuba, especially as the ex-Queen was in exile and in bad odor with the Spanish authorities. Sickles even gained the name of the "Yankee King of Spain" but it was at the neglect of his job in Madrid; and because of this, and other adverse developments in Cuba, he failed completely, as had Pierre Soulé, in his primary mission. This affair also hurt the chances of the Queen's son, Alfonso XII, to succeed his mother on the Spanish throne, and it was finally terminated by the marriage of Sickles to a young and obedient lady in waiting to the Queen named Caroline Creagh, a señorita of obvious Irish descent. Sickles returned to New York in 1871 and continued a turbulent career until his death in 1914, "old, irresponsible and cantankerous." His lasting monument is Central Park, which he successfully obtained for the city in 1852 while serving as a member of the State Legislature.

Caleb Cushing of Massachusetts, an eminently respectable and able jurist, succeeded Dan Sickles but no further serious effort was ever made to buy Cuba from Spain. If variety is the spice of life, the Spaniards certainly have no reason to complain about the diversity of types of the American ministers to their country. Before and soon after Cushing, there were such illustrious Americans as the men of letters, Washington Irving of New York and James Russell Lowell of Massachusetts; and the statesmen and men of affairs, Charles and Thomas Pinckney of South Carolina, David Humphreys of Connecticut, John H. Eaton of Tennessee (husband of the famous Peggy, who basked in Madrid society during her four-year stay there), Carl Schurz of Wisconsin, Hannibal Hamlin of Maine (Lincoln's Vice President), John W. Foster of Indiana (who was later Secretary of State), and Perry Belmont of New York.

During the same year (1855) in which Pierre Soulé returned home from Spain, a Cincinnati physician formed a secret political organization called "The Knights of the Golden Circle" which was a pro-slavery and expansionistic society with one of its principal objectives the conquest of Mexico and presumably other countries to the south. During the Civil War this organization became a rallying center for Copperheads and other Southern sympathizers but what efforts it made to help William Walker, who made his initial landing in Nicaragua in June of that year, seem to be unknown. It was a misty, nebulous society and is a worthwhile subject for serious research.

After all these preliminary bouts we at last come to the main event—to William Walker, the grand master of the filibustering profession . . . the man who nearly succeeded.

141

CHAPTER VII

William Walker: King of the
Wild Filibusters

CONSIDERING the amount of screaming publicity which he received in his time, William Walker is an astonishingly unknown man today. He was truly a headline figure of world interest during the five years before the Civil War; the vortex of furious and reckless deeds in battle and of frantic disputes and debates in cabinets, chancelleries, and legislatures. And always his actions were headlines on the front pages of all newspapers. He was (and still is) used as a threatening ogre to frighten naughty children into obedience in Central America; and he was carried on shoulders, amidst hysterical cheers and tears of emotion, by welcoming crowds in the cities of the United States. He was the hero who almost —almost but not quite—put over the great and successful filibuster. If he had won out—and he might well have done so but for his shortsighted stubbornness—he would unquestionably have changed the subsequent histories of the United States and of our Latin American neighbors; yet, today, his name is usually met by a puzzled look. And even

142

worse, the word "filibuster" is now generally understood in its degenerate meaning of a political windbag who uses obstructionist tactics to block undesired legislation instead of in its original sense of a freebooter—almost a pirate. Walker, however, did not like the term "filibusters" for his followers, and he usually called them "liberators."

William Walker was a strange personality. Of unprepossessing appearance, he made an almost negative first impression, but he possessed an iron will, he was entirely ruthless, and he almost never compromised or changed his mind. These qualities helped him to the heights of Nicaragua and then, when he was pitted against vastly more experienced and craftier enemies in the greater world outside, they led to his complete downfall.[1] One young American adventurer met him in Guaymas, Mexico, the seaport of the state of Sonora, before he had embarked on his first filibuster, and later wrote his impression of him:

His appearance was that of anything else than a military chieftain. Below the medium height [Walker was only about five feet, five inches], and very slim, I should hardly imagine him to weigh over a hundred pounds. His hair light and towy, which his almost white eyebrows and lashes concealed a seem-

---

[1] There are many books for those who want to read in further detail about William Walker and his men, most of which are given in the bibliography. Three are outstanding: Walker's own book, *The War in Nicaragua*, Mobile, Alabama, 1860 which, while strongly prejudiced, is generally acknowledged to be so factually accurate that it is accepted unquestionably by hostile Central American historians; secondly, William O. Scroggs, *Filibusters and Financiers*, New York, 1916, a scholarly and readable book; and finally, Laurence Greene, *The Filibuster*, Indianapolis-New York, 1937, which is written in a popular vein. Incidentally, a recent novel, Darwin Teilhet's *The Lion's Skin*, New York, 1955, while having the usual love story slanted at Hollywood, gives an excellent description of the Nicaraguan countryside by an author who has actually been there.

ingly pupilless, grey, cold eye and his face was a mass of yellow freckles, the whole expression very heavy. His dress was scarcely less remarkable than his person. His head was surmounted by a huge white fur hat, whose long knap waved with the breeze, which, together with a very ill-made short-waisted blue coat, with gilt buttons, and a pair of grey, strapless pantaloons, made up the ensemble of as unprepossessing-looking a person as one would meet in a day's walk. I will leave you to imagine the figure he cut in Guaymas with the thermometer at 100°, when every one else was arrayed in white. Indeed half the dread which the Mexicans had of filibusters vanished when they saw this their Grand Sachem—such an insignificant-looking specimen. [The observer was writing in retrospect, for Walker's record at that time was as innocuous as his looks.] But anyone who estimated Mr. Walker by his personal appearance, made a great mistake. Extremely taciturn, he would sit for an hour in company without opening his lips; but once interested, he arrested your attention with the first word he uttered, and as he proceeded, you felt convinced that he was no ordinary person.[2]

Walker's uncanny, piercing eyes were his striking feature and all noticed them. He became known later in Nicaragua as "the grey-eyed man of destiny" which was probably to fulfill an old legend that such a man would one day deliver the Indians from their centuries of bondage.

His ancestry was that of the most daring pioneers, the spearheads of the frontier—Scotch and Scotch-Irish, as were, for example, Daniel Boone, Davy Crockett, Samuel Bowie, Andrew Jackson, Sam Houston and countless others of that restless, turbulent breed who were the cutting edge of civilization. Superb in adversity and amidst hardships, they could not always stand prosperity; and success and comfort often caused their downfall. Walker's father was a native Scot who

---

[2] T. Robinson Warren, *Dust and Foam.* New York, 1859, pp. 212-13.

had settled in Nashville, Tennessee, and became successful in the mercantile and insurance businesses. He married a Kentucky girl, Mary Norvell, and there were four children, three boys and a girl, of whom William, born in 1824, was the oldest. The other two boys later followed William to Nicaragua but Norvell proved dissipated and incompetent and the youngest, James, died there of cholera.

In his boyhood William impressed some of the neighbors as being something of a "mama's boy" and a bit effeminate; but those who best knew him did not consider him a prig. His mother became an invalid and her devoted son spent much time reading aloud to her for her diversion, which was in no sense an unmanly habit. A woman friend of his mother's later said of him, "He was very intelligent and as refined in his feeling as a girl. I used often to go to see his mother and always found him entertaining her in some way." [3] The boy was not much of a student but he kept a passing grade in the local school and then graduated from the University of Nashville when but fourteen years old. However, this university was only about the equivalent of the modern high school so that young Walker was not quite so precocious as he sounds. But he received a rigid course in moral training at the university and bowed for prayers eight times on weekdays, with Sundays crowded with additional religious services and Bible study. All the lighter pastimes were forbidden, and no organized sports existed. It was a grim and serious atmosphere which produced the greatest filibuster and a far cry from the romantic concep-

---

[3] Jane H. Thomas, *Old Days in Nashville, Tennessee.* Nashville, 1897. pp. 78-79.

tion of how a young Southern cavalier was educated. Probably it was typical of the Calvinistic background which caused so many Tennessee boys to dive into the excitement of the frontier as a reaction to this all-work-no-play education.

Walker's parents had intended him for the ministry and he actually joined the Christian Disciples Church (an extreme branch of Presbyterianism), but upon graduation he decided upon a medical career and finally received an M.D. degree from the University of Pennsylvania in 1843. After that he spent over two years in Paris and in other European cities in advanced medical studies. Then, for some reason or other, he dropped medicine and turned to the study of law. After reading law in a local office for several months he suddenly pulled stakes and went to New Orleans—which meant additional legal preparation, for Louisiana followed the Napoleonic Code instead of the English common law. However, before too long he was admitted to the bar and hung out his shingle on famous Canal Street. He was not a success. His reserve and coldness of manner prevented his gaining friends or clients and finally he shut down his law office and, turning to journalism, became an editor of the New Orleans *Crescent*. This was an ultra-conservative newspaper which ridiculed the filibustering attempts into Cuba by Narciso Lopez, and the more extreme and hot-headed Southern expansionists even called it a "Yankee paper." It did not prosper and by the autumn of 1849 young Walker was again out of a job.

But during his stay in New Orleans he was said to have fallen in love with an attractive and well-educated girl named Helen Martin who, however, was handicapped by being stone deaf from birth. The young couple carried on their courtship in the sign language but this romance ended sadly in the death of Helen, who was a victim of one of the city's periodic yellow fever epidemics. This loss was believed to have changed the serious young Walker from his studious ways to a rash ambition and a complete indifference to human life, and, combined with the loss of his job, to have set his foot on the path of reckless adventure.

The obvious way to forgetfulness in the fateful year of 1849 was blazoned across the skies. Walker joined the great rush to the Golden West and, in June, 1850, he was in San Francisco. There he again became a journalist and an editor of the *Daily Herald*. A few months later he became involved in a controversy with an unpopular local judge whom he had attacked in the *Herald* for his leniency to certain criminals. The judge found Walker guilty of contempt of court and fined him a sizable sum which the latter refused to pay and went to jail. Popular indignation over this reached a fever pitch; thousands of citizens marched from a protest mass meeting to cheer him in jail; and finally he was released by a superior court to find himself the hero of the moment. If Walker had possessed personal magnetism he might have ridden this popular wave to political prominence, but his cold personality lacked the basic requirements for vote getting.

Walker's restlessness then took him to the growing town of Marysville where he returned to the practice of law for the years 1851-1852. Here news arrived of the French expeditions into Sonora under de Pindray and Raousset-Boulbon and these stirred the unsettled and restive young lawyer into plans for action and adventure of his own. After Count Raousset had agreed to evacuate the captured city of Hermosillo and left Mexico, Walker and his law partner went to Guaymas in June, 1853, to solicit a colonization grant similar to those of their French predecessors.[4] Their reception, quite naturally, was a cold one. The Mexicans had experienced enough trouble with the so-called French colonizers and were certainly not going to extend any similar privileges to the infinitely more dangerous gringos who, they felt sure, had plans eventually to absorb the rest of their hapless country. So Walker and his companion failed completely to obtain official sanction for any colonizing project. But Walker had keenly observed conditions and returned convinced that many Mexicans would welcome American settlers to protect them from the Apache raids and the rapacity of their own officials. Before he arrived in Guaymas, his friends in San Francisco had marketed bonds of the "Republic of Sonora" signed by him as "Colonel of the Independence Regiment," which certainly was a dead give-away of his true intentions to establish an independent republic on Mexican territory.

Despite Walker's failure to obtain official Mexican approval, he went ahead with his plans for leading an illegal expedition into Mexico. After various difficulties with the authorities in San Francisco, who were now aware that he planned some kind of an outright filibuster in violation of the Neutrality Act of 1818—an act which forbade the armed invasion of a friendly country by bands of marauding Ameri-

---

[4] The impression of Walker (p. 143) was gained on this trip.

cans—Walker slipped out the harbor with forty-five followers on the brig *Caroline* in the early morning fogs of October 16, 1853.

What manner of men were these filibusters who set out with Walker? They must have been pretty much of a type on all these expeditions. And why did they go? There was always a varying proportion of drifters along, bar flies and dock rats, but the officers and the hard core of these volunteers must have been a splendid set of men. As one old ex-filibuster recalled his comrades, years afterwards:

In the 50's men looked upon life from a more romantic viewpoint than they do now. There was more sentiment, more singing of songs, and more writing of love verses to sweethearts; grace and gallantry lent a charm to society, as perfume enhances the beauty of the rose; the cavalier, with his plumes and ribbons, had not departed, and the music of the troubador still tinkled amidst the sounds of revelry. Those were the days when the ardor for adventure by land and sea was hot in the breasts of men. In the vast regions of the West, the stars shone upon a primeval wilderness, where there was lure of gold, and where hunger and conflict and even death challenged those whose daring and hardihood defied the vicissitudes of fortune in their search for El Dorado. Men had not outgrown the customs of their forefathers, and if they resorted to the *code duello* in defense of their honor, and the honor of women, they were moved by sincerity, and surrounded by traditions still too potent to be cast aside. Such were the men who took service under Walker, and were led by him in his desperate struggles to make real a dream that might have dazzled the great Corsican himself.[5]

An English explorer, who was in Nicaragua after Walker's final expulsion from there, gave his impressions of some of Walker's men who remained in that country. He wrote:

---

[5] James Carson Jamison, *With Walker in Nicaragua*. Columbia, Missouri, 1909, pp. 11-12.

Tall, upright, broad-shouldered men they were nearly all. Their heads were well set on, hands and feet small, muscles like iron. Every movement was quick and decided: there seemed to be a restless activity about them which kept the deck in a continual bustle. Their language was a compound of extravagant humor and improbable blasphemy. . . . We were among the very pick of the Western States—men highly thought of even there for reckless daring. . . . They were simply the most good-natured, good-tempered fellows I ever met with.[6]

Walker decided to establish first a base in Lower California whence he could operate across the Gulf of Mexico into Sonora when the proper time came. That long, narrow, mountainous, arid peninsula was so remote and so sparsely populated that he would be free from interference by Mexican authorities while he waited for reinforcements and supplies for a big foray into rich Sonora. And so, sailing around the extreme tip of the peninsula, the *Caroline* turned up into the Gulf of California and reached the territorial capital of La Paz near the end of October. Walker rushed his men ashore, captured the astounded governor, and replaced the Mexican flag by a one-starred design of his own which purported to be the banner of the independent Republic of Lower California. All this was bloodlessly accomplished in about a half an hour. He then resorted to his most adept weapon, the pen, and turned out the first of his many resonant and rhetorical proclamations in which he announced the birth of this new nation with himself as President. So far it had all been easy.

But La Paz was found too distant from his supporters and

[6] Frederick Boyle, F.R.G.S., *A Ride Across a Continent: A Personal Narrative of Wanderings through Nicaragua and Costa Rica.* 2 vols., London, 1868. Vol. I, p. 77.

hoped-for recruits in California and too far south for an expedition into Sonora, and so, after only three days in the town, Walker re-embarked his men, taking along as prisoners the old governor and a new governor whom he had captured as he sailed into the harbor. Just before he left he had his first skirmish with the natives, with considerable shooting but no known casualties. The *Caroline* then sailed back toward upper California to Ensenada about a hundred miles south of San Diego on the Pacific coast. Here they landed again, established a new headquarters, and Walker finished the paper work of forming the new government with the result that every fourth man of his command became a cabinet official or a commissioned officer.

Before the end of November he issued a proclamation to the people of the United States in which he declared that Lower California had been shamefully neglected by the Mexican government because of its isolation and that its independence was necessary for its proper development, the implication, of course, being that eventual annexation to the United States would benefit all concerned. This was a popular appeal to Americans because many people, especially in the South, believed that the annexation of Lower California and northern Sonora, particularly the area around the mouth of the Colorado River, should have been included in the terms of the peace treaty ending the Mexican War and that this might have been accomplished fairly easily with a prostrate Mexico. This territory might even have been included in the Gadsden Purchase of the following month, December, 1853, if Walker's rash foray had not excited and antagonized the Mexicans. Certainly his acts were of no

151

help to James Gadsden, laboring in Mexico City to purchase additional land on the southern boundary of what are now the states of Arizona and New Mexico for the building of a transcontinental railroad. Gadsden obtained this needed land, now known as the Gadsden Purchase, but any efforts to buy the other desirable area were nullified by Walker's irresponsible filibuster. Later, Walker more or less did the same thing to Nicaragua, which might well have been the site for our transoceanic canal instead of Panama if he had not devastated the country and raised an undying distrust there for the United States. So, in the long run, Walker proved a distinct liability to our empire builders.

Soon afterwards the Mexicans made their first attack on these invaders but were driven off with a few casualties on both sides. During the fighting the *Caroline* suddenly sailed off without warning, carrying most of the provisions and the two captive governors, who may well have bribed the crew to take them southward to liberty. But on December 28th a new ship, the *Anita*, arrived from San Francisco carrying arms and two hundred recruits but no food. This meant that Walker's men would have to live off the country and he used the attack of the Mexicans to justify this drastic action. So on the day after the arrival of these reinforcements a raid was made on a nearby village, where his men seized a large number of cattle and horses belonging to a famous outlaw who was alleged to have led the initial attack on the Americans. With these provisions, and others confiscated from neighboring ranches, Walker then prepared to march across the desolate peninsula and invade the state of Sonora, his true objective, by crossing the Colorado River near its mouth.

Before setting out on this bold venture he issued several proclamations on January 18, 1854. It was fortunate that the Gadsden Purchase had been signed the previous month, for these proclamations and his subsequent foray might have upset all of James Gadsden's efforts in Mexico City. By these incredible decrees he annexed Sonora to his republic of Lower California and changed the name of this enlarged country to the Republic of Sonora, consisting of the two states of Lower California and Sonora, with, of course, William Walker as *Presidente* of this new nation. An additional star was added to his flag which easily covered that situation. The editor of the newspaper *Alta California* aptly noted: "It would have been just as cheap and easy to have annexed the whole of Mexico at once, and would have saved the trouble of making future proclamations." It was an utterly ridiculous act on the surface but Walker had a deadly and grim determination which made his announcements by no means funny to those immediately concerned.

In the meantime his men had become restive with the monotonous diet of fresh beef, corn, and high-sounding pronouncements, and a number of them were on the verge of mutiny. Finally Walker demanded an oath of obedience from them all—a sort of swearing-in which gave him complete power of life and death—and about fifty malcontents refused to commit themselves and, after much excitement and many mutual threats, marched out of the camp and across the boundary to San Diego. Other causes reduced the army to about one hundred and thirty men and, leading these, Walker left Ensenada on February 13, 1854, to cross the narrow peninsula.

A short way out, at the village of San Vicente, he called a convention of the native Mexicans and by force or persuasion administered an oath of allegiance to some of these bewildered people. He made this quite a ceremony with his men drawn up in formation, and a few Germans, who had brought their instruments with them from California, played appropriate martial music.

But desperation indeed was closing in on him. A Mexican man-of-war, with the co-operation of American naval vessels, had cut off his seaborne supplies and recruits from California, and the only course for Walker seemed straight eastward to Sonora. Desertions were increasing and native hostility rising every day. It was then that he initiated the harsh discipline which was ever after to mark his leadership. He had had absolutely no military experience of any kind and all his knowledge of fundamentals, such as drill regulations and the daily routine of an armed force, must have come from books or from his officers, many of whom were veterans of the late war with Mexico. Probably he had read various lives and memoirs of the military great and somewhere he had gained a fixed belief in harsh discipline and the strictest punctilio in military etiquette. These would probably have been all right with seasoned troops but his men, fresh from the uncontrolled liberties of the mining camps, were not used to discipline or even, for that matter, to much self-control, and Walker's unyielding harshness seems to have often done as much harm as good. He started off his rule of the iron rod by ordering two men shot and two others flogged who had attempted to desert.

Then, leaving about twenty men behind at San Vicente to guard his base and headquarters, he led about a hundred others on a rugged trek across the rough trails of the Sierras of northern Lower California. During this rash and hard march he lost some of the driven cattle and his treacherous Indian guides stole still more. After many privations, Walker and his men reached the west bank of the Colorado River at a region of steaming mud flats about six miles above its mouth. The men managed to cross the swift and deep stream on makeshift rafts but the cattle which they tried to drive across were all drowned. They could not go forward without food, their clothing and shoes were in rags and tatters or completely gone, and a quick retreat became imperative. About fifty more men deserted at this point and made their way north upstream to Fort Yuma which lay about seventy miles away, just over the United States boundary.

Walker then led his remaining followers, in a retreat of horror, back over the way they had come which was, in fact, the only thing he could do to keep his expedition alive. About the middle of April they staggered into San Vicente to find that the Mexicans had massacred the small garrison left behind. From then on the hostile natives closed in on this forlorn band to harass them day and night by encirclement and constant sniping. The Mexicans offered them a safe conduct to the boundary if they would lay down their arms but Walker was too wary of such promises to meet the fate of the later over-gullible Henry Crabb and his unfortunate men.

Again only one sane course of action remained, a fighting retreat to the boundary, and Walker led out his miserable and dejected men and headed north for the United States border and safety. Mounted Mexicans galloped continually around them at a safe distance and hurled jeers and insults at the dejected army of the Republic of Sonora as it shambled along. Occasionally each side would take a random pot shot at the other but the Mexicans kept too safe a distance for these to be effective. News of Walker's approach reached San Diego and many spectators came to the nearby boundary line where they obtained front row seats on a hill to watch the climax of this drama. And this came when the Mexicans placed themselves between the oncoming filibusters and the United States line. When Walker saw this he ordered his men to charge, and with yells and cheers the handful of remaining Americans rushed at their tormentors. The mounted Mexicans decided that a battle at this point would not be worth the casualties and, spurring their horses, galloped off. As soon as he was over the line, Walker surrendered his followers to waiting officers of the United States Army and he and all his men—only thirty-three were left to him as he thus ended his term as President of Sonora—gave their parole to report to the federal authorities in San Francisco under charges of violating the neutrality laws of the United States. The day was May 8, 1854, which also happened to be William Walker's thirtieth birthday. Few of the spectators would have wagered that this humiliated young leader of filibusters would soon rise like a phoenix from the ashes of this ignominious debacle.

CHAPTER VIII

The Immortals

GOING to California from the settled portions of the United States was a long, tough trip before the opening of a transcontinental railroad in 1869. During the frenetic days of the gold rush of 1849, and the succeeding years, there were several routes. For people who lived in what we now call the Middle West and for those west of the Mississippi River the overland route was the logical choice despite the dangers from Indians and bandits, and the great natural hazards and hardships. It was usually the slowest way but often the surest. However, for people on or near the salt water of the Atlantic Ocean or the Gulf of Mexico, passage by ship was a logical choice. There were several routes to choose from: the all-water, no-change one around Cape Horn which was long and rough, but at least a passenger remained on one ship; the way of the Isthmus of Panama which meant down on one overcrowded ship, a miserable up-and-down crossing on muleback over a rugged trail across the fever-ridden isthmus, and then passage on another pack-jammed ship up the Pacific Ocean to California. In 1855 a railroad was opened across Panama which replaced the trip by mule and made this eventually the most popular and practical route. A few people went by water to Mexico, usually to the southern Isthmus of Tehuantepec, crossed by land, and then took ship on the Pacific side to California, but this seems to have been an irregular and especially hazardous way. And then there was the way which especially concerns us, across Nicaragua, which, being nearer the United States, was somewhat shorter than the Panama way and about equally popular. It had the advantage of crossing the country by small steamboats upon river and lake with only a mere twelve miles or so by land on a good highway as the last stretch to the Pacific. Also the scenery was magnificent, the climate mild, and the trip far pleasanter than through the steaming malarial jungles of Panama; so that until the opening of the Panama railroad and the arrival of William Walker and his filibusters, both of which occurred in 1855, the Nicaraguan route probably got most of the trade going both ways.

Nicaragua had had quite a history. The Spaniards conquered the native Indians in 1522 and soon afterwards established settlements along its Pacific slope. This was a beautiful and fertile land, with such superb natural scenery that an early English monk named it "Mahomet's Paradise," which all observers agreed was an apt title with the perfumes of its orange groves and myriad wild flowers sweetening its gentle airs like unto the Moslem heaven. To the east of these early settlements lay Lake Nicaragua which, with smoking volcanoes rising as islands from its waters and with others towering along its western shore, was strikingly scenic. The outlet from this lake was the San Juan River which flowed into the Caribbean. At its mouth was a drab settlement named San Juan del Norte, or Greytown[1] as it was called by the British when they forcibly occupied it for a while—for the purpose, as Americans believed, of preventing the United States from controlling an interoceanic canal.

Commodore William Vanderbilt was the driving force behind the Accessory Transit Company which controlled the ocean steamships and the river and lake boats which served this route to and from California. The ocean steamers landed and picked up passengers at Greytown on the Caribbean side and at San Juan del Sur on the Pacific coast, the latter being a port developed by the company. Arriving at Greytown, the passengers transferred to specially designed shallow-draft river boats which steamed up the river, bucking several rapids at which the passengers often landed and walked or rode around by land to re-embark above or to transfer to another boat. When Lake Nicaragua was reached they boarded a larger craft, resembling somewhat a New York ferry boat, and on this they steamed some forty miles across the lake to Virgin Bay on the west shore. When the first of these lake boats arrived at the river from New York it was reported to Commodore Vanderbilt that it was impossible to get it up the river over the rapids. Vanderbilt then went to Nicaragua and brought it successfully up the river himself. From Virgin Bay the passengers rode comfortably in coaches on an improved road (built at company expense) to San Juan del Sur where they embarked on the ocean steamers for California. Passengers going the other

---

[1] To be called Greytown hereafter to prevent confusion with San Juan del Sur.

way, of course, reversed the process but had a somewhat easier trip by going downstream from Lake Nicaragua on the San Juan River. This company had obtained its grant by agreeing to construct eventually an interoceanic canal across Nicaragua, if possible, and by promising to pay the government a percentage of its profits. The latter clause caused trouble and was used by William Walker as an excuse for his later seizure of the company's properties within the country.

Nicaragua had sleepily and peacefully existed for almost three hundred Spanish colonial years as a province of the captaincy-general of Guatemala which had its capital at Guatemala City. A captaincy-general was a political division of lesser importance than a viceroyalty such as Mexico and Peru but maintained direct relations with Spain. When Mexico declared its independence in 1821, this captaincy-general became nominally a part of the independent empire of Mexico proclaimed under Agustin de Iturbide, but this ended with the Emperor's downfall in 1823, in which year the former captaincy-general of Guatemala (with the exception of the province of Chiapas which remained permanently with Mexico) proclaimed itself an independent republic under the name "United Provinces of Central America." Five provinces formed this new country—Guatemala, Honduras, Salvador, Nicaragua, and Costa Rica, all of which today are separate republics.

As in most of the other new Spanish-American republics, revolution soon broke loose in the new country and in 1838 it dissolved into the present-day five republics. However, in 1824, before general anarchy broke out, the new country of

YUCATAN SOLDIER

NARCISCO LOPEZ

FILIBUSTERS AT VIRGIN BAY

PIERRE SOULÉ   GENERAL HENNINGSEN

WILLIAM WALKER

THE BATTLE OF RIVAS

FILIBUSTERS RESTING AFTER BATTLE

THE FEVER HOSPITAL AT GRANADA

Central America passed a decree abolishing human slavery which is notable as the first emancipation measure in the western hemisphere; also because of William Walker's later repeal of this decree, thereby re-establishing slavery in Nicaragua.

Nicaragua as an independent country continued on an even more lawless and bloody course with constant revolutions and fighting drenching the country with blood and destroying its economy and much property. Two factions fought constantly for political control, the Conservatives with their headquarters in the city of Granada on the northwestern shore of Lake Nicaragua, and the Liberals who centered about the old provincial capital of Leon, a city about eighty miles to the north. It was something like the constant intercity warfares of ancient Greece. During one period of six years the distressed republic had fifteen presidents, which is a fair example of its anarchic condition. In 1855 the Conservatives, or Legitimists, or Serviles as they were often called, held nominal control of the government, but the Liberals or Democrats were in open rebellion and controlled Leon and the surrounding area. It was the perfect opportunity for a band of American filibusters to enter the country as paid mercenaries for one side or the other. And this is exactly what happened and how William Walker managed to enter Nicaragua.

Ever since the first opening of the transit line across the country, travelers had noticed its fertility, its good climate, and its great natural resources and, of course, the depressing destruction and neglect which the constant revolutions had brought to this Mahomet's Paradise. Certainly all American instincts for material progress were outraged by this utter waste of such good material and the belief spread that all Nicaragua needed was stability to become a second Eden. The natives were obviously incapable of accomplishing this and it seemed that this was another place marked for the Manifest Destiny of the United States to take over and bring order out of chaos.

Up in California, William Walker had stood trial for violation of our neutrality laws. He acted as his own attorney and stated that he had been morally supported during his privations in Lower California and Sonora by the consciousness that he was upholding justice and humanity and emulating the Pilgrim Fathers by rescuing the country from savages to make it fit for civilization. One of his recruiting agents had already been found guilty and fined but the jury took only eight minutes to return a verdict of not guilty for Walker, this same agent's principal. The result was that the federal authorities, notably General John E. Wool, a grizzled old soldier who had been the principal mover against the filibusters, became so disgusted that the subsequent filibustering expeditions were allowed to organize and sail off without interference. It was almost impossible for a military man to enforce an unpopular law with no civilian co-operation. Walker then became an editor of a San Francisco newspaper, the *Commercial Advertiser,* one of whose owners was Byron Cole, from the State of Maine, who had a great interest in Nicaragua and who persuaded Walker to forget any further plans of returning to Sonora and to concentrate on the far more promising possibilities of Nicaragua. Shortly afterwards, this newspaper stopped publication. Walker then went to another editorial job in Sacramento and Byron Cole sailed to Nicaragua to explore the possibilities there for some kind of an American expedition.

Cole sailed on a Transit Company steamer from San Francisco in August, 1854, accompanied by another New Englander, William V. Wells, a grandson of Samuel Adams the Boston firebrand of the Revolutionary War, who afterwards wrote a very pro-Walker book, published at the height of the latter's success.[2] Cole returned with a contract from the revolting Liberals, or Democrats, of Nicaragua to bring in three hundred Americans to serve as soldiers with that faction. But when he showed this to Walker the latter's legal eye saw that it was too flagrant a violation of our neutrality laws and might make endless difficulties with the government. Cole then sailed back to Nicaragua and secured a new contract to bring three hundred colonists, with the privilege of bearing arms, into the country. Walker accepted this, quit his newspaper job and moved to San Francisco to prepare for his second filibustering expedition. He took the precaution of securing the approval of the federal officials for this new contract and reported that even crusty old General Wool read it and then, shaking hands, wished him luck.

It took four months of patience and disappointments to prepare this expedition, the main troubles being financial. But finally enough money was scraped together and a picked lot of recruits assembled, many of them veterans of the late Mexican War, some survivors of Lopez's disastrous foray into Cuba, and even one case-hardened veteran of Walker's catastrophe in Lower California. They chartered a leaky old

---

[2] *Walker's Expedition to Nicaragua.* New York, 1856.

brig, the *Vesta*, placed men and supplies aboard, but just as all was ready for sailing, a deputy sheriff appeared who attached the ship for a debt owed by its owner. This might have been the last straw for some men but Walker overcame this block by enticing the deputy into the cabin where he plied him with liquor until that representative of the law acquiesced. A steam tug towed the vessel outside the harbor, incidentally bringing back the agreeable sheriff's deputy, and early on the morning of May 4, 1855, the *Vesta*, spreading her sails, set a course to the southward. Walker had fifty-eight followers on board and these intrepid men were afterwards called "The Immortals." It had the makings of one of the most important events in all United States history; and had Walker won permanent success in his venture such a title would not have been inappropriate.

★ 2 ★

On June 16, 1855, over six weeks after leaving San Francisco, Walker and his men landed at Realejo,[3] the northernmost Pacific port of Nicaragua which served the Democratic stronghold of Leon. They were welcomed, as Walker described it, by an officer who was

—a light, active young fellow, with a bright red short-cloak thrown gracefully over his left shoulder—. The soldiers all wore the red ribbon with the words "Ejercito Democratico" [Democratic Army] printed on it; and although without uniform or any music except that made by a very indifferent drum, they had a good military carriage, and their step, unimpeded by shoe or sandal, was excellent. As the Americans passed up the street to the quarters assigned them, the women, with their best

---

[3] Since superseded by the port of Corinto.

dresses and most pleasing smiles, stood at the doors and windows saluting with much natural grace the strangers who had come to find a home in their midst, and to share the fortunes of the party with which their husbands and lovers, and fathers and brothers, were identified.

The next day, Walker started for Leon to see the leader of the Democrats and was much impressed by the "country for which nature has done much and man little; and the effect of even what little man had done was marred by the constant signs of revolutionary violence." Leon was on a vast plain which seemed endless to the south but was hemmed in to the north by a lofty and picturesque chain of volcanoes. It had been the capital and largest city of the old Spanish colonial province of Nicaragua, and was supposedly more progressive than its hated conservative rival Granada to the south, but the constant internal wars had wreaked havoc and destruction on it and its population was probably only about twenty thousand, about a third of its former size, when Walker arrived.

The "Provisional Director" Castellon, of the Democratic faction, received Walker with great cordiality, as the fortunes of his party were on the wane, and the newcomers were given the name of the American Phalanx (or Falange), under, of course, the command of Colonel Walker, and the men wound the distinctive red ribbons around their slouch hats. Soon afterwards, most of the Americans became Nicaraguan citizens by a simple declaration of intention which put them officially on the payroll and made them eligible for certain grants of land as a bonus. Walker thought Castellon a rather weak character who might be influenced by certain officers jealous of the American volunteers, and decided on quick action to establish his own prestige. And so he almost immediately afterwards re-embarked his men (who had practically drunk the countryside dry) on the *Vesta*, and, with a hundred odd native allies, sailed southward down the coast to seize the Transit Road across the narrow strip of land between the Pacific Ocean and Lake Nicaragua. He knew full well that this would be his supply line for future recruits and equipment from his supporters in California and the East and that it was absolutely vital for his success.

Walker landed his men about eighteen miles north of the Transit port of San Juan del Sur and headed across country, through torrential rains with consequent hard going, to attack the town of Rivas, which lay a little north of the Transit Road and about midway of its length; which strategic location gave it control of all passing traffic. The Legitimists had been told of Walker's coming—through the treachery of one of the jealous Democrat officers in Leon, he afterwards believed—and had strongly garrisoned the town with over five hundred men.

The next morning as the command neared Rivas "a scene of beauty and of splendor burst upon their vision" which "almost made the pulse stand still," and "an exclamation of surprise and pleasure escaped the lips of all" as the weary American *falanginos* gazed out over Lake Nicaragua to the east from whose waters rose the graceful cone of the volcano Omotepe. For a little while the men enjoyed this lull before the storm.

Then, about noon, Walker led them on a reckless frontal charge into the expectant town. At the first shots, his native allies turned tail and left the fifty-odd Americans to fight ten times their numbers. The *falanginos* met a steady and deadly fire as they charged toward the central plaza with wild yells and cheers (the usual head-on tactics of filibusters) and were soon forced to take shelter in several adobe houses where they were surrounded by the enemy. The American rifles took a fearful toll but Walker's two ranking officers, Lieutenant Colonel Achilles Kewen, who had been with Lopez in Cuba, and Major Timothy Crocker, who had endured Walker's Lower California campaign, were both killed, and three other officers were wounded. Among the men five were dead and twelve wounded. The Legitimists then set fire to the sheltering houses and an immediate retreat became imperative to save the survivors. The Americans sallied forth with cheers and shouts and, before the enemy could meet this unexpected offensive, pushed through the streets to the outskirts of the town. Several of the wounded were too seriously hurt to move and these were immediately butchered by the Legitimists and their bodies burned. The enemy losses, however, were ten times those of the Americans and thereafter no sober natives ever wanted to shoot it out at close range with the gringo invaders.

It was a badly beaten-up and exhausted group of survivors who reassembled in a cacao plantation outside the town. Led by native guides, they stumbled along a trail in the dark until they neared the Transit Road about midnight. The ground was muddy and sticky and the men sank into it over their boots, the wounded suffering untold tortures. But there was no sign of pursuit and the exhausted *falan-*

ginos finally dropped in their tracks when they reached a deserted hut which gave some shelter. The next morning they marched safely into the port of San Juan del Sur, limping, battle-stained, filthy and ravenous. It was a bad beginning. But depressing as were the prospects, two Americans in the town enlisted in the Phalanx and this somehow raised the morale of all. It was an example of how this seemingly unfeeling leader attracted men and held their astonishing loyalty throughout the most adverse circumstances.

The schooner *Vesta* was nowhere in sight, so Walker seized a Costa Rican ship in the harbor and loaded his followers aboard. They met the missing *Vesta* soon afterwards and, transferring to her, arrived at Realejo two days after the battle at Rivas.

Walker immediately went inland to Leon where he made vehement accusations of treachery by his native allies at Rivas and blamed this on the machinations of a jealous Democratic general. Then, turning on his heel, he returned to the *Vesta* where he sulked on board for ten days, letting the powers at Leon worry about a Legitimist attack. Finally, he gave in to the frantic pleas from these Democratic leaders and went again to see them, accompanied by Byron Cole of Maine, the original promoter of the expedition, and a former Prussian cavalry officer, Bruno von Natzmer, who later became a valuable officer in the Phalanx.

In Leon, Walker proposed a second attack on the Transit route but could not obtain official consent because of opposition by the same general who he believed had previously betrayed him. The tactful Byron Cole, however, secured another contract to bring in three hundred more Americans for military service and, even more important, he obtained from the harassed Provisional Director Castellon complete authority for Walker to settle all differences between the republic and the Accessory Transit Company, and this power was to prove most important later.

In the middle of August, 1855, without any authorization, Walker embarked his men again on the *Vesta*. This second expedition to the Transit route was in direct disobedience to Walker's nominal superior, Castellon, and was in fact a sort of revolution within a revolution—all in the best Latin-American tradition—and showed his adaptability to local customs and methods. With him went a colorful part-Indian colonel named José Maria Vallé, a battle-scarred veteran of many revolutions, who had conceived a great admiration for the Americans and who brought along a hundred and twenty native followers. Colonel Vallé immediately started a card game of monte on the deck, which he kept going day and night with the final result that he won the shirts off the backs of his native followers and many from the Americans during a voyage of six days to San Juan del Sur. Evidently Walker, despite his military punctilio, did not object to an officer gambling with the enlisted men.

On the night of September 2nd, Walker marched his followers the entire length of the Transit Road from San Juan del Sur to Virgin Bay on Lake Nicaragua. As the weary men were getting breakfast after their arrival, they were suddenly attacked by six hundred Legitimists who had descended from Rivas. In command of these attackers was a

Guatemalan general [4] called Guardiola the Butcher who was renowned for his ferocious cruelty. On this occasion he had distributed generous rations of native brandy to his troops before giving the order to charge the gringos and their native allies with greased bayonets which could be quickly withdrawn from a finished foe. With their rifles the Americans took a frightful toll of their half-drunken enemies who came on with reckless courage to within easy shooting range. The enemy finally broke and left the field, upon which over sixty of their dead were found. And, as Walker reported: "The empty demijohns which were picked up on the road after the action looked like huge cannon-balls that had missed their mark." The Falange had none killed although several were wounded. It was a heartening victory for the Americans.

During this battle many of the native women and children had found refuge in the Transit Company's building under the protection of its agent who was none other than Cortlandt[5] Cushing, from Indiana, who had been the United States Chargé d'Affaires in Guayaquil, Ecuador, a little over three years before, and whose house there had been shelled by General Juan José Flores' attacking fleet. One can wonder what brought this adventurous Hoosier to Nicaragua to become again an innocent bystander in the midst of a storm of shot. Certainly those jobs could not have paid well enough to make the position of a perennial target worth while. Probably he had succumbed to the lure of the easy-going

---

[4] The Central American republics all had the same political divisions and it was common enough for a Democrat or Legitimist of one country to bring aid to his political brothers in another republic.

[5] Spelled this way, instead of Courtland, by Walker.

Latin-American countries as has many a man before and since. If he kept a journal of his adventures it has never come to light, which is a pity for it is the accounts of the man on the spot which are usually of the best value. Anyway, because of Cushing's precautions in arranging a protective barricade of trunks and boxes none of the refugees were hurt. Walker wrote that, during the fighting, all within "maintained a silence which might be the result of revolutionary training. After the danger had passed, however, their tongues were unloosed, and the squalling of babies, mixed up with the shrill tones of the mothers, soon brought even the smooth-tempered agent into the open air."

After this battle at Virgin Bay, which took place, incidentally, on September 3, 1855, Walker ordered that the enemy wounded be as carefully cared for as his own men. The astonished and grateful prisoners repaid him for this civilized treatment by giving him as much information as they could about the Legitimist forces. But, alas, his enemies did not always reciprocate when they captured American falangists. Usually they butchered these on the spot by shot or bayonet.

The next afternoon Walker marched his followers back to San Juan del Sur where he received word of the death by cholera of his nominal superior, Provisional Director Castellon. This dreadful disease was the scourge of Central America and, for that matter, often enough of the United States as well a century ago. The succeeding director was simply a figurehead and thenceforth Walker was a law unto himself and acted as he saw fit. A few days later a Transit steamer arrived from San Francisco bringing thirty-five re-

171

cruits, the first to arrive, under the command of Colonel Charles Gilman of Baltimore, who had lost a leg in Walker's Sonora venture. With him was another veteran officer of that disastrous campaign, Captain George R. Davidson of Kentucky. The flame of adventure must have burned strongly in these two men and it is sad that both of them met death in about two months. More native recruits arrived at the same time and swelled Walker's force to about three hundred and fifty men. This allowed him to take a strong offensive. He always refused to impress the natives into his army, as was the usual local custom, and would enlist only volunteers so that his followers were truly picked men, eager for action.

Walker now decided on the one really brilliant stroke of generalship in his career. The entire Legitimist army was in Rivas, leaving the city of Granada, about thirty miles north, almost undefended. On October 11th, he suddenly marched his whole force back across the Transit Road to Virgin Bay. With them for the first time were two small pieces of artillery. When the Transit steamer on Lake Nicaragua anchored off the port that night, Walker sent a detail of his men aboard to seize and hold her. The next afternoon he loaded his entire force aboard despite the protests of her captain and Mr. Courtland Cushing, who claimed her as a ship of the United States. Walker easily answered their objections by some of his legal rationalisms which were offered only as a courtesy, as he had the force to do anything he desired. At his direction the vessel steamed north that night with lights out, up the lake to a point a short distance beyond Granada where the men landed. Then, behind their mounted leader,

172

they marched in a silent column toward the unsuspecting city. They surged over an undefended barricade at the beginning of the first paved street and rushed at the double into the main plaza with only a few scattered shots from the surprised skeleton garrison who then turned and fled. In a short time Walker was complete master of this Legitimist stronghold at the cost of one native soldier killed. The families of most of the Legitimist officers lived in this city and there the civilian machinery of that faction's government was located, so that the victorious Walker held all the vital hostages. It was an amazing *tour de force* and in effect he was master now of Nicaragua as well. Never before had an American filibuster gained so many trump cards so quickly in the game with destiny.

CHAPTER IX

President Walker of Nicaragua

WALKER, by his capture of the city of Granada, put himself into a key position in Nicaraguan politics, a position which might very possibly have led in time to his dominance of all Central America and even, just possibly, to the eventual conquest of Cuba as well, and its consolidation into a Central American-Caribbean empire of sorts which, based on slavery, would be a firm ally to the Southern states of the United States. It was a stirring prospect and the chances are that Walker dimly sighted this glittering objective. His failings, however, were a stubborn refusal to heed the advice of experienced advisers and an overwhelming impatience, the occupational disease of almost all dictators, who seem to believe that destiny bids them quickly pyramid one success upon another. And these faults betrayed him.

However, for a while he played his newly won high cards with considerable skill. First, he released about a hundred political prisoners rotting in chains and dungeons under the great Cathedral of Granada. This act generally pleased his followers of the Democratic faction but he antagonized some by forbidding any looting of the hated city or physical

174

mistreatment of the local Legitimists, as was the time-honored Nicaraguan custom. Not only had the spoils always belonged to the victors but the lives of the vanquished as well. On the other hand, this humane treatment quite naturally gained him the gratitude of the defeated Legitimists so that he rode the two political horses fairly well for a time. The day after the capture of Granada he attended Mass at the cathedral, accompanied by many of his officers, and soon won the powerful support of the clergy by his respect for church property and traditions. That same day the city officials petitioned Walker to accept the presidency of the country, which he modestly declined but suggested that they offer this high position to General Ponciano Corral, commanding the frustrated Legitimist army outside the city. He hoped thereby to effect an immediate peace by compromise. The American Minister to Nicaragua, John H. Wheeler, of North Carolina,[1] went to Rivas as an emissary of peace but the Legitimists spurned his offers at first, and, in fact, treated him with insults and indignities. The time was not ripe for the Legitimists to swallow the bitter pill of such a quick change of fortune.

But events and Walker's iron ruthlessness soon brought his sulky opponents to terms. A Transit steamer arrived at San Juan del Sur from San Francisco carrying sixty American volunteers, led by Parker H. French, who was wanted for forgery in the States, although this was not known to Walker at the time. French led these recruits across the

---

[1] Wheeler gave a collection of scrapbooks to the Library of Congress which include four compiled in Nicaragua and these present extremely interesting sidelights on the country's occupation by the American filibusters.

175

Transit Road to Virgin Bay where, on his own initiative, he commandeered a lake steamer and placed his men on board amidst the civilian passengers, of which many were women and children. Under his orders the ship then steamed across Lake Nicaragua in a foolish effort to capture Fort San Carlos, still held by the Legitimists, which commanded the outlet of the lake into the San Juan River. After a futile demand for the fort's surrender, French and his men decided it was too strong to capture and headed the steamer for Granada where they reported to Walker. The steamer then returned to Virgin Bay and landed about two hundred and fifty passengers who were sheltered in the company's buildings, and there they were fired upon by prowling Legitimists who killed and wounded several. It was difficult for a native Nicaraguan to distinguish between filibuster and innocent passenger. To make matters worse the now tense and trigger-happy Legitimist garrison at Fort San Carlos fired on the next steamer coming up the river from the Caribbean and killed an American widow and her baby among the passengers from the Atlantic States. This necessitated the closing of all traffic on the Transit route and threatened Walker's supply lines. But he, instead of punishing Parker French for his ill-advised acts, used these incidents as an excuse to punish the opposing faction. He picked out the most prominent of his Legitimist hostages in Granada, a former cabinet member, and ordered his execution in reprisal. This completely innocent man was taken to the main plaza of Granada and shot by a firing squad of gloating native Leonese. It was a nasty business which caused resentment among the Granadinos and doubts among some of the

Americans. But it certainly brought the stubborn Legitimists to terms when they understood that their families in the city would be expendable as future hostages for their behavior.

The Legitimist commander, General Corral, recognized defeat and came into Granada, on October 23, 1855, to arrange a peace. Walker put on a great show for his entry by lining the streets and the plaza with his heavily armed followers and also armed and paraded a large number of male passengers who were stranded in the city because of the closure of the Transit route. Corral seemed to be impressed by his enemy's strength and quickly proceeded with the peace negotiations.

The final result was a treaty which ended hostilities and named Patricio Rivas, an innocuous Legitimist, temporary President of the united republic. It abolished the distinctive white and red ribbons of each faction in favor of a blue ribbon to be worn by all, and finally and most fatefully appointed William Walker as Commander-in-Chief of the combined armies. The Legitimist garrison at Fort San Carlos and another farther down the San Juan River then abandoned their posts and the Transit line was again open to free movement. Landing with fifty-eight men, William Walker had, in effect, captured Nicaragua in a little more than four months.

About a week later the peace was consummated by a sort of public love feast when General Corral paraded into Granada at the head of his army. Walker's men were drawn up in battle array in the main plaza—it was a tense situation and an accidental shot might have started a pitched battle —and he and his former enemy embraced in the best Spanish manner in front of the cathedral. Then, arm in arm, they entered the church for a religious service conducted by Padre Augustin Vigil, a prominent native priest who thenceforth enthusiastically supported Walker in his efforts to bring law and order to that distracted land.

Shortly afterwards there was more pomp and ceremonies for the inauguration of the puppet President, Patricio Rivas. Again Walker and Corral attended in style and both took an oath to support the new regime and observe the peace treaty. It was rumored that Corral hoped that Walker, as a non-Catholic, might quibble over the required kneeling and the religious form of the oath, but, if so, Walker disappointed him by serenely following all the required forms and promises. Corral, however, was evidently seething inwardly with bitterness and frustration over Walker's triumph and, with his oath of loyalty barely past his lips, began to plot for the overthrow of this dangerous Yankee intruder.

Walker fully realized his precarious position, despite his apparent triumph, and immediately began strenuous efforts to induce more Americans to emigrate to Nicaragua and by their numbers entrench him against the inevitable onslaughts of his enemies. He had found printing equipment in the city and he now established a newspaper, *El Nicaraguense*,[2] published in Spanish and English and edited by one of his original "Immortals," a New Englander named John Tabor, who wrote enthusiastic descriptions of Nicaragua and of the glittering opportunities there for ambitious young Americans. This propaganda sheet was sent in large

---

[2] A file of this fascinating periodical is in the Library of Congress.

quantities to the United States for publicity purposes and many newspapers quoted it at length.

Less than a fortnight later, Walker was awakened early in the morning by his faithful Indian officer, José Maria Vallé (he of the continuous gambling game on the brig *Vesta*) who excitedly handed him a packet of letters turned over to him by a friendly mail courier. These proved to have been written by the treacherous Corral to Legitimist friends in Honduras imploring aid against Walker and warning that all Central America would be lost if the American leader was not soon checked in his upward career.

The Commander-in-Chief at once called a cabinet meeting, including Corral who was Minister of War, and laid the incriminating letters before its stunned members. Corral perforce admitted his guilt but Walker insisted on the formality of a court-martial which, at the accused's special request, was composed only of Americans. The court found Corral guilty of treason, but recommended mercy to the Commander-in-Chief. But this plea was in vain, for the grim and determined Walker realized that a rod of iron was best suited to rule the Nicaraguans at that particular time. Petitions for clemency came from all sides but, as Walker wrote, "Mercy to Corral would have been an invitation to all the Legitimists to engage in like conspiracies. . . ." And so, on the afternoon of November 8, 1855, General Corral, the outstanding leader of the Legitimists, was shot in the main plaza of Granada, kneeling in the usual fashion with his back to the firing squad. An immense crowd witnessed the execution and broke into cries and lamentations after the crash of the fatal volley. Many rushed forward to clip locks of hair from his head and to dip their handkerchiefs in his blood. His supporters naturally made him a martyr and probably Walker gained many new enemies. But for the time being this destruction of the most powerful Legitimist gave him unqualified power. He was now the supreme dictator of Nicaragua and the strongest man in all Central America.

After the treaty of peace, two favorable events seemed to prove that nothing succeeds like success. Two days after the execution of General Corral the American Minister Wheeler recognized the new Rivas-Walker government on his own initiative and responsibility. It was a premature act, for orders were already on their way to him from Secretary of State William L. Marcy to withhold all recognition until the new government proved its stability. When news of his recognition reached Washington the State Department disavowed Wheeler's act and reprimanded him. About a year later, when the pressure in the States really went on against Walker, Wheeler was recalled for his obvious sympathy for his fellow countryman. As a Southerner, John Wheeler unquestionably let his emotions rule his head as Walker's cause became more and more a sectional affair at home.

The other seemingly auspicious event for the filibuster regime was a loan of twenty thousand dollars in gold obtained from the agent of the Transit Company. The national treasury was empty and this advance against the annual payments made by the company to the government for its franchise allowed Walker to pay his soldiers and generally benefited the whole community. However, it was a fateful act and committed the leader to friends who indirectly brought about his downfall. It was all a matter of politics within the Accessory Transit Company and Walker rather stupidly lined up with a faction trying to oust Commodore Vanderbilt from control. At the time, Vanderbilt was in Europe and two of his company associates, C. K. Garrison in San Francisco and Charles Morgan in New York, were trying to gain control of the company by various stock manipulations to their advantage and the Commodore's loss. Walker's good will, of course, was a tremendous asset and this loan from a representative of Garrison aligned him with the plotters in their impending struggle with the old Commodore. Walker, of course, was ignorant of the connivings and machinations of financial jungle warfare and probably quite innocently thought this loan did not obligate him particularly. However, it turned out to be a fatal step downward by tying him to the losing faction in the following struggle for control of the Transit route across Nicaragua.

Soon after Corral's execution, a small delegation of Americans arrived in Granada, headed by Joseph Warren Fabens, a native of Salem and one-time student at Harvard College. They represented Henry L. Kinney, founder of Corpus Christi, Texas, who had a concession of over twenty-two million acres of land on the east coast of Nicaragua in what was called the Mosquito Kingdom, a sort of comic-opera Negro state established on paper by Great Britain to block American control of any interocean canal. Kinney had been unsuccessful in promoting emigration from the United States and decided to approach Walker for a partnership. Nicaragua had never recognized the puppet Mosquito Kingdom from which Kinney had indirectly obtained his grant, and Walker was on friendly terms with the Transit Company which was hostile to Kinney, so the filibuster leader coldly rejected these overtures and announced: "If I ever lay hands on him [Kinney] on Nicaraguan soil I shall surely hang him." Fabens and his associates then deserted Kinney's sinking ship and climbed on the Walker bandwagon. This about finished poor Kinney's venture but he and his influential friends at home (including, it was said, President Franklin Pierce) resented such high-handed methods and afterwards used their influence against Walker.

Walker's next step to consolidate and strengthen his position was to win the recognition (Minister Wheeler's premature action having been repudiated) and possibly the tacit support of the United States government. At the time it seemed to be generally accepted by Walker's followers, both in Nicaragua and at home, that eventual annexation to the United States was their leader's ultimate objective. And so it was important to send a suitable representative of the new government to Washington. For this key position Walker picked the fast-talking scoundrel Parker H. French and he could not have made a worse choice. French arrived in New York where he found himself, for a while, the popular hero of the moment, especially when he defied the federal authorities who attempted to enforce the unpopular neutrality laws. Public approval was a new sensation for this slippery megalomaniac and he basked in its rays and expanded luxuriously. But, alas, his unusual popularity was short-lived for the newspapers soon picked up reports of his earlier swindles, and this self-lauded hero of Nicaragua came to a quick end. The State Department refused him recognition and Walker was forced to recall his flashy representative and to suspend relations with Mr. Wheeler in Granada. French returned to Nicaragua where he was coldly received by Walker, who severed him from all official connection with the government. He came back to the States and capitalized on his notoriety by brazenly going on a lecture tour, but gradually he faded out and was lost in obscurity.

While all this futile seeking for recognition was going on, Walker and his supporters in the States intensified their efforts for American emigration to Nicaragua. Not only were recruits for the army wanted but also permanent settlers, especially farmers and planters who could put their roots down in the soil and become a stabilized hard core which would make Walker's regime impregnable. Two hundred and fifty acres of good land were offered to each single man with an additional hundred acres for a married man with a family. These offers were publicized by recruiting campaigns and newspaper advertising in San Francisco, New Orleans and New York with encouraging results. Recruits flocked in, especially from the landless poor in the large cities, and these were considerably below the standards of the lusty, hard-fighting "Immortals" who primarily had sought adventure and excitement. The Accessory Transit Company officials, including Commodore Vanderbilt, who had returned from Europe and regained control of the company from his plotting associates, Morgan and Garrison, gave their wholehearted support and often arranged free passage for these volunteers. Little did the Commodore suspect what further schemes were brewing between these

183

plotters and William Walker or he would never have given his help. In California there were far more clamoring recruits than could be loaded aboard the ships and those left behind often broke into rioting on the dock. In New York the volunteers were given send-offs marked with enthusiastic disorders.

Quite naturally the representatives of the other Central American republics in Washington protested vehemently to the federal authorities about these apparent breaches of our neutrality laws. By then they could clearly see the threat to their own freedoms from the horde of Americans descending into Central America. Great Britain and France undoubtedly brought pressure to bear as well against the future danger to a neutral interoceanic canal. President Franklin Pierce perforce took notice of the impending great exodus and solemnly warned that anyone who took part in any military operation in Nicaragua forfeited all protection of the United States government. Orders were sent to the authorities in the principal ports to prevent unlawful military expeditions leaving. But the difficulty was that it was almost impossible to distinguish between a recruit for Walker's army and a bona fide passenger on his way to or from California via Nicaragua. Also, public opinion was wildly in favor of the emigrants, and this gave qualms to politically appointed officials.

Federal District Attorney McKeon in New York made the first serious attempt to prevent the sailing of a group of filibuster recruits on the steamer *Northern Light* on the day before Christmas, 1855. A composite report in the New York newspapers on his efforts went about as follows:

He boarded the ship and addressed the passengers:

"Gentlemen" said Mr. McKeon, "I have here a dispatch from the President which I wish to—"

"To hell with the President!" yelled a tall ferocious-looking fellow.

"Let's duck him in the river, boys!" vociferated another.

"Throw him overboard and be d—d to him" shouted a third.

Mr. McKeon prudently withdrew to the pier and uttered a final bellow "Gentlemen, I wish to read—"

But hoots, groans, catcalls, hisses, jeers and whistles drowned him out. The *Northern Light* drew out from her pier and moved slowly out into the river.

A gallant on the pier, pointing toward the ladies on deck, called for "three cheers for the future mothers of Nicaragua!" The response was thunderous.

"Now," cried another. "Three cheers for the independent State of Nicaragua!"

"Three more," cried a third, "for the independent State of Matrimony!"

And in the midst of hurrahs and laughter the *Northern Light* pointed downstream and steamed steadily, majestically out of hearing. But the joy of some of the defiant filibusters was short lived, for the *Northern Light* was stopped farther down the harbor by the U. S. Revenue Cutter *Washington*, commanded by Captain Faunce who boarded the steamer with an armed detachment and proceeded to segregate a few obvious filibusters (without tickets) from the legitimate passengers. The *Herald* of December 26, 1855, reported:

"Come, boys," said Captain Faunce, "you might as well go on shore. You see you are overpowered here, so you might as well go peaceably. You got to go anyhow, so go quietly and say nothing more about it."

One fellow approaching Captain Faunce, said, "Who the hell are you? You h'aint nobody—'cause you got brass buttons on, you think you are some, but I've licked bigger policemen than you are; and for one, I h'aint goin' on shore, but I'm going to Nicaragua, I am."

Captain Faunce, who is a stout, heavy man, stepped up to this fellow and deliberately took him by the neck, and lifting him once or twice at arm's length, clear from the deck, coolly remarked "Why, my boy, how much do you weigh? Why, you are much lighter than I thought you were." (Here he gave him another lift.) "Come, now don't you think you had better go on shore?"

"Well, yes, I guess I had," was the reply and Mr. Filibuster walked straight on board the steam tug without as much as saying "Good-bye" to Captain Faunce.

The *Washington* landed several frustrated filibusters at the foot of Barclay Street, and one of them, a Mr. Samuel G. Mathews, later told the *Herald* reporter:

I, with another fellow, went over to Tammany Hall about 3 o'clock, to a fancy dress ball; we went upstairs, and there being no doorkeeper visible, we both walked in to take a dance. I saw one woman dressed as a shepherdess; she looked pretty neat; I went up to the young beauty and asked her if I might have the honor; she said yes; I got her on the floor for a quadrille, and my friend had another dainty piece of calico *vis à vis*. Just as the dance was commencing, an old fogy came up and put me and my friend out of the room. I then went home and got there about daylight, thinking I had gone through enough for one day.

Mr. Mathews, however, may have reached Nicaragua later by another ship, for the approaching Presidential election of 1856 made the Nicaraguan question political dynamite and few politicians wanted to enforce such an unpopular law. And so the recruits flowed on for the time being. But if Mathews, like a good boy, remained at home he probably owed his life to Captain Faunce, for when Walker's fleeting halcyon days ended many of his followers met deaths by disease or violence.

★ 2 ★

Back in Nicaragua, the Americans enjoyed this peaceful interlude and planned for the future. A steady stream of immigrants flowed in from the States, many of them skilled artisans and farmers, and these spread out through the country to put their roots down. Almost all of the native troops had been discharged from service and the regular army now consisted of about six hundred Americans who were organized into two battalions, one called the Rifles and the other the Light Infantry. Some of these men, especially in the outlying posts, were mounted on horses they had obtained from the countryside. Afterwards a definite body of cavalry called the Rangers was organized. There was no trained artillery at this time. The men usually wore dark jean or corduroy trousers tucked into heavy boots, a red or blue flannel shirt, and a wide-brimmed black slouch hat, a uniform which was pretty much the standard garb of the California mining camps. The company and regiment insignia were sewed on the left-hand shirt pocket. The Rifles, nearly all, carried that weapon, often a Sharps repeating rifle, and as many of the Light Infantry as could obtain one, the rest using the smoothbore musket. Almost all wore a Colt pistol

187

(often two) and a bowie knife (again some had a pair).
Most of the men were bearded to the cheekbones, burned
the color of mahogany, and were a husky, tough-looking lot
who were every bit as hard as they appeared. The headquarters of the Rifles (which was a picked unit) was at
Leon, toward the northern frontier. The Light Infantry
centered about Granada. Besides these regular troops,
Walker estimated that there were another six hundred
American civilians about the country, some of whom were
organized as a volunteer reserve who could be called into
service in case of an enemy attack. More settlers and recruits
were constantly arriving so that each week brought an increase in Walker's strength and a greater sense of security.
Besides the American immigrants, in the late winter of
1856 a body of two hundred and fifty Cuban volunteers
arrived under the command of D. Domingo de Goicouria
and it was tacitly understood by all that these Cubans eventually expected Walker's help, after his victory was assured,
in winning the independence of their island from the
Spaniards.

All these troops seemed to have behaved pretty well during this lull between storms. There was occasionally too
much drinking, especially among the officers, which irked
the abstemious Walker, and probably the usual amount of
"fraternization" went on, but this was as nothing to the
later excesses when things went wrong. According to the
native historians and chroniclers Walker found himself an
attractive mistress and his descendants are said to live in
Granada today. Her name was Elenita Ojaran [O'Harran],

the granddaughter of an Irishman in the old Spanish colonial service, and she was a lovely, winsome girl.[3]

There were some musicians, mostly Germans, among the arriving volunteers and these often organized themselves into impromptu fife-and-drum corps or brass bands and gave concerts in the main plaza of Granada, but they probably never equaled the excellent military bands of the native Nicaraguans, who, like all Latin Americans, were born with a flair for music. On occasion these rather informal bands would march to the quarters of their Commander-in-Chief, followed by most of the off-duty filibusters, to serenade him with such tunes as "Yankee Doodle" and "Hail Columbia." Then, following the old American custom, there would be loud cheers and calls for "Colonel Walker" to make a speech. Walker would appear on a balcony, say a few appropriate words to his "fellow citizens"; there would be cheers for "Uncle Billy" (he was thirty-two years old) and the men would gradually disperse to their *chiquitas* or the various *cantinas*.

Two events led to the breakup of this situation for the American filibusters, both taking place in February, 1856. The first was the outbreak of war with the republic of Costa Rica, lying immediately to the south of Nicaragua. This southernmost of the five Central American republics was the most stable and conservative, possibly because its citizens were almost entirely of pure Spanish blood in marked contrast to its Indian and *mestizo* neighbors to the

---

[3] Darwin Teilhet obtained this information while in Nicaragua gathering material for his novel, *The Lion's Skin*, p. 344.

north. Walker had sent Louis Schlesinger,[4] whom we met as a follower of the ill-fated Narciso Lopez in Cuba, as an envoy to Costa Rica seeking peace early in February. Incidentally, Schlesinger, for whom a definite warrant had been issued, had been a passenger on the *Northern Light*, but he had escaped the eagle eye of the efficient Captain Faunce by disguising himself as a sailor. Schlesinger and two fellow envoys were rudely turned back by the Costa Ricans and late that same month that republic, controlled by the conservative Legitimists, announced its support "for the republic of Nicaragua" and declared war on the American filibusters alone, with a pronouncement that no quarter would be given to Walker's "bandits." President Mora raised an army of nine thousand men and early in March took the offensive by crossing the boundary with about half that number. Walker at once ordered his troops to resume wearing the old red ribbon of the Democrats and moved the government to Leon, thus once again making his government a partisan one.

But even more fateful than these ominous hostilities with the neighboring Costa Ricans was Walker's abrogation of the contract with Commodore Vanderbilt's Accessory Transit Company, the seizure of all its steamers and properties in Nicaragua, and the granting of a new charter to the local representative of Charles Morgan in New York and Cornelius K. Garrison of San Francisco, the men who had unsuccessfully tried to gain control of the company during

---

[4] Walker and other writers spelled his name with two s's, but I have followed the spelling used in his own articles in *The Democratic Review*.

Vanderbilt's absence in Europe. This drastic act had been simmering ever since Walker captured Granada. He was much in their debt for certain favors, such as the free transportation of many recruits from the States, and the loan of $20,000 in gold. But he raised up a terrible and deadly enemy in Commodore Vanderbilt by this high-handed confiscation of what the old man had built up and its transfer to his business enemies. Walker justified this extreme act by one of his legal rationalizations, in which he claimed the company had defrauded the republic of Nicaragua in its yearly payments. Very possibly it had, but that did not excuse the sheer, outright stupidity of this rash action. Vanderbilt had returned from Europe, regained control of the Accessory Transit Company and was giving Walker his wholehearted support by encouraging recruiting in the States, in furnishing these volunteers free transportation to Nicaragua when necessary, and in giving freight priorities to supplies and equipment for the American filibusters. Walker had the backing of the greatest financial power in the United States and he threw it over.

The old Commodore's wrath when he heard of this rash act was said to have been terrible beyond description and he immediately suspended the sailings of all Transit ships to Nicaragua. What especially infuriated him was the departure, with his blessings but a few days before, of the two hundred and fifty Cuban volunteers under Domingo de Goicouria on one of his Transit steamships with their passages charged to his account. Thenceforth all his enormous resources were thrown against William Walker and the latter's Central American enemies could write their own ticket for money and arms to use against the filibuster leader. Walker wrote his inevitable end when he published this decree of confiscation by the hand of his puppet, President Rivas. Most probably Walker had been lulled and gulled by the agents of Vanderbilt's enemies and believed that they had the resources to withstand successfully the Commodore's onslaughts. Evidently his knowledge of the financial world, and the relative powers therein, was woefully distorted.

Vanderbilt then turned to the State Department in Washington for some kind of redress for this outrage. Just previous, he had sneered at our neutrality laws and the pitiful efforts made to enforce them, and had defied the officials of the government. Now it was the turn of the government to laugh. But Vanderbilt was no man to be stopped by a few unfavorable preliminary skirmishes. Finding that he could get no official assistance, or even sympathy, in Washington he turned all his efforts and resources to helping Walker's enemies in Central America. First, he began secret negotiations with Walker's puppet, President Rivas, through an unknown intermediary[5] who was close to both Rivas and Walker, and this probably was a major cause in the break between these two a few months later. Other agents were sent to help the Costa Ricans and these achieved successes, in time, which were fatal to the filibusters' cause. But for the present all he could do was to withdraw all the company's steamers sailing to and from Nicaragua. Garrison and Morgan, who planned to substitute steamers of their

---

[5] This traitor was never discovered. There is some evidence now that it may have been Domingo de Goicouria.

own, were not as yet ready and for six weeks Walker was cut off from supplies and reinforcements from the States.

In the meantime the Costa Rican army had crossed the border on March 11, 1856. To meet the invasion, Walker sent a battalion of four companies under the command of the newly arrived Louis Schlesinger. These men were poorly chosen for their mission because most of them were green recruits with no military experience, and one company contained only Germans and another only Frenchmen with hardly a man able to understand English. Walker wrote that he chose Schlesinger to command this heterogeneous mob because he was the only officer who could speak to each man in his own language. Why he did not send some of his case-hardened veterans on such an important assignment is hard to understand. He must have greatly underestimated the Costa Ricans. The result was a disastrous defeat for the filibusters who were skillfully ambushed and driven back in a disgraceful rout by the enemy who were commanded by a Prussian soldier-of-fortune who had once been an old comrade-at-arms of Walker's officer, Bruno von Natzmer.

Walker was ill in bed with a fever when this bad news came and was not able to return to duty for a few days. The American civilians caught the panic contagion and many sought to leave the country at once. Many officers of the army went on prolonged benders, including Walker's own brother Norvell, a captain. To stop this mounting demoralization Walker reduced Norvell to the ranks as an example, which halted the carousing; and then, so as better to protect and control the Transit Road, he moved his entire force from Granada to Rivas. In all he had about five hundred men fit for duty to meet an oncoming Costa Rican army of about four thousand. As soon as his forces were in Rivas, Walker paraded them in the main plaza and gave them a straight-from-the-shoulder fight talk which did not gloss over their peril but emphasized the need for future good behavior to overcome their overwhelming enemies. This speech had the desired effect and the conduct and *esprit de corps* of his followers noticeably improved.

Walker then impetuously moved his army back to Granada again because of rumors of an impending invasion from the north by San Salvador, Honduras, and Guatemala. The victorious Costa Ricans marched into Rivas on the heels of the retreating filibusters, plundered and burned the property of the long-suffering Transit Company at Virgin Bay, killed nine of its civilian employees, and promised death to all Americans. It was difficult for the natives to distinguish between an innocent civilian workman or traveler and a filibuster.

When news of this reached Walker he attacked Rivas with six hundred men, on April 11, 1856, in another slapdash, screaming, revolver-shooting assault which gained the central plaza. But again he was forced out by an overwhelming enemy, leaving behind his seriously wounded, whom the Costa Ricans slaughtered. It was a thoroughly bad piece of generalship on his part.

But the Costa Rican commander was even worse. Instead of burning or burying the dead, he threw the corpses of friend and foe into the wells of the town. A frightful epidemic of cholera followed and the demoralized Costa

Ricans retreated home, where only four hundred arrived out of an invading army of four thousand. The disease spread through the country and over ten thousand more Costa Ricans died in the debacle. Before leaving Rivas, however, the enemy begged mercy for the sick and wounded left behind and Walker showed his usual humanity to prisoners by giving these poor devils the same care as his own men received.

The Americans suffered far less from the cholera because of the efficiency of their surgeon general, Dr. Israel Moses, and, also, they showed more natural resistance to the dreadful disease. One of the victims, however, was Walker's youngest brother James, who had recently arrived.

Gradually the cholera wore itself out. Nicaragua was free of invaders, and Charles Morgan in New York somehow found new steamships in which a fresh stream of men and supplies arrived. In May, the encouraging news came that the priest, Father Augustin Vigil, former curate of Granada, who had been sent as minister to replace the impossible Parker French, had been formally received by the State Department in Washington, which meant the long-desired recognition by the United States. The outlook for the filibusters became more favorable than it had been since the peace treaty of the previous October.

The next step toward stabilization was an election of a permanent government and this was set for June 10th by Acting President Rivas. It was a foregone conclusion that William Walker would be the successful candidate for the presidency but behind the scenes the resentment of the native leaders was mounting. Suddenly Rivas and some of the prominent Democrats in Leon took off to the north, whence they sent appeals to San Salvador and Guatemala for help to expel the American invaders, and these countries and Honduras sent troops to Leon. Shortly afterwards, Walker's former puppet Rivas launched a blast against the filibusters to his fellow Nicaraguans, exhorting them to revolt against the invading filibusters.

Walker at once concentrated his forces in Granada, which he re-established as the capital and, amidst a great smoke screen of legal huffs and puffs, held the election on June 29th in all the districts controlled by his men, who voted as often as twenty times apiece. He was overwhelmingly elected.

On July 12, 1856, President William Walker was inaugurated in Granada. There was a parade of the filibusters behind a band and the city officials and foreign diplomats fell into line to the main plaza. After taking the oath of office on bended knees, President Walker delivered his inaugural address in English (translated into Spanish by a Cuban aide) which, besides the usual platitudes, gave a strong hint that his objective was not annexation to the United States but the establishment of an empire of Central America and Cuba. All then entered the cathedral where a *Te Deum* was sung, and afterwards attended a banquet at which only light wines were served, following Walker's temperate habits. This was just as well, for fifty-three toasts were drunk: one to the President of the United States, and another to "Uncle Billy" Walker at which the stern little president was said to have laughed heartily, a most unusual event. The avuncular title for the thirty-two-year-old president, however, was not so ridiculous as it sounded, for the average age of his officers was but twenty-four years.

The little "gray-eyed man of destiny" had reached the top in but a little over a year after he landed with his fifty-odd "Immortals." To this day, he is the only native-born American who has ever become the head of a foreign sovereign nation.

★ 3 ★

Five days after Walker's inaugural, Minister John H. Wheeler once more took it upon himself to extend the recognition of the United States to the new Walker administration. In doing this he let his enthusiasm for the filibusters carry him again beyond his instructions, for he had only been told to recognize the Rivas-Walker regime which had disappeared when President Rivas had deserted to Walker's Central American enemies to the north. Quite a show was put on for Wheeler's impetuous act, for he was given a military escort and a brass band to accompany him to the executive offices where he delivered a formal and fulsome speech to his intimate friend, President William Walker, and his assembled staff, in which he welcomed Nicaragua again into the fold of socially acceptable nations. When news of this reached Washington, Secretary of State Marcy at once recalled Wheeler and forced his resignation, and no replacement was sent to Nicaragua for the rest of Walker's sway.

On the other hand, Father Vigil was having his own troubles in Washington as the representative of the Rivas-Walker government. Although officially received by the

State Department, he met slurs and snubs from most of the diplomatic corps. The Latin Americans moved against him, almost as a body, and even drafted a tentative alliance against the filibusters which they sent home to their governments for approval. Great Britain, France and Spain also used their influences against the lonely priest and, to climax his unhappy lot, his fellow clergymen gave him the cold shoulder as well. It was too much for the sensitive padre and he returned to Nicaragua before the end of June where he soon thereafter asked for his passport and left for New Granada (Colombia). There he found a haven in a quiet rural parish. Walker replaced Vigil by Appleton Oaksmith who, like the original promoter of the Nicaraguan venture Byron Cole, was from the state of Maine. Oaksmith, who was interested in floating some bonds for the new Walker government, was a man of wealth and influence in the States, but this availed him naught, for Marcy refused to receive him. And thenceforth there were no official relations between the United States and the Walker administration.

Despite these setbacks in foreign relations, Walker turned to internal affairs with zest. His two main purposes were to induce immigration from the States and to raise money; and he combined these by confiscating, in July, the estates of those he termed "enemies of the republic" and offering them for sale to the highest bidders, with payment in cash or the military script used to pay his soldiers. This redeemed script would, of course, cancel a large part of his indebtedness, and these estates would be in the hands of his supporters. Also, he hoped to attract American capital to speculate in these attractive offerings which were sold considerably below their true values. But, naturally enough, the native landowners were considerably alarmed and gave more support to his enemies.

To make it even more difficult for the natives and more advantageous to prospective American landowners, he also issued a simultaneous decree which announced that all public documents might be written in either Spanish or English, thereby making it legal for court proceedings and the recording of deeds to be made in English, which would eventually give the Americans a great advantage over the natives in any litigation. Walker frankly admitted this in his book, *The War in Nicaragua* (p. 252), by writing: "The decree concerning the use of the two languages tended to make the ownership of the lands of the State fall into the hands of those speaking English." And then, to securely clinch this advantage, he issued still another decree which required the registry of all land titles within six months. The registry system was common practice in the United States but was completely unknown in Nicaragua and certainly only half a year was a short time for this drastic change to be effected. Also stories of how huge blocks of land had been swindled away from the native owners in California by unscrupulous gringo operators taking advantage of their ignorance of similar land laws must have penetrated into Nicaragua as they had into Mexico. Walker was brutally frank when he went on to write:

The general tendency of these several decrees was the same. They were intended to place a large portion of the land of the country in the hands of the white race. The military force of the State might, for a time, secure the Americans in the government of the Republic, but in order that their possession of government might be permanent, it was requisite for them to hold the land.

It is a wonder that he had any native followers at all after these decrees, but this amazing man always seemed to have supporters, no matter how harsh his policies. Perhaps those Nicaraguans who remained loyal to him (and a surprising number did to the bitter end) were mostly of the landless class, or perhaps he made special exceptions, off the record, for certain favored native landowners.

Supplementing these extreme decrees which so favored the Americans, Walker's agent in the States made a colonization contract, in August, 1856, with the Yankee entrepreneur William Leslie Cazneau. This contract called for the settlement, within a year, of a thousand able-bodied colonists of good character in Nicaragua, and Walker's government, on its part, agreed to establish them in settlements (presumably on state lands) of not less than fifty families each and to furnish each colonist with eighty acres of land, the title of which was to pass, free and clear, to each settler after only a year's residence. This contract, however, never amounted to anything because of the outbreak of war with all the other Central American republics. Walker also sent several of his army officers to scatter through the South and California on recruiting missions. He was said to be disgusted by the low type of volunteers, mostly foreigners, who had arrived from city slums, and instructed these officers to recruit, as far as possible, native-born Americans of pioneer stock. These men were fairly successful in obtaining recruits but later circumstances prevented their reaching Walker.

Following soon after these extraordinary fiats, toward the

end of August, came an ominous figure on the Nicaraguan stage in the person of the Hon. Pierre Soulé, one-time champion of the Spanish dueling field and certainly no harbinger of good tidings for the Nicaraguan landowners. The outward purpose of Soulé's visit was to float a loan secured by the public lands of the state. This deal was successfully arranged, for a new decree was issued about a week later allocating one million acres as security for a loan of $500,000 for twenty years at six per cent interest. A few bonds were later sold in New Orleans but nothing much seems to have come of this financial transaction before Walker's fortunes took a downward turn.

What really was interesting was the undercover influence of Soulé and its results. As we have seen, he was a fervent leader of the states-rights Southerners, a fanatical believer in the institution of slavery, and an extreme advocate of its expansion into new territory. What went on in private conversations between him and Walker is, of course, unknown, but soon after his arrival Walker issued more decrees which were of the greatest potential importance and radically changed his former policies. It does seem as if there was some kind of an organized cabal working at this time to support Walker and other potential expansionists. One can catch glimpses now and then of what seems suspiciously like concerted actions by men like Soulé, John A. Quitman of Mississippi, and other Southern leaders. Whether the secret Knights of the Golden Circle had any part in these dealings remains unknown. Probably all the records (if any) were destroyed years ago and it would be impossible to find definite proof of any such conspiracy at this late date. But, nevertheless, the writer has a very strong feeling that there was more going on in the way of organized secret support for Walker, particularly in the South, than meets the eye in published memoirs and history books.

Walker showed his wholehearted admiration for Soulé by writing:

But, although the decree for the loan was the immediate object of Mr. Soulé's visit, his presence in Nicaragua had other beneficial results. His fine head and noble air made a deep impression on the people of the country, peculiarly sensitive as they are to the charms of feature and of manner; and then he spoke the Castilian with such lofty elegance, and addressed the common people with so much kindness and insight into their wants and feelings that all listened to him with mingled delight and reverence. The docility of the native Nicaraguans, especially of the Indians, is great, and when approached with gentleness and persuasion they may be led in almost any direction. The influence of such words as Mr. Soulé spoke to them remained for a long time, and often after he left they used to ask when His Excellency, a title they give to persons they consider of rank, would return to Nicaragua.

Soulé's influence on Walker probably was the cause of the startling decrees which the President issued in the next month of September. There was no question of any legislative approval for these revolutionary changes or of any judicial review of their legality. Walker was a complete dictator and his word was law. Soulé was a visionary of boundless dreams for an American civilization based on slavery, and he unquestionably fired Walker with his zeal and inspired these drastic changes in the Nicaraguan program, which purported to secure an adequate supply of labor for any American purchaser of confiscated or state lands. For of what use were the lands without labor to till them? And under the existing system the easy-going natives would not work to meet American standards. The first decree was against vagrancy and allowed persons without visible means of support to be sentenced up to six months of labor on public works. This was followed by another decree covering labor contracts whereby a laborer was severely punished for failure to fulfill his obligations for the specified time of the contract. In effect this established a system of peonage which many observers believed worse than actual slavery, as the employer did not have the responsibilities for his laborers as did a slave owner for his slaves. This system was quite common in Latin America, especially in Mexico, and many pro-slavery advocates pointed a finger of scorn at it, probably in the hopes of diverting the attention of Northern reformers from their own peculiar institution.

But the really astonishing decree was the one which President William Walker issued on September 22, 1856. This, at first glance, appeared rather innocuous for it simply declared null and void the acts and decrees of the old government of the United Provinces of Central America —the short-lived government which had existed for a halcyon period of only fifteen years (from 1823 to 1838) before it had disintegrated into five separate republics. But it should be remembered that an act of this former government had abolished slavery in the year 1824 so that Walker's decree, by erasing all the old Federal enactments, made slavery

203

lawful again in Nicaragua. The hand of His Excellency, the Hon. Pierre Soulé, seems all too obvious in this extremely significant action of Walker.

That this decree was startling is to state it mildly. Walker, although a Southerner from Tennessee, had never identified himself in his lawyer or journalist days with the pro-slavery faction of the Democratic Party. Quite the contrary, he had even been accused in New Orleans of editing an anti-slavery, Yankee newspaper. And in California he had definitely been with the anti-slavery element of his party. Suddenly, and without any warning to his supporters, he aligned himself with the slavery extremists.

But once Walker had come out for slavery he went overboard completely. He not only declared for its re-establishment in Nicaragua but also for a revival of the slave trade to furnish the needed slaves in a country where Negroes were rather a rarity. To the twentieth century reader his arguments as set forth in his book, *The War in Nicaragua*,[6] are simply astounding. They do, however, illustrate the sincere beliefs of most Southerners of the time, and provide an authentic glimpse of that now forgotten point of view. Mostly he based his arguments on economic reasons. For example, Haiti had been the jewel of the French colonial empire until the Negroes had gained their independence, since when it had been a jungle of savagery with increasing degeneration in every way. The British possession of Jamaica had been a profitable island until the abolition of slavery in 1832, since when it, and the other British West

---

[6] General William Walker, *The War in Nicaragua*. Mobile, 1860, pp. 255-280.

Indian islands, had become poorhouses and liabilities to the mother country because of the chronic unwillingness of the Negroes to do any voluntary labor. As for the abolishment of the slave trade on the high seas, which had been accomplished under British leadership, he believed that Great Britain had finally realized her mistake and that

> . . . the frenzy of the British public against the slave-trade has exhausted itself, and men have begun to perceive that they were led into error by the benevolent enthusiasm of parsons, who knew more about Greek and Hebrew than they did about physiology or political economy, and of middle-aged spinsters, smit with the love of general humanity, though disdaining to fix their affections firmly on any objects less remote than Africa.

All verbiage aside, what Walker's new policy undoubtedly meant was that he preferred to count on the wholehearted (often fanatical) and enthusiastic support of the solid South rather than on the lukewarm and erratic backing of the United States as a whole. It meant that he had given up any plans for annexation to the United States in favor of the project of an independent Caribbean state based on slavery which would be bound by the closest ties to the slave states at home, and if and when these same states seceded from the Union, either peacefully or successfully in "the irrepressible conflict," then his Caribbean empire would act as an ally in case of war, or, if the secession was peacefully accomplished, it would consider annexation to a Southern Confederacy. Again there is the strong feeling that a coterie of intelligent Southerners had foreseen the coming struggle and were working behind the scenes for a strategic position in the Caribbean area.

But again Walker was as ill advised as he had been in his opposition to Commodore Vanderbilt. He more or less admitted this in his book (written some four years later) when he noted:

It is true the author of the slavery decree was not aware, at the time it was published, of the strong and universal feeling which exists in the Northern States against Southern society. He did not know how thoroughly anti-slavery sentiments prevail in the free-labor States; that they are taught in the schools, preached from the pulpits, and instilled by mothers into the minds of their children from infancy upward.

But then Walker, as if ashamed of this admission, went on to say: "But the knowledge of such a state of feeling would have made the publication of the decree a matter of sacred duty no less than of policy." This was written just before his last desperate filibustering attempt, in 1860, when he still counted on Southern support.

At all events, none of these drastic decrees was ever put into effect, for Walker was thenceforth so busy combatting his ever-increasing enemies that he never again had the time for internal changes in Nicaragua either in theory or practice. The strange part of it is that these decrees did not seem to diminish the loyalty of most of his Northern followers, of whom there were a goodly number, including many New Englanders such as Byron Cole (shortly afterwards killed), Joseph W. Fabens, William L. Cazneau, and Appleton Oaksmith. Very probably they were all too deeply involved by that time and, besides, they may have looked on these decrees as being only on paper, which time would eventually modify; or, in some cases, they had been converted to the belief that slavery in the tropics was a fit and proper institution which would be profitable to themselves.

Just a few days before Walker issued his decree about slavery, the combined armies of Guatemala, San Salvador, and Honduras advanced southward from the city of Leon, where they had assembled, under the command of a rather inept Salvadorian general who was hampered by the usual Latin-American jealousies. To meet them Walker now had about eight hundred men, including a small body of cavalry under the command of an able officer, Major John P. Waters, a natural cavalryman who, like poets, are born, not made. Probably this was the most efficient fighting force the filibuster leader had ever commanded but he mishandled it.

First, he withdrew his garrison from Masaya, an outlying town north of Granada, and presented the enemy with this well-fortified base. Then, he decided to recapture the place, and led one of his usual slambang, revolver-shooting attacks into the town, but soon withdrew when news came that an enemy force had slipped behind his rear and was attacking Granada. He led his men, staggering from fatigue, on a forced march back to the capital and drove out a gloating force of Guatemalans, glutted with liquor and plunder, on October 13, 1856, just a year, to the day, after he had himself captured the city by a sneak attack.

A few days later the embattled filibusters were immeasurably encouraged and strengthened by the arrival of the famous soldier of fortune Charles Frederick Henningsen, an Englishman of Scandinavian descent, who had won great renown on the side of the rebellious Carlists in Spain and with the revolutionists in Russia and Hungary. A tall, handsome *beau sabreur,* just over forty years old, and an author of considerable note, he possessed the highest military talents and henceforth Walker could count on the best technical advice. With him Henningsen brought a shipment of several thousand Minié rifles and some howitzers and ammunition, a present from his wealthy wife, the niece of Senator Berrien of Georgia.

Walker immediately commissioned Henningsen a brigadier general and made him second in command, and the energetic newcomer began the training of the men in the use of these arms. Some of the officers resented the high rank given to him. "But," wrote Walker, "his own worth and merits soon overcame most of these prejudices, though in the breasts of some officers jealousy lurked to the last."

CHAPTER X

Here Was Granada

THE city of Granada followed the regular rectangular pattern of Spanish-American cities, with its main plaza the center of a right-angled web of straight streets which ran into smaller plazas at intervals until they finally reached Lake Nicaragua on the east and the open country in the other directions. The houses were constructed of the usual stone and cement, or adobe, one or two stories high, with a forbidding front, abutting on the sidewalk, which presented only heavily barred windows and a massive, thick wooden door to the outside world. On the larger houses belonging to the wealthier families there was often a coat of arms, carved in stone over the doorway, a relic of the old days of Spanish rule. Inside, the scene was a contrast for the life of the household centered about an attractive interior patio, filled with flowers, in which a fountain often played cheerfully. The ceilings were high, which allowed a circulation of air on the hottest days, and the inhabitants would doze in swinging hammocks for their afternoon siestas, lulled by the music of a guitar or the sound of gently flowing water. One American observer believed that

the ubiquitous hammock in Nicaragua was the greatest
obstacle to modern progress; which was probably so, but it
was a delightful instrument of passive resistance. In the
larger urban houses of this sort and on the great haciendas
in the country there were families who preserved the old
customs and traditions of Spain. Many of their sons and
daughters were educated in Europe and maintained, as one
old filibuster nostalgically recalled, over fifty years later, "an
elegance and brilliancy, a delicacy and refinement, that
found expression in the grace of its women and the gallantry of its men."

In the background was the romantic setting of the country about which this same *filibustero* wrote:

The tropical luxuriance of its flowers, its sparkling sunshine,
its blue skies, and the soft languor of its moonlit nights, made
Nicaragua a land where one's heart was keenly susceptible to
romance and sentiment. While pianos were to be found in
Nicaraguan homes, yet the guitar, softer and sweeter than in a
northern clime, was the favorite musical instrument, and its
tinkling accompaniment to the song of some lovely woman filled
softly many a night at Rivas, at Granada, at Leon, and at San
Juan del Sur.[1]

The charm and beauty of these native women was celebrated in verse by General Mirabeau Buonaparte Lamar, a
former President of the Republic of Texas, who served as
United States Minister to the country soon after Walker's
withdrawal. Lamar wrote poetry in the Byronic manner
and commemorated the Nicaraguan belles in "The Daughter of Mendoza," of which one stanza went:

_____
[1] James Carson Jamison, *With Walker in Nicaragua*. Columbia, Missouri,
1909, pp. 115-116.

Here Was Granada

How brilliant is the morning star!
The evening star how tender!
The light of both is in her eye,
Their softness and their splendor.
But for the lash that shades their light,
They are too dazzling for the sight;
And when she shuts them, all is night—
The daughter of Mendoza.

General Mirabeau Buonaparte Lamar[2] was probably a better President of Texas than he was a poet but he gave the general idea of the tropical charm of the upper-class Nicaraguan señoritas.

A few of Walker's *filibusteros* gained an entree into this delightful society and a few, a very few, married the native charmers and like the lotus eaters never returned home. And, as the Nicaraguans claim, the rigid little man of destiny, William Walker, found solace in the arms of Elenita Ojaran.

But the bulk of the Americans found social relaxation amongst themselves in the local *cantinas* and with the type of women who would hang around such a place. There was

---

[2] The family ran to florid names. One, Gazaway Bugg Lamar, was a prominent Southern banker, and Mirabeau's nephew, Lucius Quintus Cincinnatus Lamar, was a Confederate officer and Congressman, the Confederate Envoy to Russia, a United States Congressman and Senator from Mississippi, the Secretary of the Interior under President Grover Cleveland, and finally, a Justice of the Supreme Court of the United States. According to Winfield Shiras in his excellent book, *Justice Shiras of Pittsburgh* (pp. 112-113), "Towards the ladies he was chivalry itself, and various stories are told of his gallantries and pretty speeches. On one occasion he was taken to task by a lady at Bar Harbor, who thought he had failed to recognize her. 'Ah, Judge,' said she, 'I am afraid you don't remember me. I met you here two years ago.' 'Remember you, Madame!' was the quick reply, with one of his courtliest bows. 'Why, I've been trying ever since to *forget* you!' 'Oh, go away,' replied the lady, laughing. 'You dear, delightful old Southern humbug!' "—all of which is irrelevant to the rough and tough filibusters.

considerable gambling and a tremendous amount of drinking with a natural consequence of quarrels and many duels; so many, in fact, that it became a serious problem to prevent the *filibusteros* from maiming or killing each other for the most trivial of disagreements. Distinctions of rank had no place in these affairs of honor and the old *filibustero* Jamison recalled one duel between Lieutenant Kelley and Private Murphy of Captain Jack Dunigan's company, of which the obliging Captain acted as second for both men. The dispute was over "a captivating damsel of Nicaragua, with whom both were in love, and upon whom they were showering their attentions. . . . Lieutenant Kelley had a small five-shooter, while Private Murphy was armed with a big dragoon six, old style."

After the duelists had taken their places and the helpful Captain was giving them instructions as to the proper procedure, the Lieutenant took a couple of practice sighting shots at his opponent, whereupon Private Murphy bawled with much agitation, "Hould on, now, Lieutenant Kelley, till the Captain says the worrd, me boy." [3]

At the given word, Private Murphy shot Lieutenant Kelley in the foot, a slight wound, which satisfied the honor of the disputants.

But many other duels did not have so light an ending and the internecine killings and maimings amongst the Americans became a very serious problem indeed. President Walker approved of the principle of dueling—he had fought several himself in the States and had once been wounded—but he believed that they should be fought only as the

---

[3] *Ibid.*, p. 109.

last resort of a serious quarrel and not over some trivial drunken argument. Idleness and liquor were the causes of most of these petty squabbles which so often ended tragically.

The antidote to this kind of demoralization was, of course, to keep the men occupied. And the arrival of General Henningsen brought this ugly habit within reasonable bounds by his program of daily drills and training which kept the men out of the saloons during the day and made them so tired that they fell into bed early at night.

President Walker boasted a navy as well. In July of that year his men at the Pacific port of San Juan del Sur had seized a Costa Rican schooner flying the American flag, whose owner was a wealthy Democrat supporter of Walker's named Mariano Salazar. That had not saved his ship when it was found it was unlawfully flying this flag, and the vessel was seized by the government. Salazar, who had a bad reputation in his business dealings, was furious and became a bitter foe of the filibuster leader, for which he was later to forfeit his life. Walker then equipped the ship with a couple of six-pounders, renamed her the *Granada* and appointed as her commander Lieutenant Callender Irvine Fayssoux, the same man who had served on the *Pampero* and the *Creole* on Narciso Lopez's two expeditions into Cuba.[4] He was an extraordinarily able seaman and officer, a small and taciturn man like his chief and equally touchy about the dignity of his position.

Later that same month Lieutenant Fayssoux captured Salazar, the former owner of his ship, on the high seas and

---

[4] See p. 53 *et. seq.*

delivered him to Walker in Granada where he paid the penalty of traitors and was shot in the plaza amidst the rejoicings of the Granadinos, who hated him for his former Democratic affiliations and for his rapacity in making money.

Lieutenant Fayssoux cruised the *Granada* up and down the Pacific coast of Nicaragua, especially in the Bay of Fonseca, where he was of great use in preventing the shipments of men and supplies to the allied enemy by sea. Late in November, off the harbor of San Juan del Sur, he encountered one evening a Costa Rican man-of-war which was armed with four nine-pound guns and manned by a hundred and fourteen men. Fayssoux at once engaged her with his *Granada,* with a working crew of twenty-three and his two six-pounders. The engagement lasted for two hours before a large crowd of spectators on the beach who could just see the gun flashes in the growing darkness and amidst the clouds of powder smoke. It was terminated by a sudden bright glare and a terrific explosion and, as Fayssoux did not return, all decided that he had blown up his ship to prevent her capture by his much stronger opponent. They had all heard him say that he would never surrender and knowing the man they had no doubt about his keeping his word. News of the supposed disaster was sent to Walker, who was in Virgin Bay with his followers at the time, and this arrived at a particularly low point of filibuster morale and thickened the gloom.

The next morning, however, the *Granada* sailed jauntily into the harbor with her decks crowded with men. These were mostly Costa Rican survivors whom Fayssoux had rescued after a shot had blown up the magazine of their ship. The Americans had only had one man killed and eight wounded. The depression of the filibusters quickly turned to rejoicing; Walker promoted Fayssoux to captain, and presented him with a large estate near Rivas which, however, the little naval captain never had the chance to enjoy. To the very end he maintained control of the Pacific coast for Walker in marked distinction to the reverses on land. Walker treated the naval captives with his usual humanity and even sent them back home (he had no food to spare for prisoners) where they spread reports of their good treatment, greatly to the concern of their government which had loosed much propaganda about the atrocities of the filibusters and which finally silenced them by direct orders. But none of these survivors could ever be forced to fight against the Americans again.

On the first of that same month of November, 1856, Costa Rica had actively re-entered the war with a blasting pronouncement against the "immigrant usurpers," and a quick striking force had seized San Juan del Sur, which was not garrisoned by the Americans, in order to control the Transit Road which they called "a highway of filibusterism." The only force Walker had in the area was his navy of one schooner under Fayssoux.

This sudden attack forced Walker to a momentous decision. The Transit Road was absolutely vital to him and he did not have enough men to control this life line and, at the same time, defend the city of Granada against the allied army at Masaya which had grown to a strength of three thousand men. He decided to evacuate Granada and move his forces to Rivas where he could control the Transit until such time as circumstances might allow him to drive his northern enemies from the country.

First, however, he executed two lightning blows to disorganize his foes and prevent them from joining forces. On November 11th, he and Henningsen led a fast-moving force of two hundred and fifty picked Rifles and two field howitzers along the length of the Transit from Virgin Bay to San Juan del Sur. This mobile force swept and scattered the Costa Ricans in all directions and so demoralized them that all immediate threat from that quarter disappeared. The next morning, leaving Fayssoux to guard the port with the navy, Walker about-faced and quickly marched his jubilant filibusters back to Virgin Bay, whence he embarked them on a steamer and reached Granada the same night.

Two days later he was again on the road to Masaya with about five hundred and sixty men. The day was broiling hot, the road dusty, and the men and pack mules tired and lagging. When about halfway, word came that the enemy had sent a flanking force to join some remnants of the defeated Costa Ricans who had gathered at Rivas. This forced Walker to detach nearly half his men and send them back to Granada with orders to take the steamer to Virgin Bay and hold the Transit at all costs. Then he pushed on with only three hundred men to attack about ten times that number holding the well-fortified Masaya. But with Henningsen's artillery he hoped to overcome these appalling odds.

As Walker approached the town, one of his most exuber-

ant officers, Major Thomas Henry,[5] who had impatiently ridden ahead of the plodding column, took it upon himself to
charge, with one companion, the enemy's outposts. Henry
was one of the incorrigible duelists of the army—as the old
filibuster Jamison described him: "Henry could no more
refrain from a duel than a boy could keep away from a
game of marbles." He was recovering from a wound received at the previous attack on Masaya and in addition
had his head in bandages where a bullet had grazed him in
a recent duel. Too weak to walk, he had mounted a mule to
accompany the column. The sight of a Guatemalan picket
so excited this lusty officer that, with a whoop and a holler,
he and his companion charged into the enemy lines, enthusiastically firing their pistols, and drove the panicked pickets
before them into the town. It was an act of derring-do
typical of the reckless bravery of the filibusters but, as often
happened in such a case, it did more harm than good for
it alerted the main body of the enemy to the approach of
the Americans.

For two days Walker assaulted Masaya. The going was
tough and slow. The fuses were timed too short and most
of the shells exploded in the air.[6] Henningsen's sappers cut
their way laboriously through from one house to another
but the overwhelming enemy kept the attackers under
constant fire and inflicted heavy casualties. After forty-eight
hours of ceaseless fighting the filibusters were within a

---

[5] He had served as a sergeant of the 7th Infantry during the Mexican
War and had risen to first lieutenant for gallant and meritorious conduct
in action.

[6] This sounds like a reflection on Henningsen but, as Walker reported it,
it was an inherent defect in the manufacture of the shells.

short distance of the plaza but all were in a state of physical collapse and a third of their number had been killed or wounded. It was even impossible to prevent the sentinels from going to sleep on their feet! There was no alternative to a retreat, and Walker withdrew his men silently at night with a long train of horses and mules carrying the wounded. The enemy let them go without molestation, by which they probably missed a golden opportunity to end the whole war, although the presence of the unruffled Henningsen with one howitzer, as a rear guard, kept the column well closed up and was a moral hazard to the shaken enemy who had, as usual, suffered far more casualties than the Americans.

Once safely within the walls of Granada, Walker decided on the most ruthless act of his entire career. He not only determined to carry out his planned evacuation of the city but to destroy it—to raze it to the ground! Granada was a beautiful old city, of many traditions, founded centuries before by the Spaniards and loved by its inhabitants with a great passion. It had probably counted about seventy thousand inhabitants until the constant revolutions had reduced it to around thirty thousand when Walker seized it. It was the capital of the republic and the headquarters of Walker's army.

Granada, however, was a comparatively unhealthy place and the mortality among the Americans there had become fearful in the weeks before this decision. The lack of hygiene, poorly prepared food, excessive drinking, and late hours and license had made the American recruits susceptible to cholera, typhoid, yellow fever, dysentery, and various tropical diseases for which no intelligent treatment was known at the time. And the ravages of venereal diseases must have been frightful. The two hospitals for the Americans were called Chambers of Horror. The wounded and the sick lay in their filthy woolen clothes on dirty cots, crawled over by swarms of flies and lice, without any competent attendants, and those who rolled onto the floor might lie there unnoticed for hours in the bedlam of groans, shrieks, and delirious ravings. The stench of these charnel houses was overpowering, and even the healthy and strong would retch and gag when they came within smelling distance. The doctors and attendants may have done their best but they certainly were not the cream of the medical profession and probably they too sought the common refuge of liquor. Each day these so-called hospitals disgorged a ghastly array of corpses which were hurried away by the burial detail to make room for new patients; for often a fourth or more of the Americans would be lying there, delirious with fever, their deadliest enemy. The medical staff estimated, at the time Walker decided to evacuate Granada, that if the mortality rate continued, every American in Nicaragua would be dead within six weeks. It is easy enough to realize why the filibusters, still on their feet, turned to strong liquors as an escape. And the decision to withdraw from the unhealthy Legitimist capital, which had been occupied mostly as a matter of prestige, was a logical one in order to concentrate on the defense of the Transit route. But the determination also to destroy the city seems like the depths of revengeful vandalism. Walker reasoned that he wanted to prevent his enemies from capturing a strong fortress and gaining the prestige of occupying intact the old Legitimist capital.

First, Walker ordered the sick and wounded to be moved to the volcanic island of Ometepe which lay in Lake Nicaragua about sixteen miles from the town of Rivas where he had determined to locate his new headquarters. Ometepe for years had been an Indian reservation with no white men allowed upon it without permission of the inhabitants, but Walker disregarded this in the emergency. A lake steamer carried two hundred patients on her decks to the island and literally dumped them on the beach in charge of a very resourceful officer, Captain John M. Baldwin, and six men, who somehow managed to move most of these wretched patients to a nearby deserted Indian village in a drenching rain. There was no food available except some soup prepared by two Indian women, there were no beds, blankets, or medicines and no doctors. The patients died like flies and a few, starving or delirious, staggered off into the surrounding woods where they terrified the fugitive Indians. Three days later a military guard of sixty men, a number of doctors, and some sixty American women and children arrived, and these did what they could for the surviving patients but all were terrified when the Indians, seeking plunder, fired into the village one night. Some of the able-bodied men of the guard stampeded at this alarm and disgracefully fled the island in canoes, leaving the helpless patients and women and children behind. Walker, on a lake steamer, picked up three of these arrant cowards and headed for the island. On the way, he met a large barge filled with forlorn women

and children; and it is a pleasure to report that some of the
women gave him a dressing-down for this affair such as no
man in his command would ever have dared to do. All the
surviving patients and women and children were soon afterwards moved to San Jorge on the mainland, where conditions were much improved. And the arrival of over three
hundred fresh recruits from California and New Orleans
bolstered the sagging morale of the Americans.

While these horrors were occurring, General Henningsen
and three hundred men were busy accomplishing a holo-
caust which developed eventually into such destruction and
sufferings that they made the experiences of all the Americans, sick and well, on Ometepe seem mild by comparison.
Walker had ordered Henningsen to *destroy* Granada and his
competent subordinate literally obeyed this order. Now, this
was no simple task for a city built of stone, and adobe neces-
sitates considerable destroying. But he organized his men
into demolition detachments and systematically began to
blow up and burn the buildings section by section. The
hysterical natives streamed out of the city toward the allies
in Masaya where soon the bugles were screaming the call
to assembly. There must be a strong instinct for destruction
in mankind which fortunately is rarely allowed free rein, but
when it occasionally is unchecked it seems to develop
quickly into a frenzied mania. Henningsen's men naturally
found loot, wines and spirits in most of the houses they
entered. It seemed a shame to waste all this fine liquor and
before long, officers and men were gloriously drunk. The
drinking soon pyramided into a sort of Bacchanalian orgy.
Henningsen was unable to restrain his officers and they, in

turn, lost all control of their men. As nightfall came, the city became an obscenity with flames shooting skywards, clouds of smoke hugging the roof tops, and groups of howling drunk, smoke-blackened filibusters screaming and reeling through the streets in an orgy of plunder and destruction. For two days and two nights this bedlam of annihilation rose to a crescendo as the crazed Americans drank and plundered, smashed and fired buildings, fell in a drunken stupor in the streets from which they would be awakened, likely as not, by the kicks of yelling and singing comrades, to rise dizzily and stagger on to smash and fire other buildings in the raging inferno of explosions and smoke—and to drink some more.

Henningsen was frantic with apprehension, for his crazy-drunk men could not possibly have withstood a surprise attack from the nearby enemy in Masaya, and word of this monstrous carousal of havoc had certainly reached them. Fortunately, the allied command was delayed by arguments and jealousies and did not act during the height of the devastation, and when they did announce their presence by a fusillade of shots from the outskirts of the city, most of the filibusters had passed from drunkenness into such terrible hangovers, although weak and shaky, that they had reached a point of irritability where they wanted to kill every man in sight and the sounds of musketry shocked them into a pugnacious sobriety.

The allies attacked the city from three different sides and one column seized the Guadalupe church which stood on the street running between the wharf on Lake Nicaragua and the main plaza where Henningsen was rallying his men.

This cut off the Americans' way of retreat to where they could have been picked up by one of the lake steamers and isolated twenty-seven American civilians who were on the wharf handling supplies, but these men barricaded themselves in the remains of an adjacent old stone fort, and withstood the enemy for two days.

Walker came in near the wharf on one of the two lake steamers, and sent provisions and ammunition to the besieged men in a boat. It was important to hold the wharf as Henningsen's way of retreat or as a means to bring him relief. Walker did not reinforce the small garrison, as they seemed confident of holding their position. But a traitor amongst them, a Venezuelan freed by the filibusters from a Granada dungeon a year before, deserted to the enemy and revealed the small number of the defenders and how they could be overwhelmed from the water side by using one of the Transit Company's barges. The next night the enemy, acting on this suggestion, surrounded the Americans and killed them to the last man.

In the meantime Henningsen was having a hideous time. He had gathered his shaky and crapulous men in the main plaza from where, after setting fire to all the surrounding buildings, he began to fight his way, foot by foot, down the street toward the wharf on Lake Nicaragua. At first, many of the Americans were still half drunk and some took to the bottle again in the face of such imminent danger. Somehow he finally got them sober and into a kind of order. A filibuster named Calvin O'Neal, whose brother had fallen in the first onslaughts, came to Henningsen in a frenzy of raging grief and asked permission to charge a body of four or five hundred Guatemalan soldiers who could be seen forming in the distance. His commander gave him thirty-two picked Rifles and, as Walker described it:

> O'Neal, barefooted and in his shirt sleeves, leaped on his horse, and calling on his Rifles to follow, dashed into the midst of the Allies as they formed near the old church. The men, fired by the spirit of their leader, followed in the same fierce career, dealing death and destruction on the terrified foe. The Allies were entirely unprepared for O'Neal's sudden, clashing charge, and they fell as heedless travellers before the blast of the simoom. The slaughter made by the thirty-two Rifles was fearful, and so far were O'Neal and his men carried by the "rapture of the strife" that it was difficult for Henningsen to recall them to the Plaza. When they did return it was through streets almost blocked with the bodies of the Guatemalans they had slain.[7]

By such acts of reckless daring was Henningsen able to average up the conduct of his command from the low behavior of some of his drunken men.

By the next morning Henningsen had concentrated his forces in the main plaza and could count his strength. He had lost twenty-three men killed or captured and mustered only 227 soldiers fit for duty; he was burdened with seventy-three wounded and some seventy women and children and sick. Why these latter were not evacuated before the destruction of the city began is another example of the usual hit-or-miss staff work of Walker's army. Probably it was no fault of Henningsen. He also had eleven pieces of artillery but very little ammunition. His problem now was to win the Guadalupe church from the Allies, which blocked his way to the lake, and in which he could find room and ade-

---

[7] *Ibid.*, p. 319.

quate protection for his noncombatants and helpless sick and wounded.

Two days later, on November 27th, after blowing up a church on the plaza and destroying the nearby buildings (Henningsen was still carrying out his orders amidst the inferno) he poured a heavy artillery fire into the Guadalupe church and captured it by an immediately following assault by sixty picked Rifles. At once he moved all his forces and supplies into this large and strong building and prepared to withstand a siege until Walker could relieve him from the lake. His men had recovered from their debauchery and were willing to work and fight for their lives and for the protection of all the noncombatants. But the crowded and unsanitary conditions in the church, the food of mule and horse meats, the night chills and rains, and the stench from the unburied enemy dead outside brought much sickness to the four hundred Americans huddled together, and cholera soon appeared as a far more dreadful foe than the allies. When this disease struck, the victim was given a heavy dose of opium and not allowed to drink water, which was considered fatal. The drug often maddened the patient, who would rave for water and crawl about the floor in his agony, grappling with other delirious victims, and falling on the wounded, who would scream with pain.

A ministering angel appeared amidst these terrible scenes, Mrs. Edward Bingham, the wife of an invalid actor who had brought his family to Nicaragua to take up one of Walker's grants of land to American settlers. From the time of her arrival she had nursed in the American hospitals, and in the Guadalupe church she constantly tended the sick and wounded with magnificent courage and complete self-sacrifice which gained her the deepest gratitude of all the soldiers. Finally, worn out and weak, she became another victim of the dreaded cholera and died within a few hours. Her children perished with her but her invalid husband survived all the horrors of the siege and eventually safely reached California. Of all the Americans in Nicaragua this splendid woman showed the finest spirit.

The allies repeatedly stormed the church and were as often beaten back by the destroying fire of the American rifles. Between onslaughts they sent, under flags of truce, pleas to Henningsen for surrender, promising to spare the lives of all the Americans and even to furnish them passports and transportation out of the country. But that experienced old veteran placed small reliance in such promises (not for him or his followers would be the fate of the gullible Henry Crabb in Sonora) and sent these emissaries of peace packing back to their commanders with answers of defiance. Henningsen never seemed to rest and was everywhere, comforting the sick and wounded, cheering the tired men on watch, and always moving about the church to watch the movements of the enemy. The enemy was constantly receiving reinforcements while sickness and deaths were weakening the Americans and daily their supplies of food and ammunition lessened. An ingenious officer, Captain Swingle, partially remedied this latter want by forming cannon balls from iron scraps piled in a clay mold over which he poured molten lead.

During these harrowing two weeks, Walker daily stood

off Granada in the lake steamer *Virgen,* praying and watching for a chance to extricate Henningsen's forces. He had only two companies of men at Virgin Bay and he could not use these without allowing the enemy to capture the Transit route, which would have sealed his doom.

Frantically but helplessly he watched the battle from the water. And then, during the first week in December, three hundred recruits arrived from New Orleans and San Francisco, well-equipped men in fine fettle and spoiling for a fight. Of these, a picked body of one hundred and sixty men were chosen as a relief force and placed under the command of the cavalry leader, Colonel John Waters (he had won a well-deserved promotion). They embarked on the *Virgen* and steamed up the lake, after dark, to the same place north of Granada where the filibusters had landed, over a year before, to capture the city.

Colonel Waters quietly landed his men and silently led them toward the city. Walker watched and listened from the *Virgen* until the sharp crack of American rifles and the answering roar of the enemy's muskets told him that Waters had reached the allies' lines. His intense concentration was interrupted by a cry from the lake and a naked, swarthy youth was pulled aboard who turned out to be a Hawaiian, called Kanaka Joe, one of the original "Immortals" who had sailed with Walker from California. This dauntless man had been swimming in the lake for hours[8] and bore a note in a

---

[8] This was an exceedingly brave act, for Lake Nicaragua is infested with man-eating sharks who are believed to have come there up the San Juan River from the Caribbean. It was, and still is, extremely dangerous to swim away from the shallow waters near the shore.

sealed bottle from Henningsen which reported his condition and asked that certain signals be given from the ship when a relief force landed. The requested signals were given at once but the confusion and fighting on shore prevented their being seen. This, however, made little difference as by dawn Waters had stormed over all the enemy barricades and had joined Henningsen, with a loss of about a fourth of his men. The gallant cavalryman had led his followers with such verve and *élan* that he had convinced the enemy leaders that his relieving force was much larger than it actually was and they soon abandoned their positions blocking Henningsen's way to the lake. The Americans, who had been slowly extending their lines from the Guadalupe church down the street toward the water, quickly seized the wharf and embarked the survivors on the *Virgen* without enemy opposition.

Thus ended the greatest and most prolonged battle of the war. Of 421 Americans in Granada (military and civilian) when the allies attacked, only 135 were rescued, which meant a loss of 286 people by death, capture, or desertion in the seventeen days of the siege. Of the 277 soldiers available to Henningsen at the beginning of the fighting only 111 safely reached the *Virgen*, which was a casualty loss of sixty per cent. There were 144 civilians, largely women and children, and of these only twenty-four survived, a loss of over eighty-six per cent. Henningsen stated, and probably correctly, that the allied losses far exceeded those of the Americans. Only a soldier of Henningsen's infinite skill and fine leadership could have saved this handful of American survivors from a besieging enemy force of originally three to four thousand men.[9]

The grand old Spanish city of Granada was destroyed. Of the inhabitants, Walker wrote: "They had for their chief city a love like that of woman; and even after years have passed tears come to their eyes when they speak of the loss of their beloved Granada."

General Henningsen, before he boarded the rescuing steamer, cast one last look back at the ruined city. Then he thrust a lance into the ground and to it attached a piece of rawhide upon which he had written, *Aqui fué Granada*—"Here was Granada."

---

[9] Walker in his book, *The War in Nicaragua,* in a footnote to p. 318, gives credit for his account of the fighting in Granada to the *Personal Recollections of Nicaragua* by General C. F. Henningsen. The writer, after an exhaustive search, is convinced that no such book was ever published—unless it was a private printing. What probably happened was that Walker read this book in manuscript form and assumed that it would be published shortly thereafter, but the outbreak of the Civil War the next year prevented this. The writer also tried to find if such a manuscript exists, and advertised in the usual library and museum bulletins, but with no success.

CHAPTER XI

The Path of Glory

THE good steamship *Virgen* carried the survivors from Granada southward down Lake Nicaragua to the lakeside village of San Jorge, which was only about three miles away from the inland town of Rivas. The Allied troops, mostly remnants of the Costa Ricans scattered by Walker and Henningsen the month previous, quickly left the latter town when they learned of the arrival of Henningsen and his artillery, and struck off across country to join the main army of the allies at Masaya. Walker then established his headquarters at Rivas and took stock of his situation. It was not too bad. On New Year's Day, 1857, his army, with recent reinforcements, counted a little over nine hundred men of whom about two hundred were on the sick list. Rivas was a well-fortified town which controlled the Transit Road by three trails diverging upon it from the town like a fan, and it was within easy distance of the lake ports of San Jorge and Virgin Bay. The Americans controlled all the steamers on Lake Nicaragua and on the San Juan River, and both the terminal ports on the Caribbean and Pacific coasts. Walker had shortened his lines to defend the Transit

Road and now it became a matter of waiting for the reinforcements which were known to be on their way. With
these, and his proverbial luck, he could again successfully
drive the enemy, weakened by disease and dissension, out
of the country.

But unknown to Walker and his hopeful followers there
were ominous movements behind the scenes which brought
the direst consequences to the filibusters. The cause of these
was the vindictive Commodore Vanderbilt who had been
biding his time for an opportunity to strike where he knew
it would hurt the most—at the Transit route. The Commodore had sent aid and encouragement to the presidents of
the four other Central American republics and urged them
to unite against the common enemy. Having accomplished
this and seeing that Walker was encircled, he played his
master cards in the game of revenge. Early in the autumn
of 1856 he dispatched two secret agents to the Costa Rican
government with a well-planned scheme to strangle Walker's
lifeline. One of these men was an Englishman but the other,
an American named Sylvanus H. Spencer,[1] was the guiding
spirit. Spencer had been an engineer on one of the Transit

---

[1] He was said to be a son of a former Secretary of War, John Canfield
Spencer, and a brother of Midshipman Philip Spencer, whom Commander
Alexander Slidell Mackenzie had hanged for mutiny without a trial on the
brig *Somers* in 1842, which was the only time an officer of the United States
Navy has been so executed. The midshipman's father was Secretary of War
at the time and the consequent repercussions were enormous. Mackenzie
was court-martialed but exonerated. It was probably the most controversial
affair in the history of the U. S. Navy. Mackenzie (he had taken his wife's
family name), was a brother of John Slidell, the Confederate agent to
France, and the father of General Ranald Slidell Mackenzie, whom many
consider a more able cavalry officer and a better Indian fighter than George
Armstrong Custer.

Company's boats and knew all the ins and outs of its route on the San Juan River and across Lake Nicaragua, and he was well acquainted with the American crews.

Spencer and his companion reached San José, the Costa Rican capital, before the end of November, 1856 (while Henningsen was fighting for his life in Granada), and quickly gained the enthusiastic co-operation of the president of that republic, who furnished them an expeditionary force of a hundred and twenty men, officered by an English and a French soldier-of-fortune but under Spencer's orders. About the middle of December Spencer embarked his followers in canoes and on rafts on the San Carlos River which flows northward from Costa Rica and enters the San Juan River about sixty miles above Greytown on the Caribbean sea. To the east another river, the Serapiqui, also flows north from that republic into the San Juan which it enters about twenty-seven miles downstream from the San Carlos, at the mouth of which the American filibusters maintained a small garrison at a place called Hipp's Point, to prevent Costa Ricans from entering the San Juan. Spencer and his followers reached the San Juan River and floated down this to a point about two miles above Hipp's Point where they landed and silently surrounded the Americans, who were conscientiously watching the Serapiqui and did not dream of an enemy force coming down the San Juan. At a signal the Costa Ricans opened fire on the Americans who were at dinner, with no sentinels posted, and with their guns in a rack some distance away. In practically no time the Costa Ricans had killed or captured the whole garrison.

After leaving a guard of forty men at Hipp's Point, the

fast-moving Spencer took the rest of his men on down the river to Greytown where he seized four Transit Company river steamers before daybreak. He soon won over the crews to his service by promising to pay them well and, hoisting the Costa Rican flag, he headed the captured boats up the river. The agent of Morgan and Garrison in Greytown made frantic appeals for protection of this property to the commander of a British squadron in the harbor, but that officer discreetly refused to interfere.

When Spencer came again to the mouth of the San Carlos River he sent a steamer up that tributary to announce his success to a large force of approaching Costa Rican reinforcements who were armed with Minié rifles and ammunition sent by Vanderbilt, and commanded by General José Joaquin Mora, brother of the president of the republic. As the steamer came into sight, a detachment of these soldiers on a raft who had never seen such a craft were so frightened that they plunged into the river and were drowned. Mora took command of the combined forces of nearly a thousand men and, proceeding on up the San Juan, he captured two more river steamers off the ruined, old Spanish fortress of Castillo Viejo. Spencer then took one steamer and, continuing upstream, sighted the larger lake steamer, *Virgen* (which had recently evacuated Henningsen's forces from Granada), lying at anchor about thirty miles from the lake. Hiding his soldiers below decks, he brought his small craft alongside without causing any suspicion, and easily captured her. Placing his men aboard the larger vessel, he steamed on up the river to Fort San Carlos which commanded the outlet of Lake Nicaragua into the San Juan River.

The *Virgen* gave the recognition signal (which had never been changed) as it neared the fort and the whole garrison trooped down to the shore to welcome the usual passengers from the States and glean the latest news from home, for theirs was a monotonous life. The Commandant put out in a rowboat, was hauled aboard the steamer, and immediately made a prisoner. Spencer then threatened his life to compel him to order his men to surrender and Fort San Carlos was taken without firing a shot. Walker's enemies now completely controlled the whole length of the San Juan River and had cut off all his communications with the Atlantic ports of the United States. But he still retained the *San Carlos*, the larger and the faster of the two lake steamers. Spencer now laid plans for her capture, which would give him a clean sweep of all the filibusters' water transportation except for their dauntless navy, the *Granada,* on the Pacific coast.

He took the *Virgen* ten miles down the river and waited— but not for long. On January 2, 1857, a steamer from San Francisco landed a number of passengers at San Juan del Sur and these were transported as usual over the Transit Road to Virgin Bay where they embarked on the *San Carlos.* The steamer crossed Lake Nicaragua and, receiving the regular go-ahead signal from Fort San Carlos, entered the river where it was trapped between the guns of the fort and Spencer and his Costa Rican soldiers on the *Virgen.* Spencer stopped the steamer and demanded her surrender but her captain at first refused to comply and wanted to run back to Virgin Bay through the artillery fire of the fort. But a son-in-law of Charles Morgan's, named Harris, ordered the skipper not to risk the lives of his passengers and the doughty captain reluctantly obeyed. Spencer sent the passengers on to Greytown where they met a crowd of recruits and California-bound travelers who had just arrived from New York and New Orleans. The New York passengers boarded the newly arrived New York steamer and went safely on their way; those bound for California were sent to Panama and from there to San Francisco on Harris's orders, which cost the partnership of Morgan and Garrison an additional $25,000 over their regular expenses. The recruits for Walker's army remained in Greytown awaiting developments.

Spencer had been completely successful down to the last detail in his well-planned and -executed coup. If ever a man could boast "Mission accomplished," it was this efficient agent of Commodore Vanderbilt's. And even Walker admitted: ". . . the success of Spencer was the reward of a rashness which, in war, sometimes supplies the place of prudent design and wise combinations. The fortune which proverbially favors the brave certainly aided Spencer much in his operations." [2]

Soon after the *San Carlos* was captured, Spencer returned to his home in New York and it would be interesting to know what became of him later. If William Walker had only had Sylvanus H. Spencer on his side and had properly used his abilities the whole history of Central America might have been drastically changed.

After Spencer's brilliant coup hundreds of recruits for

[2] *The War in Nicaragua*, p. 349.

Walker arrived in Greytown. Among them were many of his veterans who had been home on leave, some picked volunteers from Texas, and a hundred and eighty so-called "Border Ruffians" who had been terrorizing Kansas in the slavery cause. These men attempted to reopen the San Juan River and actually recaptured Hipp's Point but bungled an attack on Castillo Viejo. Finally, dogged by bad luck, by British interference at Greytown, and by sickness and calamities, they were forced to give up and returned to the States, except for a handful who reached Walker by way of Panama. One, William K. Rogers, who had been foraging from Rivas when cut off, reached San Juan del Sur from Panama by forcing two natives at pistol point to take him in an open skiff across the five hundred miles of open sea.

Walker was thus left in Rivas with all communications cut to the Caribbean sea but he stubbornly held out, hoping against hope that his recruits in Greytown would somehow cut their way through. The allies, however, now under the command of the energetic Costa Ricans, took full advantage of their newly won control of all water transportation and energetically moved up to encircle the American filibusters.

Walker and Henningsen (who had been promoted to major general for his magnificent stand at Granada) led attack after attack against the ever-tightening circle of the enemy, but gained nothing and suffered heavy casualties. Among the killed was the gallant boy Calvin O'Neal who had led the wild charge of the handful of filibusters against five hundred Guatemalans in Granada. And often in the front of battle was the incredible Colonel Thomas Henry

(another well-deserved promotion). Convalescing from
more wounds, on one occasion he rose again from a hospital
bed to mount a mule and dash into battle and, once more,
like a magnet, he attracted another bullet before returning
to bed with a fresh wound.

The Costa Ricans now reversed their former policy and
instead of proclaiming death to the gringo invaders they
promised the best of treatment to deserters and, as conditions worsened for the besieged filibusters, desertion became
an epidemic. Whole companies went over as a unit, even a
brass band which then serenaded their former comrades
with nostalgic tunes of home.

By April, 1857, the filibusters were completely on the
defensive in Rivas with only a few over three hundred men
fit for duty and two thirds as many in the hospital. Word
arrived that Morgan and Garrison had discontinued all sailings to both coasts and to top this came the bad news that
the recruits in Greytown had given up all attempts to fight
their way through. All knew then that the end was near
but the stubborn Walker refused to discuss surrender.

An American naval officer, Commander Charles H. Davis,
finally allowed Walker to save face in this hopeless situation
by accepting his surrender with the cheerful consent of the
Central Americans, who primarily wanted the filibuster ogre
out of the country at all costs. On May 1, 1857, William
Walker embarked on the U.S.S. *St. Mary's* and arrived
some four weeks later to a tumultuous greeting in New
Orleans where the crowd carried him on their shoulders
through the streets. Later he received a hero's welcome in
New York and in many of the Southern cities. Of his loyal

followers many were brought back, ragged and verminous, destitute and sick, to New York where the newspapers featured their pitiful condition and drew a moral on the fate of filibusters.

Walker or his leaders attempted thrice more to invade Nicaragua. The first attempt, the following November, after an initial success at Greytown, was broken up by the intervention of the United States Navy. After this there was an interim of quiet while Walker wrote his book *The War in Nicaragua*[3] but there must have been many secret connivings and one can wonder again if a definite secret organization such as the Knights of the Golden Circle was passing the word along to the scattered ex-filibusters and to new recruits smitten by the fateful disease. During this time, Walker, a born Scotch Presbyterian, joined the Roman Catholic Church and his enemies claimed this was but to win favor in Central America.

About a year later, in December, 1858, an advance party of filibusters sailed to establish a beachhead in Honduras where Walker undoubtedly planned to join them, but they were wrecked on a coastal reef and rescued by a British man-of-war which carried them ignominiously back to Mobile.

The third and final attempt came when Walker and that untamable man of iron Thomas Henry led a landing, in August, 1860, of about a hundred men on the north coast of Honduras where they seized an old, semi-ruined Spanish fort

---

[3] It is an accurate and well-written account, told in the third person, of all his experiences from Lower California to his surrender to Commander Davis at Rivas, and it is accepted as an authoritative source by even the hostile Central Americans.

guarding the port of Trujillo. The plan was to use this as a base where recruits could land and whence they could march south across-country to Nicaragua.

But everything went wrong. The incomparable Colonel Thomas Henry, well laced with brandy, casually entered the ammunition magazine smoking a cigar. Always ready for a fight, he attacked the officer who ordered him out and, in self-defense, this officer shot him in the face, the bullet carrying away his lower jaw. For days Henry survived a wound that would have finished an ordinary man in hours, watched over constantly by his old commander, who neglected his other duties to care for him.

Meanwhile, a British warship, the *Icarus*, appeared in the port and the sound of her anchor chain was the knell of this rash expedition. Her commander, Norvell Salmon, notified Walker at once that he had seized a port on whose customs duties the British had a lien and demanded that he return the duties, surrender his arms, and leave at once. Salmon promised safe conduct home to the filibusters after they had complied. Walker quibbled in further correspondence and under cover of this delay he left his sick men and the dying Henry behind, and led out his remaining followers into the jungle. Those left in the old fort expected the natives to rush in at any moment to massacre them, but their surgeon next morning notified the British who at once placed them under protection before news of Walker's flight reached the town. The indomitable Colonel Henry was said to have swallowed a fatal overdose of morphine to end his sufferings when he heard of his chief's flight.

The British and the Hondurans brought Walker's forlorn

hope to an end when they shortly afterwards surrounded him a ways down the coast to the east. Walker specifically surrendered to the British commander, who placed the worn filibusters on his ship and returned them to Trujillo where he handed over Walker to the Honduran authorities but held the rest of the men, about seventy, under British protection until they could be shipped home. Walker protested against his deliverance to the Hondurans after his surrender to the British commander but to no avail. He was imprisoned in the same fort he had captured a few weeks before.

After a confinement of six days he was led out on the morning of September 12, 1860, to face the death he had dealt to so many enemies. Two priests accompanied him as he walked quietly and erect, surrounded by soldiers, to a place outside the town. A great crowd of natives fell in behind the procession, almost unbelieving, to see with their own eyes the end of the terrible Walker. A squad of soldiers fired at the signal as he stood before an adobe wall; a second group stepped forward and poured another volley into his fallen body; and then to be sure that this superman did not live, an officer fired the *coup de grâce*, a shot into the head.

Many of Walker's men went on to fight again in strange places. One of them, Frederick Townsend Ward from Salem, Massachusetts, wandered to China where he rose to the chief command of the Imperial Army in the Taiping rebellion and became one of the greatest men in the old Manchu empire. Others fought on both sides in the Civil War, mostly for the Confederacy, and among these were C. C. Hornsby, Edward J. Sanders, Frank P. Anderson, Callender Irvine

Fayssoux, Chatham R. Wheat, Robert C. Tyler, and Charles
Francis Henningsen. Years later Henningsen compared his
experiences in the two wars and what he said of those
Homeric men of Nicaragua is a fitting epitaph:

I have heard two greasy privates disputing over the correct
reading and comparative merits of Aeschylus and Euripides. I
have seen a soldier on guard incessantly scribbling strips of paper, which turned out to be a finely versified translation of his
dog's-eared copy of the "Divina Commedia."

I have often seen them marching with a broken or compound-
fractured arm in splints, and using the other to fire the rifle or
revolver. Those with a fractured thigh, or wounds which rendered them incapable of removal, often (or, rather, in early
times, always) shot themselves, sooner than fall into the hands
of the enemy. Such men do not turn up in the average of every-
day life, nor do I ever expect to see their like again. I was on the
Confederate side in many of the bloodiest battles of the late war;
but I aver that if, at the end of that war, I had been allowed to
pick five thousand of the bravest Confederate or Federal soldiers
I ever saw, and could resurrect and pit against them one thousand of such men as lie beneath the orange trees of Nicaragua, I
feel certain that the thousand would have scattered and utterly
routed the five thousand within an hour. All military science
failed, on a suddenly given field, before assailants who came on
at a run, to close with their revolvers, and who thought little of
charging a battery, pistol in hand.[4]

After the soldiers came the politicians. The Buchanan administration in Washington was naturally desirous of dis-
pelling the suspicions and ill will toward the United States
which Walker's filibusters had created in Central America;
and to do this the State Department sent a special agent to

---

[4] James Jeffrey Roche, *The Story of the Filibusters*. London, 1891, p.
153.

Nicaragua soon after Walker's withdrawal. The man chosen
for this delicate mission was William Carey Jones, a son-in-
law of the famous United States Senator from Missouri
Thomas Hart Benton and, of course, a brother-in-law of John
C. Fremont, the first Republican candidate for the Presidency, whom James Buchanan had defeated in the election
of 1856. A more unfortunate choice could not have been
made. According to the newspaper reports Jones hardly drew
a sober breath after his arrival and his alcoholic progress
about the country was ludicrous. As one correspondent reported: "He certainly has won for himself imperishable laurels with the sugar cane distillers. . . ." Another account
ran:

I do not think, up to date, Mr. Jones has been able to find
where the government of Nicaragua is. It is difficult to conceive
what the administration was about in selecting such a man for
the Central American mission. It is truly amusing to watch him
when navigating under full steam. I overheard him one day,
when he was brim full, discuss on the public place at Rivas the
question of international law. It is well, however, to let your
readers know that Mr. Jones was waddling at the time as a duck
does in a gutter, and turning up his eyes after the fashion of
that biped in a thunderstorm. He had been sent (said he) to
Nicaragua to negotiate with its government—had been looking
for it for a period of three months, and he would be d—d if he
had yet been able to find one. "D—n," said Mr. Jones, "all international proceeding—all diplomatic mission. Boys, lets us have a
drink. That's the policy of harmony!" Says Mr. Jones, "Nicaragua
for ever!" Mr. Carey Jones' proposition was unanimously adopted
and he, and his aides, disappeared in a small groggery; and there
they stuck till they all got fairly blind.

The Path of Glory

Space and time, regretfully added the correspondent, would not permit a detailed account of Mr. Jones' adventures—from being confined in the calaboose, and threatening war to all Central America, to being lost for three days on Lake Nicaragua in a canoe, wrapped up in the Stars and Stripes.

CHAPTER XII

The Female of the Species

GENERAL WINFIELD SCOTT did not like the biting, whistling "Northers" which howled down on the American Army before the Mexican port of Vera Cruz—the city of the True Cross—in March 1847; neither did his officers and men, for the gales filled everyone's tents, clothes, hair, and eyes, from general to private, with a coarse sand like granulated sugar. It was impossible to get a mouthful of food without a condiment of grit, and the grinding and gnashing of teeth at the soldiers' messes rivaled the sound of the surf on the beach. With the flying sand came a legion of fleas which enjoyed the novelty of gringo meat and attacked from all quarters. The Americans scratched themselves and cursed the ceaseless whine of the chilling wind but instead they should have given thanks for, while it bore fleas and sandy discomfort, it blew away the mosquitoes from the surrounding swamps and the dreaded *vomito,* the yellow fever, had not appeared as it usually did at this time of year. But nobody in those days knew that mosquitoes caused yellow fever and the immediate distress of the Northers was reviled, to a man, by Scott's army of ten thousand.

244

The Female of the Species

Early in that same month the General had landed his men from the fleet commanded by Commodore David Conner on the beach below Vera Cruz and, quickly extending his lines through the sand dunes to the north, he had invested the city by land. Extensive trenches were dug, gun emplacements constructed, all roads leading into the besieged city blocked, and the water supply cut off. General Scott was now ready for either an assault or a heavy bombardment to capture Vera Cruz.

The war with Mexico was not quite a year old and this landing was the initial step of a bold plan to march up through the towering sierras, following in the footsteps of the great conquistador, Hernando Cortez, of over three centuries before, to capture Mexico City, lying on the high inland plateau, nearly three hundred miles away by road. It was hoped this daring design would end the war by paralyzing the nerve center, the capital, of the enemy. But before a move could be made up the old Spanish National Highway to the capital it was absolutely necessary to capture the well-fortified and strongly garrisoned city of Vera Cruz for a seaport base of supplies; then to get the army away into the healthy highlands before the dreaded yellow fever appeared. Scott was a harassed and hurried general in a race with time.

On March 20th, he had completed his entrenchments and was debating with his ranking officers and his staff whether to take the city by storm or to pound it into submission by an artillery bombardment of heavy naval guns which would have to be borrowed from the men-of-war and dragged to the land emplacements. These perplexities were interrupted by an orderly who announced that an American lady, a Mrs. Storms, would like to see General Scott, for whom she bore important information. Now the appearance of an American lady at that time and place was almost in the nature of a supernatural visitation and General Scott, welcoming a break to his problems, hurriedly brushed the sand out of his white hair, donned his best dress uniform and assumed his courtliest manner. He was a splendid-looking man, even in his sixty-first year, standing six feet four inches, straight as a ramrod, and perfectly turned out in dress. Opinions varied considerably about his military ability but all agreed he was the epitome of martial glamor in his appearance and cut the finest figure of how a soldier should look; and such was his insistence on military punctilio that he was universally known as "Old Fuss and Feathers." His manners matched his looks, for even in the florid 1840's he was called "a gentleman of the old school" and none could equal him in courtliness to the opposite sex. But this magnificent lady-killer led a blameless personal life. A prominent phrenologist of the time had discovered an outstanding bump of amativeness upon his head and the General had once confided to a young aide that all his life he had had to discipline his amatory impulses, or as he put it, "The professor did not mistake me, but I have always curbed my mutinous appetites." This, then, was the resplendent man who curiously awaited the entrance of his mysterious caller.

Never was a man more pleasantly surprised as there entered his tent a mature but shapely and vivacious brunette with snapping black eyes set in a face of dark and haunting beauty and with good breeding and winsome manners to

match. The General and his staff must have been astounded
at the appearance of this lovely apparition. The staff officers
were a picked lot; among them the two captains of the Corps
of Engineers, Joseph G. Totten and Robert E. Lee, and that
strange mystic-soldier, Ethan Allen Hitchcock, the Inspector
General of the invading army. These men were about the
same age (forty) as this fascinating and mysterious visitor
and there was probably wistful thinking of what a pity it
was this charming caller had to listen to the heavy gallantries of General Scott, a man old enough to be her father.

It was soon apparent that Mrs. Storms had bravery and
brains as well as beauty, for the information she brought
was of the greatest interest and value. She said she had come
to Mexico the previous autumn as a secret agent of the
United States. Previously she had been a newspaperwoman
connected with the New York *Sun* and when President Polk
and Secretary of State James Buchanan had sent the pro-
prietor and editor of that paper, Moses Yale Beach, on a
special mission to Mexico City, she had accompanied him
and Mrs. Beach to the capital.[1] Their purpose had been to
approach the Catholic hierarchy and other powers about
peace, and she, being a converted Catholic and speaking
Spanish, was the guiding spirit. They had made their way,
under British passports and amidst the greatest dangers, for
the country was aflame with anti-American sentiment, to
that city where they had discussed peace terms with top
officials of state and church, about which she was now on
her way to report in Washington. Leaving Mr. and Mrs. (or

---

[1] It is not altogether clear whether his wife or daughter was with Beach
but it was all conventional enough.

Miss) Beach in Mexico City, she had ridden alone down the bandit-infested National Highway from Mexico City to Vera Cruz to help the newly landed American army. It was an extraordinary act of courage and daring and General Scott was more than impressed.

The information she brought of great immediate value was that the inhabitants of the small city of Jalapa, seventy-four miles away in the mountains, were favorably disposed toward the Americans, and that much-needed forage and supplies were plentiful there; and she strongly advised General Scott to take that route to Mexico City instead of the alternative way through Cordoba. Scott had been greatly concerned about the lack of supplies in the barren country back of Vera Cruz and puzzled about which of the two roads to follow to the capital after he had captured the seaport, and this information was exactly what he needed to make a decision. When Vera Cruz surrendered on March 29th, following a devastating bombardment, he followed Mrs. Storms' advice and, after decisively defeating a blocking Mexican army under General Santa Anna at Cerro Gordo in mid-April, he moved his headquarters to healthy and hospitable Jalapa whence he later successfully marched on to capture the Mexican capital in the following September.[2] Mrs. Storms' courageous services to Scott's army were of inestimable value.

One can wonder what she thought of General Scott. Henry Watterson, the famous editor of the Louisville *Journal-Courier,* years later wrote in his memoirs that she heartily disliked him (as did many others) and gave him the

---

[2] See p. 16.

nickname "Old Fuss and Feathers," which was probably untrue as he appears to have been called that for years previous; Watterson also states that it was she "who dubbed
William Walker 'the little gray-eyed man of destiny'" which
is also doubtful.[3] When in Vera Cruz, and this is pure con-
jecture, she may have called on Scott's best fighting general,
Major General William Jenkins Worth, who was a sort of
prototype of General George S. Patton. He was from Hudson, New York, near her home city of Troy, and his wife
was from a prominent Albany family. He commanded the
First Division of regulars before Vera Cruz, and Scott had
his headquarters in his divisional area. What makes one
think that she may have talked to Worth is because her
newspaper, the New York *Sun,* the following August boomed
Worth for the Presidential nomination on the Democratic
ticket; and Worth wrote Secretary of War Marcy, from
Mexico City in October, giving his wholehearted support to
the annexation of all Mexico, which was her pet project.
Also, in June 1848, on his way home from Mexico City he
was offered command of an impending filibustering expedition into Cuba,[4] which Narciso Lopez had planned, and Mrs.
Storms was said to be deeply involved in Lopez's plots to
free that island. On her way to Mexico she had stopped off
in Cuba with the Beaches and there she may have seen
some of the native conspirators. Later, in Mexico City, Scott
and Worth became involved in the most rancorous quarrel
in the annals of the United States Army and the New York

---

[3] *"Marse Henry": An Autobiography.* New York, 1919, pp. 56-58.
[4] See Edward S. Wallace, *General William Jenkins Worth, Monterey's Forgotten Hero.* Dallas, 1953, pp. 169-170 and 185.

Sun strongly supported Worth. There seems a very good chance that she spoke with Worth at Vera Cruz.

From Vera Cruz, Mrs. Storms returned to Washington where she labored long and hard for the annexation of all Mexico and, as Senator Thomas Hart Benton grumpily noted:

> In the course of the summer [1847] a *"female,"* fresh from Mexico, and with a masculine stomach for war and politics, arrived in Washington, had interviews with members of the administration, and infected some of them with the contagion of a large project—nothing less than the absorption into our Union of all Mexico. . . .

Senator Benton went on to say that the *"female"* went back to Mexico "with high letters from some members of the cabinet to the commanding general [Scott], and to the plenipotentiary negotiator [Nicholas Trist]; both of whom, however, eschewed the proffered aid." [5] "Old Marse" Henry Watterson quoted Benton as saying that Mrs. Storms had more to do with making and ending the Mexican War than anybody else.

Just who was the extraordinary Mrs. Storms and why has she been lost in obscurity? These are moot questions and exceedingly difficult ones to answer. If not exactly an adventuress, she was the most adventurous of any American woman on record and deserves far more than the oblivion which has been her fate. Her Mexican venture was but one of a series of daring undertakings in which she met more failure than success, but never did she cease to gamble along lines far removed from staid conformity in her quest for an

---

[5] Thomas Hart Benton, *Thirty Years View*. 2 vols. New York, 1856. Vol. II, p. 704.

elusive fortune. Henry Watterson, whom she had befriended when he was a cub reporter on the *Washington States* in the 1850's, said further about her:

A braver, more intellectual woman never lived. She must have been a beauty in her youth; she was still very comely at fifty; but a born insurrecto and a terror with her pen. God made and equipped her for a filibuster. She possessed infinite knowledge of Spanish-American affairs, looked like a Spanish woman, and wrote and spoke the Spanish language fluently. Her obsession was the bringing of Central America into the Federal Union.

Never did this captivating woman actually participate in a pistol-shooting charge of the filibusters; in fact, she was probably never under fire. But as a behind-the-scenes wire-puller, as a power behind the throne, she well deserved Watterson's title of "filibuster" and a place with Lopez, Walker and others of that lost profession.

The accounts of her life are fragmentary and fleeting but by patching these together a bare outline can be traced. Her maiden name was Jane McManus and she was born near Troy, New York, in 1807. Her father William T. McManus was a fairly successful lawyer and politician who, after acting as surrogate and district attorney of Rensselaer County, was elected a United States congressman and served in Washington from 1825 to 1827. He was a friend of the influential William L. Marcy and of Aaron Burr, and the latter's influence considerably affected his career and that of his daughter. Young Jane's girlhood seems lost in obscurity. She had an aunt with the somewhat imperial name of Brittania McManus who married Lemuel Hawley Sherman and went to live in his home village of Brookfield, Connecticut. To make things really confusing, Brittania McManus Sherman adopted two girls named Jane and Jeanette McManus and it would logically seem that our Jane was one of these two, especially as she later dedicated one of her books, *Eagle Pass; or, Life on the Border*, written under her usual pen name of Cora Montgomery, to Mrs. Lemuel Hawley Sherman whom she describes as the "dearest guide of my youth." But, no, it appears the adopted Jane was a cousin, who later married, in 1844, a staid New Haven man named Birdsey Curtis Lake and lived a conventional life in the Elm City until her death in 1890. But our Jane, the colorful one, judging from her dedication, must have often visited her aunt in Brookfield, and the confusion with her younger (by some seventeen years) cousin is considerable. Today nothing whatever seems to be known in the lovely little hill town of Brookfield about the two Janes or even about those life-long residents, the Lemuel Hawley Shermans.

Our Jane married young, probably sometime between 1823-1825, a man named William F. Storms, and had a son by him. This marriage probably ended in divorce and until she was married again, to William Leslie Cazneau just before 1850, she called herself, at various times and places, either Mrs. Storms or Mrs. McManus. There is no mention of her young son on her many trips and adventures, possibly she left him in the care of Aunt Brittania back in quiet Brookfield.

Following the very dim tracks of this young matron we next find her involved with the ever-fateful Aaron Burr in a colonizing venture into Texas, which was still part of the Republic of Mexico at the time. Her father had lost most of his money and the family wanted to recoup their fortunes by a venture in new lands. On the advice of Aaron Burr they decided to investigate the possibilities in Stephen Austin's new settlements in Texas and young Jane was chosen to report on the situation there. She sailed with her brother from New York in the autumn of 1832 for New Orleans, whence it may be presumed she went to see Stephen Austin in Texas, and possibly on to Saltillo, the capital of the Mexican state of Coahuila-Texas, or even to Mexico City. Aaron Burr sent her a letter of introduction, calling her Mrs. McManus, to his friend Judge James Workman of New Orleans, in which he wrote:

Allow me the liberty, my dear Sir, to introduce to your acquaintance *A Lady!*—be not alarmed, for it is not intended that she should tax your Hospitalities nor, but very slightly, your gallantry; for she is a woman of business and has great enterprise in view.

. . . She has in an eminent degree that peculiar discernment or tact in the Character and dispositions of men—a talent peculiar to her sex but she has also (which is more rare) courage, stability and perseverance and I pledge myself for her good faith and her candour.[6]

The next year, in 1833, at the age of seventy-seven, Aaron Burr married a rich widow, Madame Eliza Jumel, who was fifty-seven—not too great a discrepancy in years for their time of life—and obtaining some of her money he invested it in a scheme to settle German colonists in Texas in which venture the McManus family, the father William, daughter Jane, and a son, Robert, were his partners; so it can be assumed that Jane brought back a favorable report about

---

[6] In the Moses Austin Bryan Papers, University of Texas. This letter and the details of the Texas venture seem to have been missed by all of Burr's biographers.

the prospects in Texas. While Burr remained in New York, the McManuses accompanied the prospective German settlers to Matagorda, Texas, that same year.

There is a brief account of Jane's stay in Matagorda (but no mention of her father and brother) in the memoirs of an early settler who was a young girl at the time, and whose family had just moved there from Pennsylvania.[7] S. Rhoads Fisher, the father of this family, persuaded two obliging young men, who kept the only store in town, to let him temporarily shelter his family in a small house they had built, and in return the Fisher family boarded their hosts and became very friendly with them. One of these men was William Leslie Cazneau from Boston. Soon afterwards there arrived a young and handsome "woman adventuress," who went by the name of "Mrs." McManus, bringing with her a colony of German emigrants whom she planned to settle on an "eleven-league grant of land" from the Mexican government. The Germans, however, refused to go any farther and settled in Matagorda. The attractive woman stayed with the Fishers for months, making herself so useful and agreeable that they all became very fond of her. So did the young Bostonian, for "she seemed possessed of much fascination and Mr. Cazneau became romantically in love with her." But it was to be some sixteen long years before William Cazneau was finally to marry the fascinating Jane. The colonization venture was a failure and Jane and her father returned East, but her brother Robert remained, and his descendants live in Texas today. When the war for Texas's

---

[7] "Memoirs of Mrs. Annie P. Harris," edited by Ethel Mary Franklin, *Southwestern Historical Quarterly*. January, 1937, pp. 231-246.

independence from Mexico began in 1836, Mrs. Fisher and the children fled to New York for safety and Jane McManus repaid their hospitality by her kindness to them in that city.

Aaron Burr lost all the money he had taken from his wife for this venture and she, described as "ill-bred, ill-tempered, ill-minded," sued for divorce in 1834, alleging various adulteries on his part and specifically one at his house in Jersey City with Jane McManus in August, 1833. A servant of Burr's named Maria Johnson, who had once worked for Madame Jumel and whom Burr's counsel called "a well-coached half-wit," swore that she had witnessed some highly indelicate behavior between the couple, particularly once when they had rung the service bell accidentally; and when she entered the room in answer to this summons, Jane McManus, she said, was so covered with embarrassment that she could only utter "Oh la! Mercy save us!!!" Mrs. Burr was granted her divorce.

Burr swore in court that this testimony was completely untrue but his general behavior in the whole matter, according to Jane, was contemptible. Certainly this alleged incident was in strong contradiction to her character—at least in later life, for Henry Watterson remembered her in the 1850's as being a much respected member of Washington society in the 1850's. At the time Jane was twenty-six and Aaron Burr was seventy-seven. Burr was a fascinator, a satyr, and a devil with the women, but over fifty years' difference in their ages was a ridiculous discrepancy for a woman of her intelligence and strong character. She made many political enemies by her initiative and audacity but, with one exception, nobody seems to have raked up this old scandal, which Christian forgiveness seems a bit unusual if it had been true.

The one exception was when she returned for a while to Matagorda in 1838 and visited Colonel and Mrs. Ira Randolph Lewis. The Colonel, a native Virginian who had served in the Texas Army, was greatly enraged when a committee of six men who were running the local "Cotillion Party," given in November, 1838, failed to ask his house guest "Mrs." McManus to the ball. The good Colonel considered this an insult to himself, as the lady was under his protection and had already suffered misfortune and injustice "until she has devoted herself, almost, to the life of a recluse." And, stated the Colonel, she actually possessed "preeminent claims to the first station in the best society." Lewis indignantly denied certain vague rumors about her and, not receiving satisfactory answers to several angry letters which he wrote during two days, he ended by challenging all six men to a duel, beginning at the top of the list as printed on the committee's stationery. This ultimatum was delivered by Jane's previous host in Matagorda, S. Rhoads Fisher and by William Cazneau, which shows that those who knew her were devoted to her. The committeeman at the top of the list immediately left town and the results with the others seem unknown—probably they apologized to Jane McManus.[8]

Jane McManus, however, married again after this and moved around a great deal, so the Burr affair may have been buried and forgotten. There was undoubtedly something strange about the whole matter, for years later, in 1882, after Jane's death, Dr. John E. Stillwell of New York saw her in-

---

[8] These letters are in the Moses Austin Bryan Papers.

timate friend Mrs. Ann S. Stephens, the authoress, and reported:

Mrs. Stephens likewise told me a story, which if true, would reflect strongly against the character of Burr. It bore upon his divorce from Madam Jumel and the use of a lady's name as corespondent. It was embellished with many circumstantial details, as told by the lady implicated, and was apparently accepted by Mrs. Stephens as truth.[9]

After Jane McManus Storms' return from Texas she became a journalist and began her connection with the New York *Sun*. In its columns, and with the support of its editor Moses Yale Beach, she carried on a strenuous campaign in behalf of the annexation of Texas, which had won its independence from Mexico in 1836 and become an independent republic. In March, 1845, her campaign came to a successful conclusion, after many setbacks, when the United States annexed Texas. The result was the war with Mexico in 1846, for that country had given fair warning that the annexation of her former territory (whose independence she had never recognized) would be tantamount to war. Upon the successful conclusion of that war, in 1848, Mexico perforce officially recognized this annexation.

Jane Storms then turned her energies to the cause of Cuban annexation to the United States and is reported to

---

[9] *The History of the Burr Portraits*. New York, 1928, p. 102. According to Stillwell's notes of this interview (now at the New York Historical Society) Jane McManus told Ann Stephens that she was in Texas at the time of the alleged adultery. She claimed that Burr had agreed to his wife's demand for a divorce on condition she named a corespondent who would be a credit to his manly charms and the absent Jane was chosen as the dupe. If true, and it was not by any means out of character with some of Burr's actions, it was about as slimy a trick as a man could play. All of Burr's apologists and biographers seem to have missed this episode.

have edited an annexationist Spanish-English newspaper, published in New York from 1848 through 1853 and illegally distributed in Cuba, which was called *La Verdad*. Under the pen name of Cora Montgomery she wrote the English section of this paper and strongly supported Narciso Lopez and his ventures. However, it is hard to understand how she did her editorial stint all this time for she was again in Texas from 1850 to 1853.

Between 1848 and 1850 Jane McManus Storms, whose husband had either died or been divorced by her, married William Leslie Cazneau, the young Bostonian who had first fallen in love with her in Matagorda in 1833. Since then he had prospered. He became a friend of Mirabeau Buonaparte Lamar, who succeeded Sam Houston as the third President of Texas, and Lamar appointed him as Commissary General of the Texas army which gave him the title of General for the rest of his life. In 1847 he went into partnership with Henry L. Kinney (whom Walker later threatened to hang in Nicaragua) and later he served in the Mexican War. Also he seems to have been in New York City for some of the time, for a William L. Cazneau is listed in that city's directories as a shipmaster, with addresses on or near Wall Street, from 1839 through 1845. Perhaps he wanted to be near the fascinating Jane. In 1850, after their marriage, they became two of the first settlers of Eagle Pass, Texas, on the Rio Grande.

They were pioneers in wild country. Two miles up the Rio Grande there was a small infantry garrison at Fort Duncan, across the river a small Mexican military post at Piedras Negras, a handful of other American settlers, and a scatter-

ing of Mexicans. Around them the wild Comanches, lords of
the open plains, rode at will on their fierce raids back and
forth to Mexico, but almost miraculously never bothered the
Cazneaus who lived in a glorified dugout. Occasionally a
wandering band of Seminole Indians, led by their famous
chief Wild Cat, would wander by and stop in for a friendly
visit. The government had transported these Indians from
Florida after their final defeat a decade before and settled
them in Arkansas, but the Seminoles had hated that section
and had sought a refuge in Mexico. From there they carried
on a ceaseless feud with the ravaging Comanches whose
hand was against all men, and Wild Cat would stop to call
on the Cazneaus when he led his band that way.

Jane McManus Cazneau wrote of these experiences on the
wild frontier in her book *Eagle Pass* under her pen name of
Cora Montgomery. She did not seem in the least fazed by
the raiding Comanches, the hostile Mexicans across the Rio
Grande, the primitive living conditions, or by snakes or wild
beasts. But a woman who had had the superb courage to
ride alone through nearly three hundred miles of hostile
Mexican country to see General Scott could take frontier
hardships and dangers in her stride. She harped on the horrors of the Mexican system of peonage for debt which she
considered far worse than slavery in the States and remarked
that, after all, moral opposition to slavery was largely geographical. Slavery, she thought, would eventually be confined to a few states and that there was too much fuss and
furor about it. And she decided it would be a blessing for
Mexico if that distracted land were annexed to the United
States, but if such a grandiose scheme was not practical she

favored the idea of a new independent republic of the northern Mexican states to be called Sierra Madre or the Republic of the Rio Grande. This visionary country was talked about frequently along the border in the 1850's, and a sizable filibuster to achieve this might have materialized had not the Civil War drawn away all the interest and fighting blood in Texas.

★ 2 ★

In 1853, William and Jane Cazneau left Eagle Pass and the General was appointed, in November, a special agent of the United States to the Dominican Republic (also called Santo Domingo). This little Caribbean republic, which occupied the eastern two thirds of the island of Hispaniola, was Spanish-speaking and had a greater proportion of white blood than the adjoining French-speaking Negro republic of Haiti. After Haiti had gained her independence from France her armies had overrun the more sparsely settled Spanish section until in 1844 the Dominicans had driven out the invaders and proclaimed an independent republic of their own. From then on there were the usual Latin-American revolutions and resulting semi-anarchy. The administration of President Franklin Pierce undoubtedly had an eye on this island as well as on Cuba as a possible field for expansion, and Cazneau's mission was to report on conditions there.

It was rumored that Mrs. Cazneau had some influence in this appointment because of her father's old friendship with Secretary of State William L. Marcy and also, gossip said, she had been friendly with President Franklin Pierce in Mexico City when he served with the army there as a briga-

dier general. Thus began an intimate association of the Cazneaus with the Dominican Republic and for the next twenty
years or so they acted as sort of contact agents between the
two countries and made their home in that isle for a large
part of the time.

On this first mission, some of the New York press hostile
to the Pierce administration accused Cazneau of plotting for
the annexation of the island republic to the United States,
or, at least, for acquiring Samaná Bay which was an excellent harbor at the northeastern end of the republic as a naval
base. The anti-slavery leaders sensed plotting, and Senator
Charles Sumner of Massachusetts was particularly apprehensive of such a political move. John Bigelow, then an editor
of the New York *Evening Post,* was in Santo Domingo City
(now Ciudad Trujillo) at the time and, discovering Mrs.
Cazneau was a Roman Catholic, became convinced that the
Papacy was behind the whole scheme for the United States
to annex Cuba, the Dominican Republic and other Latin-
American countries, and wrote warning letters to the *Post.*
Great Britain and France were also bitterly opposed to any
American expansion but they were so occupied in fighting
the Crimean War against Russia that it seemed a golden
opportunity to the American expansionists to move into the
Caribbean area. Public sentiment in the United States was
strongly pro-Russian, strange as this may sound to American
ears a century later. But General Cazneau failed to secure
even a commonplace and innocuous treaty of amity and
commerce with the Dominican Republic because of the
frantic opposition there of the British and French representatives, aided by the Spaniards who were shivering in their

261

boots in Madrid over the attempts of Pierre Soulé to secure the cession of Cuba. Finally, in June, 1855, Cazneau admitted the failure of his mission but he and his wife had completely fallen under the spell of the country and returned there as soon as possible for some extraordinary activities.

An interesting sidelight on Cazneau's first mission to this country was the appearance there of Captain George Brinton McClellan of the U. S. Corps of Topographical Engineers to make a survey of Samaná Bay and select the best site for a naval base, which was the reason given by the Pierce administration for its interest in the island. Young McClellan had just previously worked on a survey for a transcontinental railroad near the Canadian border under the direction of Governor Isaac Ingalls Stevens of Washington Territory, and Stevens had considered him somewhat overcautious and dilatory, which was his reputation later in the Civil War as commanding general of the Army of the Potomac. But, curiously enough, Cazneau thought that McClellan had acted with rash haste in making this survey and antagonized the natives by not waiting until certain formalities were observed. McClellan, however, was in a rush, did not follow Cazneau's advice and completed his report in a few days.[10] Cazneau was a true prophet of evil tidings, for the British and French used McClellan's impetuous disregard for the amenities as an example of American contempt for the Latin-American peoples, and it was a factor in Cazneau's failure.

The next year, in August, 1856, General Cazneau nego-

[10] Published as House Exec. Doc. 43 of 41 Cong. 3 Sess.

tiated his contract with William Walker to ship a thousand able-bodied Americans to Nicaragua to serve in the filibuster army and to be paid in land. He does not appear to have gone to Nicaragua and probably made this contract through one of Walker's agents. Jane Cazneau's part, if any, in this recruiting scheme is not clear and she probably confined her efforts to favorable articles and letters to the newspapers.

Although she was with her husband on his ventures to Eagle Pass and the Dominican Republic, she also seems to have spent much time in New York and Washington during the 1850's, as she had in the previous decade. Quite naturally she moved in literary circles and her friends were well-known writers in their day. Among them was Ann S. Stephens from Derby, Connecticut (not too far from Jane McManus's childhood haunt of Brookfield), who later told Dr. Stillwell about the Burr affair and who was famous as a romantic author and editor of ladies' magazines. Also there was Mrs. E. D. E. Southworth of Washington, D. C., a prolific and much-read novelist whose works were published in an edition of forty-two volumes, fair samples of which were *The Maiden Widow* and *The Missing Bride*. Another was the writer of Western thrillers, Charles Wilkins Webber, who died fighting for William Walker in Nicaragua; and Richard B. Kimball, a lawyer-author of New York who edited two of her books, *The Prince of Kashna* and *In the Tropics, By a Settler in Santo Domingo*, which she sent him in manuscript from the West Indies. Then there was the poet-president of Texas, Mirabeau Buonaparte Lamar, a close friend of both the Cazneaus, who was often in and about New York and Washington. He even dedicated a volume of his poems, *Verse Memorials,* published in New York in 1857, to C.M. which, of course, were the initials of Jane's pen name of Cora Montgomery. Malicious gossip had it that she was more than a friend to the Byronic Lamar.

Certainly she had a warm attachment to the third President of Texas, for she had written as early as 1845 an article for the March issue of *The United States Magazine and Democratic Review* entitled "Texas and Her Presidents" which is a most sympathetic account of his career and glows with warmth toward the poet-president. In describing his predecessor, Sam Houston, who did not get on with Lamar, she goes to the other extreme and lambasts old Sam with scorn, contrasting his drunken bumbling in office and elsewhere, with the nobility, high ideals, and efficiency of Mirabeau Buonaparte Lamar. History and posterity, however, have not upheld her favoritism and the years have enhanced the true greatness of old Sam Houston.

In 1850, a small book, *The Queen of Islands and the King of Rivers* by Cora Montgomery, was published in New York and was described as a few chapters from a forthcoming larger book to be titled *Our Mother Land.*[11] As can be guessed from the title, it is about Cuba and the Mississippi River with more emphasis on the former. It is largely an argument, based on economics, for the annexation of the island which, she says:

. . . stands interferingly in the way between the Atlantic ports and the Gulf terminus of the short land route to California, on our own soil, now in course of survey by the United States Engineers and which a pioneer merchant train of 80 wagons is now

---

[11] This book never appeared.

traversing under General W. L. Cazneau, with a view to pene-
trate to the markets of Northern Mexico by the new and direct
line from the Gulf.

She was reputed to have been an enthusiastic supporter
of Narciso Lopez and his two unsuccessful filibustering expeditions into Cuba in 1850 and 1851, although she could
not have been too active from far-off Eagle Pass where she
was supposed to have been for most of those years. But
nothing was impossible for Jane Cazneau. She was reported
to have gone previously to Cuba in Lopez's interests, before
his expeditions, to spy out the land and act as a go-between
with his native sympathizers, although this may refer to her
visit on the way to Mexico with Moses Yale Beach. Again
there is a disappointing lack of definite information about
her actions, probably because it was necessarily all very
secret at the time and in after years she kept quiet to protect those who had helped Lopez's cause, for Spanish vengeance would have been swift and sure, and Cuba did not
free herself from Spanish rule until twenty years after her
death.

In 1859 the Cazneaus were again in the center of affairs
in the Dominican Republic, this time with the very best of
backing. Jane Cazneau, writing as Cora Montgomery, in a
book called *Our Winter Eden*, published years later in 1878,
describes a meeting in the library of the White House between President James Buchanan and her husband in which
General Cazneau expounded the advantages of a free port
at Samaná Bay. Secretary of State Lewis Cass came in during the discussion and listened with interest as the General
declared he was returning to Santo Domingo to work for

this project either as a private enterprise or with the help of the United States government if possible. Cass invited Cazneau to call on him the next day and the result was that he was again appointed, on April 7, 1859, the Special Agent of the United States to that country. It is said that Jane Cazneau was some kind of a cousin of President James Buchanan and certainly her report of this interview in the White House indicates a considerable degree of intimacy with him.

The Cazneaus left at once and soon were as active as before in promoting a deal to obtain Samaná Bay as an American naval station. But again they failed for as the threats of sectional secession grew at home the European powers, in their turn, took as much advantage as possible of these distractions in the United States. The Cazneaus' enthusiasm for their new home, however, was unbounded and the General reported to Cass about the unlimited possibilities in the republic for American capital and enterprise but warned, in March, 1860, that Spain was planning to reoccupy this former colony. Again his dire prediction became all too true for in March, 1861, the peaceful reannexation of the Dominican Republic to Spain was announced by the president of the extinguished country. The reason for this docile surrender of Dominican independence was promised Spanish help against the forces of Haiti which had been sporadically invading the country.

An old friend now joined the Cazneaus, Joseph Warren Fabens, who had been with Henry L. Kinney on his Mosquito Coast venture in Nicaragua but had deserted that luckless promoter to join the forces of William Walker. Born in Salem, Massachusetts, of an old seafaring family, he had entered Harvard College in 1838 but had left in his sophomore year because of poor health. He then became U. S. Consul at Cayenne in French Guiana where his father had interests, but left there for Texas where he was commissioned a colonel in the Texas army. He and Cazneau first became associated there through Kinney. Fabens was an author of sorts and his book, *The Camel Hunt*, was published in Boston and Cambridge in 1851. It is a romantic novel about a voyage from Boston to Mogador on the Atlantic coast of Morocco, whence a cargo of camels was transported to Panama; colorful sheiks gallop about the desert rescuing captive maidens through its pages, but the narrative is mainly about the introduction of camels into Panama from Morocco. And this is interesting because, a few years later, 1857-1858, Secretary of War Jefferson Davis brought over two shiploads of these beasts to Texas as an experiment which was initially successful but was ended by the outbreak of the Civil War. Later Cazneau and Fabens imported a lot of these "ships of the desert" into the Dominican Republic. The locale of the book, Morocco, is another place where Jane Cazneau was said to have spent some time and there is the possibility that she actually accompanied Fabens and her shipmaster husband on some such trip, before or after her marriage to him. It is another tantalizing blind spot of her life.

Fabens and the Cazneaus now went into land promotion and speculation on a large scale in Santo Domingo, in a way which has never been quite equaled. They used every bit of their official positions as representatives of the United

States to further their own interests, and for these activities they have been criticized as unscrupulous. But it should be remembered that ethics were considerably different in the business world of the 1860's and 1870's, during which years most of the great fortunes of this country were started, and these Yankee *entrepreneurs* were merely hoping for commensurate rewards for their daring and foresight in a new field.

Having made an agreement with the returning Spaniards, they started their promotions by organizing in 1862 the "American West Indian Company" with the intention of attracting American settlers who wanted to exchange the evil furies and excitements loosed by the Civil War at home for the bliss of a tropical paradise. A glowing prospectus of the company's properties in the Dominican Republic was printed, promising a good and full life, tax-free for ten years, for purchasers of land in this Elysium. Jane Cazneau (Cora Montgomery) wrote *In the Tropics, By a Settler in Santo Domingo*,[12] published in London in 1863, which described the raptures of an American settler who had taken advantage of this rare offer and was living an idyllic life in this lush Arcady. Fabens also broke into print with an enthusiastic brochure, *Facts about Santo Domingo Applicable to the Present Crisis*, and read a colorful paper on the "Resources of Santo Domingo" before the American Geographical and Statistical Society of New York in 1863, in which he praised the progressive policies of the "Young Spain" in her reannexed colony, this modern Isle of the Blest.

---

[12] This book has been attributed to Fabens but the evidence points to Cora Montgomery.

But alas for all these optimistic presumptions, some of the enticed settlers found actual conditions in this promised Paradise far different from their anticipation, and the American Commercial Agent at Santo Domingo City sadly reported that nine out of fourteen settlers sent out by the company had died of fever, and the rest, except for two who had gone home, were not expected to live. To cap this, the Spaniards, completely unmindful of the praises heaped upon them by these exuberant promoters, had the ingratitude to destroy the splendid estate of the Cazneaus in 1865 when they evacuated the island rather than contend with a resurgent revolution for independence. The Cazneaus withdrew from these disorders for a while to the island of Jamaica, to an estate named Keith Hall, near Kingston, where Jane wrote another romantic novel, *The Prince of Kashna: A West Indian Story*, which was published in New York in 1866. The Cazneaus for the rest of their lives strove to obtain an indemnity for their losses from the Spaniards but with no success.

All this was discouraging but not daunting to this trio of intrepid speculators and they returned to Santo Domingo on the heels of the retiring Spaniards. Thenceforth instead of appealing to the individual settler their united efforts were given toward the annexation of the whole Dominican Republic to the United States; but they first obtained ownership or control of the choicest lots of land in the right places (such as on the harbor of the proposed naval base at Samaná Bay) and concessions for the most promising mineral and timber rights. Annexation would bring stability and prosperity and the Fabens-Cazneau partnership would cash in on their foresight in the biggest sort of way.

Jane Cazneau advocated, as an initial step, the establishment of a free zone on the island, in a letter which indirectly reached Secretary of State William H. Seward. Seward, who was exhausted and depressed by the strain of his office during the recently ended Civil War—by illness, by the injuries received from the attempt on his life on the same day Lincoln was assassinated, and by the recent death of his wife—welcomed a chance for a convalescent Caribbean trip on official business and he arrived at Santo Domingo City on January 14, 1866. The Cazneaus met Seward at the dock and never let him out of their sight, introducing him to the president and other notables, and keeping him away from any uncongenial people.

The ascetic Seward, sixty-five years old, was evidently enthralled by the vivacious and intelligent company of the fifty-eight-year-old Jane Cazneau, for he was completely won over to their ideas and projects. Some cynical bystanders thought that General Cazneau especially wanted to impress the new president by his intimacy with Seward in order to further some of his pet projects and in this he certainly succeeded. The United States had not as yet recognized the revivified republic and the president was most anxious for this to happen. Anyway, the Cazneaus gained considerable local prestige from Seward's visit. When the refreshed Seward returned to Washington he influenced President Andrew Johnson to nominate General Cazneau as the United States Commissioner and Consul-General to Dominica. Certain unfriendly Americans in that republic made such a protest that the Senate never confirmed this nomination; but this did not discourage the indefatigable General who continued to keep Seward informed about developments in that re-established island republic, and in the autumn of 1866 its government was formally recognized.

The finances of the little republic, however, were in a weak state, and a loan was desperately needed. As security for American help the old plan of selling or leasing a United States naval base soon rose again. This time Joseph Warren Fabens, Cazneau's partner in the Isle of the Blest, wrote Secretary Seward trying to interest him in a naval base at Monte Christi on the northwest coast, near the Haitian border. The adventurous promoters had imported thirty camels from Africa to improve Dominican transportation, and placed them in that area in which they also undoubtedly owned property. Negotiations and dickerings rose in a crescendo for the much-wanted naval base, with the Samaná Bay again becoming the favored site. Secretary Seward became more and more enthusiastic but just as an agreement was reached, a revolution in the republic postponed the negotiations.

Cazneau and Fabens became especially friendly with President Buenaventura (Welcome) Baez who began his third term (not consecutive) in December 1865. He appeared to live up to his first name and to welcome a chance to make a little money, along with his two American intimates, out of his position. There now began to be talk far beyond any lease or sale of Samaná Bay but instead of annexation of the whole republic to the United States, and the two intrepid *entrepreneurs*, ably aided by the capable Jane

Cazneau, put forth all their efforts in that direction and she cheerfully predicted that the republic would prove a second California.

To make short a long and exceedingly involved story of striving and scheming, nothing definite was accomplished during the balance of President Johnson's administration, but the hopes of the Fabens-Cazneau combine soared when Ulysses S. Grant succeeded him in 1869 and Hamilton Fish became Secretary of State. Grant became an extreme imperialist and his pet project the annexation of the Dominican Republic to the United States, although Fish was considerably reluctant about this. The villain in the piece who ruined Grant's dream of an American empire in the Caribbean was Senator Charles Sumner of Massachusetts, who before the Civil War had blocked the plan to acquire Samaná Bay as a naval base. Grant and Sumner hated each other instinctively; the President particularly loathed the parochial narrowness of the Bostonian and Sumner abominated Grant's bluntness and the corruption of some of his associates.

Fabens and the Cazneaus in the meantime had secured about every worthwhile concession in the republic that was not nailed down, from their friend President Baez, including mineral rights on a tenth of all the land in the country; in addition Cazneau controlled several promising copper properties and a lease of a large part of the waterfront of the capital, Santo Domingo City, while Fabens owned a large water frontage at Samaná Bay. They enlisted the support of New York capitalists in founding the National Bank of Santo Domingo and in establishing a steamship line between New York and the ports of the republic. Incidentally, among those interested, at one time or another, in the grandiose projects of these super-promoters were General Benjamin (Beast) Butler of Civil War notoriety and C. K. Garrison who with his partner Charles Morgan had unsuccessfully tried to buck Commodore Vanderbilt for control of the Accessory Transit Company in Nicaragua. Another was Richard B. Kimball, the New York author-lawyer friend of Jane Cazneau. The one bird-of-a-feather missing among these speculators was the notorious General Santa Anna of Mexico who, curiously enough, was living in exile in the town of Santiago deep in the heart of the Dominican Republic in the year 1869. All these ventures and concessions were ample to secure a large fortune to Fabens and the Cazneaus if the United States annexed the little republic.

But back in Washington, Senator Charles Sumner took a very contrary view. He was chairman of the all-powerful Senate Committee on Foreign Relations and was in a position to kill any proposed treaty. The reports he received about the activities of Fabens and Cazneau in feathering their own nests while furthering these treaties upset him, and his innate antipathy to President Grant strengthened his opposition to Grant's keen desire for annexation. Despite terrific pressure from the White House he took a firm stand against ratification of these agreements.

General Cazneau and his wife, however, took the ratification by the Senate for granted because of Grant's enthusiastic backing, and turned their efforts to securing an affirmative vote for annexation in the Dominican Republic in a plebiscite held there in February 1870, of which the results were 90 per cent favorable. It probably helped when President Baez threatened to shoot or exile any man who voted against the proposal.

The Cazneaus, flushed with this success, started another campaign to attract American immigrants: propaganda material was poured at the press, and letters were written describing the golden opportunities and claiming that an American with only a little capital had but to buy "a few acres of land and a small outfit to be certain of a fortune in a few years." Also Cazneau endeavored to secure further large grants of land and other special privileges to increase his already enormous holdings. He failed, however, to win over the American Commercial Agent to his side and this man, Raymond H. Perry, who had purposely been picked by Grant to further the whole plan, became convinced that Cazneau was "a trickster and dishonest man" and so reported to Washington.

The result was that Sumner's committee reported adversely on the treaty in March, 1870, and the Senate later failed to ratify it by the necessary two-thirds vote. Grant was furious and finally forced Sumner's resignation from his committee but the harm was done and the treaty finally languished to death.

And so Charles Sumner ended the hopes of his fellow Bostonians, William Cazneau and Joseph Fabens (also a fellow Harvard man), for a great fortune. For Jane Cazneau it was another failure to win when the stakes were high—just when fortune seemed around the corner. She and her husband appear to have moved again to Jamaica and quietly lived there until he died in 1876.

Two years afterwards, Jane McManus Cazneau met a violent death at sea. She and her Southern daughter-in-law, Mrs. William M. Storms, sailed from New York on December 10, 1878, on the steamer *Emily B. Souder* bound for Jamaica. Two days later they ran into a frightful gale east of Cape Hatteras and the ship began to sink. The four women passengers aboard were loaded into the first lifeboat launched, under the command of the first officer, and this had hardly pulled away before it capsized. Only two seamen were later rescued, afloat on a life raft, and these survivors told of the horrible screams of the women as they were hurled into the waves and the helplessness of the onlookers. Jane Cazneau was seventy-one years old at the time and it is probable that the screams were not hers.

So ended in dramatic violence the career of this amazing woman. If only she had written her memoirs or left some record of her undercover activities in Texas, in Cuba, in Mexico, possibly in Nicaragua, and, of course, in the Dominican Republic. All her books are, curiously enough, replete with romantic descriptions of quiet and idyllic rural life but tell little of her own experiences, and contain only occasional flashes of her intrepid spirit and restless initiative. She must have been that rare combination of gentle femininity and reckless audacity which reaches the heights or depths; something which would have been more fitting to Renaissance Italy than mid-Victorian America. She covered up nearly all traces of her own adventures and it is almost impossible to piece together a true description of her extraordinary life.

CHAPTER XIII

The Halls of Montezuma Again

AFTER William and Jane Cazneau left Eagle Pass, Texas, the pleasant little town on the Rio Grande gradually expanded through the 1850's; but it was not a quiet growth, for the border was aflame with raids and forays by the hostile Indians and lacerated by American and Mexican bandits, and Eagle Pass was right on the main road for these hit-and-run depredators. The meager garrisons of the scattered United States Army posts did their best to stem the disorders but the numbers of troops were too few to hold back the wave of destruction which ebbed and flowed across the border. As a result, the Texans often took the law into their own hands and on one occasion, in October 1855, James Hughes Callahan led a punitive force of over a hundred men, ostensibly chasing Indians, across the river from Eagle Pass to capture the Mexican town of Piedras Negras. There were rumors that this was the prelude of a filibustering expedition to seize northern Mexico, possibly to establish the much-talked-of republic of Sierra Madre. The Mexicans, however, rushed up reinforcements and Callahan, after looting and burning the town, recrossed the Rio Grande under cover of a battery of United States field artillery, brought from nearby Fort Duncan, which stopped Mexican pursuit. It was an outrageous act, all over in no time at all, and it certainly did not improve good-neighbor relations along the border. Years later the United States indemnified the Mexicans whose property had been destroyed. If it was intended as a serious filibuster (which is extremely doubtful) it was the shortest and quickest one on record.

During the Civil War Eagle Pass had many an anxious day for, after the withdrawal of Federal troops, West Texas became a land without law and the raiding Indians and bandits rode back and forth almost unchecked. The Confederates were too busy elsewhere to give more than token protection. But somehow the town survived and even did quite a business in importing supplies from Mexico for the Confederacy, which was blockaded by sea. When news of the Confederate collapse arrived the bottom fell out of the contraband business and Eagle Pass anxiously awaited the arrival of Federal forces to replace the Confederates who had scattered to their homes.

A few weeks later, on a hot June day, a slowly rising and approaching cloud of dust denoted the approach of a sizable mounted force from the east. Some of the townspeople rode out to meet it and to their astonishment and poignant joy found that it was not a body of blue-coated Yankee troopers but a brigade of Confederates, the remnants of the Missouri Cavalry Division, led in person by the famous General Joseph Orville Shelby, who had refused to obey the surrender order of General E. Kirby-Smith, commanding the Confederate forces west of the Mississippi River. The men were a young and hard-bitten lot, for the married and older men had mostly chosen to return to their homes when "Fighting Jo"[1] Shelby had given them that choice or of following him across Texas to take service as a unit with one of the warring factions in Mexico, for, as he said, "Surrender is a word which neither my division nor myself understand."

In Mexico the Emperor Maximilian, supported by the native Conservatives but actually upheld by French troops sent by Napoleon III and by Austrian and Belgian volunteers, controlled all the larger cities, but the opposing Liberals, led by Benito Juarez, lurked in the mountains and jungles and carried on a ceaseless guerrilla warfare against these foreign invaders. The French Emperor had taken advantage of the distractions of the Civil War in the United States to flout the Monroe Doctrine and had invaded the Mexican Republic with French troops to place the Austrian Archduke on the throne of a newly formed empire. The United States had bitterly resented this but had been powerless to act during the war; now, after victory, Federal troops were pouring toward the Mexican border to stage a powerful show of force and to help unofficially the Mexican Liberals in every possible way.[2]

"Fighting Jo" Shelby, a native Kentuckian, was in his thirty-fifth year and had been an outstanding cavalry leader

---

[1] The name Joseph seemed to bring the nickname "Fighting Joe" (or Jo). Besides Shelby, there were "Fighting Joe" Wheeler, C.S.A., and "Fighting Joe" Hooker, U.S.A. However, Joseph E. Johnston, C.S.A., the best general of all, somehow escaped it.

[2] This was often done by leaving large, unguarded supplies of arms and ammunition in a convenient place and then quietly sending word to the Juaristas to come and get them.

in the merciless semi-guerrilla warfare in Arkansas and Missouri where the infamous William Clarke Quantrill, ably assisted by Frank and Jesse James, had operated under his command. Shelby has been ranked in ability with Jeb Stuart, by an enthusiastic biographer, which seems a bit extreme, but he was undoubtedly an unusually able cavalryman.[3]

The exact number of men who chose to follow Shelby into Mexico is uncertain. One trooper reported only a hundred and fifty but Shelby's exuberant adjutant, Major John Newman Edwards, estimated some five hundred.[4] The number varied along the way from day to day as new recruits joined and others fell out. The original volunteers for Mexico had formed a regiment at Corsicana, Texas, and unanimously elected Shelby as Colonel; several unpopular officers, however, did not fare so well and were demoted to privates in the balloting, which they accepted with good grace. There was no trouble about equipment, for Texas was one vast supply depot of guns, ammunition, and provisions which had avoided the Federal blockade by way of Mexico. These had all been abandoned upon news of the collapse of the Confederacy and they were Shelby's for the taking. He plentifully supplied his followers with arms and ammunition, so much so that each trooper bore four Colt repeating revolvers apiece. Ten brand-new howitzers of French manufacture

[3] Daniel O'Flaherty, *General Jo Shelby*. Chapel Hill, 1954, p. 3. The outstanding Confederate cavalryman was the natural genius Nathan Bedford Forrest.

[4] The trooper was Thomas Westlake, who wrote an account of his adventures which is now in the Western Historical Manuscripts Collection at the University of Missouri. He left the expedition at Monterrey, Mexico, so it is an incomplete narrative. Edwards wrote the only published account of the expedition from start to finish.

were taken as an artillery train and all kinds of imported delicacies were obtained from an abandoned wagon train. His men had never seen anything like it and glutted themselves with fancy food and equipment.

This force of defiant Rebel cavalrymen started on the last filibuster when they rode into Mexico, and it might well have been the greatest of all if the Emperor Maximilian had so chosen; for Shelby could probably have made his band the cadre for an army of fifty thousand Confederate veterans, with unpredictable results. As it was, Shelby and his troopers fought their way down from Eagle Pass to Mexico City through nearly a thousand miles of hostile, bandit-infested country, through deserts and mountains, to offer their services as a unit to the astonished Emperor Maximilian as the climax to their anabasis.

The story of it is told by Shelby's adjutant, Major John N. Edwards, in a rare book, *Shelby's Expedition to Mexico,* which is the only published account of the strange adventures of these irreconcilable Rebels who chose exile rather than life under Yankee rule. Edwards was a Virginian who had gone to Missouri before the war to edit a newspaper, and to this he later returned after his wandering adventures were over. He had a style which appears to stem from Sir Walter Scott's Waverly Novels, Sir Thomas Malory's *Morte d'Arthur,* Lord Alfred Tennyson's *Idylls of the King,* and Edmund Spenser's *Faerie Queene,* all shaken well together and topped off with a strong dash of Lord Byron. The result is an almost incredible mixture of murky rodomontade and historical inaccuracy. Everybody moved in a golden cloud of medieval chivalry, drunken brawls were described as courtly jousts, knights errant galloped off in all directions, virtuous womanhood was always on a pedestal, valor triumphed over fearful odds, a fair maiden was rescued from a wicked ogre, and about the only thing missing was a fight with a real, fire-breathing dragon—but perhaps Edwards realized, subconsciously, that the limit had been reached without that. Strangely enough, it is withal a good story simply because of the bare facts which he could not completely smother, and it could even have been a great one if simply and truthfully told.

From Corsicana Shelby's new regiment rode to Houston, where was the largest Confederate supply depot, to find the town in a state of semi-anarchy with looters and discharged soldiers about to break into a government warehouse. Shelby's advance guard stationed themselves before its door and the commander shouted "Disperse! We are Jo Shelby's men. We are Missourians, we are leaving Texas, we have no homes, but we have our orders and our honor." As Major Edwards reported it, the mob glared back with "wild, vicious eyes . . . red and swollen by drink" but they dispersed.[5] The same sort of scene was repeated in two small towns on the way to Austin in one of which a knight errant sat himself on a powder keg and threatened to blow up a warehouse and all concerned rather than deliver it to a mob. And when he held a match over a fuse "the mass of marauders surged back as if the earth had opened at their very feet."

---

[5] All quotations are from Edwards unless otherwise noted.

281

They came into Austin to an ovation of grateful citizens and were welcomed by Governor Murrah, a man dying of consumption, whose fatal signs

. . . were seen in the hectic cheeks, the large, mournful eyes, the tall, bent frame that quivered as it moved. Murrah was a gifted and brilliant man, but his heart was broken. In his life there was the memory of an unblessed and an unhallowed love, too deep for human sympathy, too sad and passionate for tears.

That night a band of robbers (they certainly picked an inopportune time) attacked the Confederate sub-treasury in the town which contained three hundred thousand dollars in specie. Word was rushed to Shelby's camp across the Colorado River and "there arose on the night air the full, resonant blare of Shelby's bugle sounding the well-known rallying call." Into the town galloped the gallant Missourians to surround the treasury inside which the robbers were "gorging themselves with gold." At the command, "A sudden, pitiless jet of flame spurted out from two scores of Sharp's carbines; there was the sound of falling men on the echoing floor, and then a great darkness. From out the smoke, and gloom, and shivered glass, and scattered eagles, they dragged the victims forth—dying, bleeding, dead."

That ended the villainous attempt of these dastardly robbers. Shelby placed his men about and "a stern guard took his post, immutable as fate, by the silver heaps and the blood puddles. In walking his beat this blood splashed him to the knees."

The grateful Governor Murrah came to Shelby in the morning to insist that he take all the money for his troopers as they were the last body of organized Confederates in the state and were about to leave it; certainly they had the best claim, as they had to the ordnance and supplies they had found. "The temptation was strong and the arguments were strong" but Shelby never wavered; "I went into the war with clean hands, and by God's blessing, I will go out of the war with clean hands" he replied. "We are the last of the race but let us be the best as well." What his war-weary followers, who had probably not been paid for months, thought of this quixotic decision is not reported by the lofty Edwards; perhaps they never knew about it or perhaps it only happened under his golden quill.

Thence on to romantic San Antonio—the city of the sun. On the way another band of desperadoes tried to rustle some of the fat, well-conditioned mounts of the command but they were met by a terrible fire from Shelby's valiant knights of Missouri. As Edwards described it: "A red cleft in the heart of the midnight—a murky shroud of dun and dark that smelt of sulphur—a sudden uprearing of staggering steeds and staggering riders—a wild, pitiful panic of spectres who had encountered the unknown"—in other words, the dastardly varlets were foiled. Incidentally, rarely did Edwards allow Shelby's knights errant to spend a peaceful night or make a day's ride without attack.

Then San Antonio: "To the hungry and war-worn soldiers of Shelby's expedition it was a Paradise," but, alas, first they found that fugitive desperadoes "had taken immediate possession of the city and were rioting in royal fashion, sitting in the laps of courtesans and drinking wines fresh through the blockade from France." This was just one too many for Shelby's frustrated men-at-arms and the courtly Missourians soon chased the pampered bandits off the laps of those motherly courtesans and showed just who sits on whose lap in the golden world of chivalry.

The Menger Hotel (which Edwards called the Mingo) was the focus of fleeing Confederate bigwigs, many of them making for the Mexican border, who spent the heat of the day in its famous bar for, as Edwards wrote, "Fugitive Generals had gathered here, and fugitive Senators, and fugitive Governors, and fugitive desperadoes, as well, men sententious of speech and quick of pistol practice." And outside this oasis, after Shelby's men had pushed the sybaritic bandits from the courtesans' laps, "Peace came upon the city as the balm of a southeast trade-wind, and after the occupation there was an ovation. Women walked forth as if to a festival. The Plaza transformed itself into a *parterre*. Roses bloomed in the manes of the horses—these were exotic; roses bloomed in the faces of the maidens—these were divine. After Cannae there was Capua."

One balmy evening in the rose-scented plaza of the Texas Capua, Shelby's band serenaded General Edmund Kirby-Smith who had quietly slipped into town incognito and, after registering at the Menger under an assumed name, had retired to a room with drawn shades. As Edwards described his arrival, "an ambulance drew up in front of the Mingo House. Besides the driver, there alighted an old man, aged, bent, spent with fatigue, and dusty as a foot soldier." But he added: "Old men need air and sunlight; they do not commence hibernating in June," and the estivation of the despondent General was broken by the stirring sounds of "Dixie" played under his window.

The Halls of Montezuma Again

The sweet, familiar strains rose up, rapid and exultant, filling all the air with life and all the pulses with blood. . . . The blinds flew open, the curtains were rolled up, and in plain view of this last remnant of his magnificent army of fifty thousand men, Gen. E. Kirby-Smith came forth undisguised, a look full of eagerness and wonderment on his weary and saddened face.

Poor old General E. Kirby-Smith had reached the advanced age of forty-one years (six years older than Shelby) when this stirring demonstration renewed his lost youth.

General Smith joined the party and all was joy in San Antonio. To complete this happy fiesta an outsider was annexed, "an Englishman who was a mystery and an enigma" but "an elegant and accomplished linguist, an extensive traveler, a soldier who had seen service in Algeria with the French, and in the Crimea with the British," and was "singularly winning and fascinating in his intercourse with the men." He had an unusual desire, an overwhelming wish to be in a railroad accident, and he had traveled over two continents in unsuccessful pursuit of this passion. Shelby was fascinated by him and persuaded him to join his force although it was headed far away from railroads and the chances of a glorious accident.

Another recruit was the famous General John Magruder (known throughout the land as "Prince John") who had commanded the Confederate forces in Texas before the collapse. Magruder was a fabulous character: a native Virginian, he had graduated from West Point in 1830 and served with distinction as an artilleryman in the Seminole War in Florida; and during the Mexican War, Stonewall Jackson had received his baptism of fire under "the restless and hot-tempered Magruder." Later he had done his share of frontier duty in California and Texas. Going with the Confederacy, he had served under Lee in Virginia but from October 1862 he commanded the district of Texas (which included New Mexico and Arizona). In January, 1863, he had recaptured the port of Galveston from the Federals, taking also the Revenue cutter, *Harriet Lane*, in a daring and skillful attack. In appearance he was the perfect *beau sabreur*, and probably the brightest social light ever to grace the United States Army. Edwards described him lyrically:

He had a figure like a Mars divested of immortality. He would fight all day and dance all night. He wrote love songs and sang them, and won an heiress rich beyond comparison.[6] The wittiest man in the old army, Gen. Scott, adored him. [Actually Scott was pretty heavy and bombastic.] His speech had a lisp that was attractive, inasmuch as it lingered over its puns and caressed its rhetoric. Six feet in height, and straight as Tecumseh, Magruder, in full regimentals, was the handsomest soldier in the Confederacy. Not the fair, blonde beauty of the city, odorous of perfume and faultless in tailor-fashion, but a great, bronzed Ajax, mighty thewed, and as strong of hand as strong of digestion. He loved women, too, and was beloved by them. After Galveston, with blood upon his garments, a bullet wound upon his body, and victory upon his standards, he danced until there was daybreak in the sky and sunlight upon the earth. From the fight to the frolic it had been fifty-eight hours since he slept.

---

[6] *The Dictionary of American Biography* is wrong and Edwards, for once, is right. Prince John married Henriette von Kapff (aged 16), daughter of the German Consul in Baltimore, in 1831. His wife and their three children went to Europe after the outbreak of the Mexican War in 1846. Mrs. Magruder never returned to this country. Her husband visited them twice in Florence, Italy, before the outbreak of the Civil War, and his wife brought the children over to Mexico for a short time in 1866. She then returned to Florence where she died. One daughter eloped in Italy to Leghorn with Dr. Reggin Buckler of Baltimore and a granddaughter of this marriage lives in that city today. Incidentally, "Prince John's" bride's father had a snug fortune but nothing beyond comparison.

The Halls of Montezuma Again

Taking the usual discount of Edwards' purple prose, it is still apparent that "Prince John" Magruder was quite a fellow, a *bon vivant* and a gallant of the first water, and this opinion is confirmed by many reliable witnesses, one of whom, Major General Alexander Watkins Terrell C.S.A.,[7] told of a dinner party given in New York by Magruder to a visiting English admiral, which was served on borrowed gold plates. The Admiral was so impressed that he asked Magruder what his salary was. "James," said the host turning to the butler, "what is my salary?" It appeared that he gave his army pay to his servant. When stationed at Fort Adams in Newport, Rhode Island (a great summer resort for Southerners before the Civil War) he had delighted Newport society with his entertainments and colorful military drills, and his flair for displays was just as keen on the frontier with Indians, Mexicans, and frontiersmen as an appreciative audience. All in all John Bankhead Magruder was rightly dubbed "Prince John" and was a giant among the colorful leaders of the Confederacy.

From San Antonio, Shelby's brigade (evidently he had picked up enough recruits along the way to form two regiments) rode through the dusty mesquite and chaparral country to Eagle Pass on the border. On the way, according to the redundant Edwards, they beat off attacks by horse thieves and defied a pursuing Federal force to stop them, and, of course, exterminated a band of robbers who had

---

[7] General Terrell was a Texan who went to Mexico for a while after the war and wrote of his experiences in *From Texas to Mexico and the Court of Maximilian in 1865*. Dallas, 1933. He returned home to become a prominent judge and served as Minister to Turkey during the second administration of President Grover Cleveland, 1893-1897.

been preying on the defenseless settlers. But finally they rode triumphantly into Eagle Pass, watched by two thousand Mexican soldiers, "quaint of costume and piratical of aspect," in Piedras Negras, just across the Rio Grande, under the command of Governor Biesca of the State of Coahuila, a man "who quoted his similes and italicised his gestures" and who was holding the town for the Juarista Liberals.

There was considerable high-flown and courtly palavering between the two commanders and the Governor offered Shelby the military command of the Juarista forces in the Mexican border states, with the right to recruit an army of fifty thousand Americans. This appealed to Shelby and very probably he had a vision of eventually forming an independent republic along the border, a plan many Confederates favored after the peace. He put it to a vote of his men. But fighting for Democracy in the "land of garlic, stilettos, and straw hats" under the leadership of the Indian Benito Juarez was not what these men, starved for pomp and pleasure, wanted after four years of campaigning in the arid Bible Belt of Arkansas, Missouri and Texas. For them the gorgeous trappings and color of empire, the promise of exotic women, French wines, and easy morals in Mexico City had far more allure, and, to a man, they voted to march to the fleshpots of the capital and join Maximilian. Shelby acquiesced with good grace and notified the Governor of the decision. That dignitary shrugged with "a muttered *buena*, a folded cigarrito, a bow to the invisible," and offered to buy Shelby's artillery as the next best possible deal. As his men needed money more than artillery, Shelby cheerfully agreed to this offer from what was now technically his enemy; and receiving it in cash he deposited it in Briesca's custom house for safekeeping, thus preserving the amenities.

Before they left Piedras Negras, however, Shelby and his men assembled on the bank of the Rio Grande to lower reverently their Confederate battle standards, weighted with stones, into the roily waters. Then for a final celebration before setting out on the long, long ride into Mexico.

The men scattered in every direction, careless of consequences, and indifferent as to results. The cafés were full, wine and women abounded. Besides the bronzed faces of the soldiers were the tawny faces of the señoritas. In the passage of the drinking-horns the men kissed the women. Great American oaths came out from the *tiendas*, harsh at times, and resonant at times. Even in their wickedness they were national. . . .

. . . which all added up to trouble with the surrounding Mexicans.

Suddenly it came. "Some revolvers were being fired. These, in the white heat of the afternoon, sounded as the tapping of woodpeckers." "The rally! the rally!—sound the rally!" Shelby cried to his bugler. "We have eaten of their salt and they have betrayed us; we have come to them as friends, and they would strip us like barbarians. It is war again—war to the knife."

The bugle sobered "all who were drunk with drink or dalliance" as Shelby's men poured out of the saloons. One crusading Missourian drew a bead on a young Mexican captain;

It looked as if he was aiming at a flower—the dark olive beauty of the Spaniard was so superb.

"Spare him!" shouted a dozen reckless soldiers in a breath, "he is too young and too handsome to die."

289

In vain! A sharp, sudden ring was the response; the Captain tossed his arms high in the air, leaped up suddenly as if to catch something above his head, and fell forward upon his face, a corpse. A wail of women arose upon the sultry evening—such as may have been heard in David's household when back from the tangled brushwood they brought the beautiful Absalom.

At this point the Mexicans awoke from their siestas, and

. . . Women went wailing through the streets; the church bells rang furiously; windows were darkened and barricaded; and over all the din and turmoil—the galloping of horses, and the clanking of steel—arose the harsh, gathering cry of the Mexican long roll—sullen, hoarse, discordant.

In the melee sixteen other Mexicans and two Americans were killed before Governor Briesca and General Shelby, storming and threatening their men, finally restored order. And then, "Laughter and songs issued again from the wine-shops." For once, Edwards stooped to understatement when he wrote, "The day had been full of surprises."

★ 2 ★

On the morning after the disturbances in Piedras Negras, Shelby led his chastened troops out on the road to Monterrey where was stationed the nearest garrison of Maximilian's Imperial Army. They rode through a desolate land, devastated by the French troops and Juarista guerrillas, and what little these warring factions spared, the Lipans (a branch of the Apaches) and Mexican outlaws destroyed. The column came to a village just visited by these ravaging jackals which was a horror:

Men hung suspended from door-facings literally flayed alive. Huge strips of skin dangled from them as tattered garments might hang. Under some a slow fire had been kindled, until strangulation came as a tardy mercy for relief. There were the bodies of some children among the slain, and one beautiful woman, not yet attacked by the elements, seemed only asleep.

Edwards wrote that "a deep silence fell upon the column, rear and van" as they cleared this ghastly hamlet.

The next morning, on the Fourth of July, 1865, they reached the Sabinas River. A dark and mysterious stranger had galloped out from Piedras Negras to warn Shelby upon his departure, "Beware of the Sabinas!" and he sensed a trap from the outlaws who had plundered the village behind him. Scouts sent ahead reported back that at least eight hundred men lay in ambush on the farther bank. But Shelby led his followers in a splashing charge through the stream and, falling on the hidden foe like a hurricane, routed them with great slaughter.

The railroad-happy Englishman, whom Fighting Jo had annexed in San Antonio, rode by the leader's side, "a battle-light on his fair face—a face that was, alas! too soon to be wan and gray, and drawn with agony." Twenty-seven of Shelby's men fell in the charge and one bullet carried the little Englishman's name. That was grist for Major Edwards' mill and, of course, the dying Englishman confessed that he was in reality a nobleman's son who had once been an officer in the British army but had been forced to leave after he had killed a brother officer in a duel over the favors of a beautiful maiden. Since then he had wandered an outcast over the face of the world until his meeting with Shelby in San Antonio. Then:

He lifted himself up and turned his face fair to the west. Some beams of the setting sun, like a benediction, rested upon the long blonde hair, and upon the white set lips, drawn now and gray with agony. No man spoke in all the rugged band, flushed with victory, and weary with killing. In the trees a little breeze lingered, and some birds flitted and sang, though far apart.

On rode Shelby and his intrepid men, on to Monterrey the bastion of the Imperial troops in northeastern Mexico, constantly skirmishing with prowling guerrillas (Edwards always called the Liberals either guerrillas or bandits) until they reached the town of Lampazos, halfway to Monterrey; and there one of the men fought a deadly duel with a Mexican. Shelby had confined his followers to camp outside the town because he felt "unwilling to trust his men to the perils of so much nakedness" which he had observed in passing through. But the men naturally felt otherwise and a sizable number slipped into town that night. One of them rudely accosted a native belle on the street and in a scuffle her *rebosa* came off "leaving all her bosom bare, the long, luxuriant hair falling down and over it as a cloud that would hide its purity and innocence." The brother of this outraged maiden came directly to Shelby demanding satisfaction. That somewhat harassed leader agreed to a duel with knives and the offending trooper killed the noble brother amidst the most dramatic scenes. There was never a dull moment according to Major Edwards.

The Halls of Montezuma Again

Colonel Jeaningros held Monterrey with some five thousand French and Mexican troops which included four regiments of the Foreign Legion and one of Zouaves who were as tough a crowd of cutthroats as the worst of the Mexican guerrillas, and Edwards reported that their commander ruled them with a rod of iron. He received Shelby's column cordially and gave a banquet of sixteen courses for the officers and other Confederate dignitaries, who had previously arrived by different routes, which General Terrell said was long remembered for its contrast to Confederate war rations. Among those present were General Magruder (who had preceded Shelby), General E. Kirby-Smith (the old man), and an assorted lot of ex-governors, ex-senators, and ex-almost-anything of importance in the Confederacy. Also there was Major General Alexander Watkins Terrell C.S.A. from Texas, and thanks to him an element of sanity now entered the picture because his memoirs[8] of these events are accurate and a healthy antidote to some of Edwards' high-flown hyperboles. At the dinner Shelby asked his host what kind of a man Maximilian was and Jeaningros, who was flushed with wine, replied:

More of a scholar than a king, good at botany, a poet on occasions . . . believing more in manifest destiny than drilled battalions . . . honest, earnest, tender-hearted and sincere, his faith is too strong in the liars who surround him, and his soul is too pure for the deeds that must be done. . . . He knows nothing of diplomacy. . . . his days are numbered; nor can all the power of France keep his crown upon his head, if, indeed, it can keep that head upon his shoulders.

[8] See footnote, p. 287.

Edwards was sensible enough in this quotation but it may have been a case of perfect hindsight, for his book was published five years after the execution of the tragic Maximilian.

Shelby was convinced by what he learned in Monterrey that Maximilian's only hope was to enlist a large army of Americans and that the best place to recruit these would be at the Mexican ports of Guaymas or Mazatlan on the Pacific coast where adventurous Californians could flock to his standard although these ports would certainly be inconvenient for Confederate veterans to reach. Perhaps Shelby, like William Walker, counted on California as the best reservoir for filibustering. Jeaningros, however, cheerfully gave him permission to march through the Imperial lines to the Pacific to raise a corps of Americans.

Shelby set out for Saltillo to the southwest (which Edwards describes as northward) and, according to his valiant chronicler, made his first camp on the battlefield of Buena Vista upon which about four thousand Americans under old Zach Taylor had turned back some twenty thousand attacking Mexicans led by General Santa Anna in February, 1847, in the most bloody encounter ever fought by an American force before the Civil War. This day's march was possible but it would have been an unusual ride, for Saltillo is nearly sixty miles from Monterrey, uphill and rough going all the way, and Buena Vista lies another seven miles south of Saltillo in a mountainous defile. Edwards gave a description of the moonlit battlefield in which he depicts the eerie ghosts of slain American and Mexican soldiers flitting about the mountain peaks "as grave after grave gave up its dead, and as spirit after spirit put on its uniform and its martial array." But the moonshine on the field of honor was as nothing to that flowing from his impassioned quill.

From there these wandering crusaders rode on westward to Parras, having, of course, the usual desperate fight with bandits (Liberals) on the way. They were inhospitably received by an alcoholic French officer who, acting on orders from Marshal Bazaine, commander of all French troops in Mexico, rudely forbade their further way to the Pacific and ordered them to ride immediately to Mexico City. To add insult to injury, "pointing to Shelby's hat, he ordered fiercely:

"'Remove that.'

"'Only to beauty and to God' was the stern, calm reply; "'to a coward, never.'"

The French officer by a supreme effort controlled himself and shouted "'Retire—retire instantly—lest I outrage all hospitality and dishonor you in my own house.'"

Naturally a duel was in order but this never came off, for the next day Jeaningros clattered into Parras with four squadrons of Chasseurs d'Afrique and, learning of the quarrel, ordered his subordinate officer to apologize to Shelby and so all ended well.

Nevertheless, Shelby had to obey Bazaine's order and perforce turned south toward Mexico City. Soon afterwards the irrepressible Edwards described an act of chivalry which was a must with all knights errant—the rescue of a captive maiden in distress. The wonder of it all is that he only mentioned one such noble act on the entire journey. Reading between the lines it would seem that some of the troopers got drunk and broke into a ranch house—which has happened in other armies before and since. But under Edwards' magic pen it appears that these chivalrous rescuers had been told that a beautiful American girl (who was, of course, "a pearl of great price") was being held in durance vile by a rich and wicked landowner in his castle-like hacienda—"an adobe eyrie." Naturally these valiant men went to the rescue and, breaking down the doors of the hacienda, they proceeded to shoot up the place in royal style. The result was the death of several Mexicans and of five rescuing Americans. Shelby was quite rightly furious with the self-appointed zealots but magnanimously forgave the survivors. The American girl, Inez Walker, "came into the presence of Shelby, a queen," but "the liquid light of her large dark eyes had long ago been quenched in tears." She joined the column and Edwards reported that she was seen later riding in the royal coach by the side of the Empress Carlota in Mexico City. What happened to the ranch owner is not quite so clear.

A bit farther along, at Matehuala, a city of twenty thousand north of San Luis Potosí, the Juaristas were attacking a much inferior French garrison but were driven off by a surprise charge on their rear by Fighting Jo's Iron Brigade, approaching from the north. The grateful commander of the relieved garrison made the city a Paradise for the men and "There were days of feasting, and mirth, and minstrelsy; and in the balm of fragrant nights the men dallied with the women."

Then on ever southward and "Adventures grew thick along the road as cactus plants," meaning daily and nightly alarms and excursions from lurking bandits. They reached the large city of San Luis Potosí where General Felix Douay accorded the Missouri Cavalry Division a lavish welcome and Fighting Jo promised in return to raise a corps of fifty thousand Americans to fight under Maximilian.

But at this point a cool wind of sanity blows aside some of Edwards' gorgeous poppycock, for General Terrell also happened to be in the city and he reported that he met General Shelby there with several officers "and a few of his men, all in bad plight and with horses poor," and that Fighting Jo was so stony broke that he tried to sell him two ivory handled six-shooters. Very probably Terrell told the truth and this deflation of Edwards' purple prose should proportionately be applied to his whole epic of the trek to Mexico City, which is in such marked contrast with William Walker's terse and accurate narrative of his Nicaraguan adventures. Actually, Edwards does General Shelby considerable disservice because one begins his incredible narrative with bewilderment, which rises to hilarity, and finally drops to boredom at the repetitious and impossibly noble deeds and courtly language of Shelby's knights of the Ozarks; and the natural conclusion is that Shelby was pretty much of a humbug himself, which is very unfair, for he was, in truth, an extremely able cavalryman, and his ride to Mexico City was a remarkable feat even if he arrived with only a handful of his beaten-up veterans.

At last they reached the great capital and the entry of these tough, battle-scarred Confederates, similar only in their raggedness to the exuberant Americans who had triumphantly entered the city nearly eighteen long years before, brought the cycle of filibustering to full circle. In that time the American filibusters had dared much and succeeded in nothing. The breed was back where it had all started. A battalion of Chasseurs d'Afrique met the Iron Brigade at the outskirts of Mexico City and escorted the men to a large stone barracks where they were comfortably quartered. How many of them arrived seems unknown, probably very few. If they had counted a respectable number, the exuberant Edwards would certainly have mentioned the total and it does not seem that they could have increased after General Terrell's report of their drab poverty and fewness, a short time before, in San Luis Potosí. But Mexico City must have seemed like the promised land to the remnants of the Missouri Cavalry Division, some of them veterans of over four years' bloody fighting in the wasted countryside of Arkansas and Missouri, amidst the greatest privations and hardships. Probably they had never seen a city of equal size.

Mexico City was crowded with prominent ex-Confederates, among them Generals John Magruder and Alexander Terrell and none other than our old friend Pierre Soulé, but most prominent and influential of all was Commodore Matthew Fontaine Maury, once an officer of the United States and Confederate navies, who was a world-famous and much-honored oceanographer and scientist, and the author of the renowned book *The Physical Geography of the Sea.* Emperor Maximilian had served as an officer in the Austro-Hungarian navy and was greatly pleased when the noted Maury, who had been a Confederate agent to Great Britain, sought refuge in Mexico and appointed him Imperial Commissioner of Immigration, which meant that he had full charge of inducing unreconciled Confederates to Mexico. As his assistant the Emperor chose the gallant Magruder with the title of Chief of the Land Office.

General Terrell had come direct from Monterrey to Mexico City by stage without any trouble. One of the first friends he met in the capital was the dashing John Magruder, beautifully tailored "in a cutaway suit of salt-and-pepper color, with a tall dove-colored hat, and patent leather boots." Terrell wore only his threadbare old Confederate uniform and the shocked Magruder took him in hand at once and led him to a fashionable tailor where he was outfitted with "a black frock coat of the finest cloth, pants of the same material, and a vest of black silk stuff . . . patent leather cavalry boots and a black silk hat." To go with this splendor Magruder gave him "a small cane with a woman's leg cut in ivory for its handle" and took him, fully arrayed, for an audience with Emperor Maximilian at Chapultepec Castle. Terrell was much impressed to find the Emperor dressed in a salt-and-pepper cutaway, identical with Magruder's.

The exuberant "Prince John" nostalgically recalled his previous stay in the city, during the American occupation of 1847-1848, and vividly described to Terrell the last banquet in the city of a social organization of the American officers, called the Aztec Club, which had been a wild bacchanalian revel on the stage of the National Theatre with the members served by men on horseback wearing the armor of Cortez's *conquistadores* and with each mounted waiter carrying a lance while he served, which, obviously, had made the dinner no place for a sober man.

Maury and Magruder arranged an audience for Shelby with Emperor Maximilian at which was present the French military commander Marshal Bazaine, who within a few years was to surrender the great fortress of Metz in the Franco-German War. Shelby offered to enroll his command at a unit and to recruit a corps of forty thousand Southerners who would replace as many unreliable native troops and become the bulwark of the Imperial Government, for, he said: "It is only a question of time, Your Majesty, before the French soldiers are withdrawn."

"Why do you think so?" inquired the Emperor.

"Because the war between the states is at an end, and Mr. Seward will insist on the rigorous enforcement of the Monroe Doctrine. France does not desire a conflict with the United States. It would neither be popular nor profitable. I left behind me a million men under arms, not one of whom has yet been discharged from the service. The nation is sore over this occupation, and the presence of the French is a perpetual menace."

Edwards quoted all this from memory and again one can suspect him of perfect hindsight. It was all true enough but there can be strong doubts that General Shelby knew it at the time. Anyway, what he and his men needed above all else were jobs, and it does not seem as if he would have gone in for Cassandra-like prophecies—true but disagreeable—at such a time and place.

Whatever the conversation may have been, it was nevertheless the crucial point upon which Maximilian's phantom empire hung if he had but known it. If his reply had been favorable there might have been a flood of recruits with unknown results—it might even have brought on another bloody war with the United States, or it might have stabilized his regime.

But Maximilian was overoptimistic, at the time, about the strength of his local support in Mexico, and he did not want complications with the United States; and so his interpreter, after the Emperor had left the room, replied to Shelby; "It's no use. He means to negotiate with the United States. He thinks Mr. Seward favorably disposed to him."

Maximilian signed his own death warrant with this decision and the Confederate adventurers found they had but moved from one lost cause to another.

The aftermath, however, had a short twilight glow before utter darkness. Shelby disappointedly released his followers who scattered to all points. Then he went with several other Confederate leaders and generals to establish a colony near the mountain town of Córdoba, some ninety miles west of the port of Vera Cruz. For almost a year this settlement had promise of success, for the soil was rich, the climate clement, and the transplanted Southerners worked long and hard. But an attack by the Juarista Liberals destroyed everything and soon afterwards the capture and execution of the tragic Maximilian, in June 1867, ended all hopes; and the Confederate expatriates gradually returned home to pick up the threads of their old lives.

This was the last flicker of the once raging fire of filibustering. Perhaps its embers lie dormant waiting for some cataclysm to fan a future flare-up; perhaps if circumstances should confine American energy to the Western Hemisphere again there may be another outburst of the spirit of

Manifest Destiny. Far stranger things have happened. Those exuberant and reckless filibusters were the product of an age when few Americans cared what the rest of the world thought of them—what they thought of the rest of the world was all that mattered. "Because" in William Wordsworth's words—

"the good old rule
Sufficeth them, the simple plan,
That they should take, who have the power,
And they should keep who can."

Sources

*Including those mentioned in the narrative and footnotes.
Only those actually used are listed.*

*The general references used throughout are listed immediately
below. The special sources are by chapters.*

Appleton's Cyclopaedia of American Biography. 6 vols. New
York, 1899-1900.

Cullum, Bvt. Maj. Gen. George, *Biographical Register of the
Officers and Graduates of the U. S. Military Academy.* 2 vols.
Boston and New York, 1891.

Estes, Claud, *List of Field Officers, Regiments and Battalions in
the Confederate States Army, 1861-1865.* Macon, Georgia,
1912.

Dictionary of American Biography. 20 vols. New York, 1928-1944.

Feipel, Louis N.: "The Navy and Filibustering in the Fifties,"
U. S. Naval Institute Proceedings. April–Sept., 1918.

Harper's Weekly. From January 3, 1857.

Heitman, Francis B., *Historical Register and Dictionary of the
United States Army.* 2 vols. Washington, 1903.

Leslie's Illustrated Weekly Newspaper. From December 15, 1855.

Manning, William R., *Diplomatic Correspondence of the United
States—Inter-American Affairs, 1831-1860.* 12 vols. Washington, 1932-1939.

New York *Herald.*

New York *Sun.*

New York *Times.*

Destiny and Glory

New York *Tribune.*

Register of Graduates and Former Cadets. United States Military Academy. 1802-1946. New York, 1946.

Scroggs, William O., *Filibusters and Financiers.* New York, 1916.

Williams, Mary Wilhelmine, *The People and Politics of Latin America.* Boston, 1945.

Chapters I and II

American Star. Mexico City, 1847-1848.

Ancona, Eligio, *Historia de Yucatan.* 4 vols. Merida, 1889.

Archives of British Honduras. Edited by John H. Burdon. 3 vols. London, 1935.

Bancroft, H. H., *History of Mexico.* Vol. V. San Francisco, 1885.

Baqueiro, Serapio, *Ensayo Historico Sobre Las Revoluciones de Yucatan.* . . . 2 vols. Merida, 1873.

Cline, Howard F., *Regionalism and Society in Yucatan.* Unpublished doctoral dissertation at Harvard University.

Daily North American. Mexico City, 1847-1848.

Diplomatic Correspondence of the Republic of Texas. Edited by G. P. Garrison. 4 vols. Washington, 1911.

El Fenix. Edited by Justo Sierra O'Reilly. Campeche, 1848-1849.

Enciclopedia Yucatanense. Vols. VII and VIII. Mexico City, 1944.

Fields, F. T., "The Texas Navy," *Texas Sketchbook,* published by Humble Oil and Refining Company. Houston, 1955.

Fuller, J. D. P., *Movement for the Acquisition of All Mexico.* Baltimore, 1936.

Ganoe, William Addleman, *The History of the United States Army.* New York, 1942.

Heller, Carl B., *Reisen in Mexiko in den Jahren 1845-1848.* Leipzig, 1853.

Hill, Jim Dan, *The Texas Navy in Forgotten Battles.* Chicago, 1937.

Houston, The Writings of Sam. Edited by Amelia W. Williams and Eugene C. Barker. 8 vols. Austin, 1938-1943.

Lamar, The Papers of Mirabeau Buonaparte. Published by Texas State Library. 6 vols. 1920-1927.

Sources

Menendez, Carlos R., *90 Años de Historia de Yucatan*. Merida, 1937.

New Orleans *Daily Delta*. 1848-1849.

New Orleans *Daily Picayune*. 1848-1849.

Norman, B. M., *Rambles in Yucatan*. New York, 1843.

O'Reilly, Justo Sierra, *Diario De Nuestro Viaje A Los Estados Unidos*. Edited by Hector Perez Martinez. Mexico, 1938.

Oswandel, J. Jacob, *Notes on the Mexican War*. Philadelphia, 1883.

Polk, The Diary of James K. Edited by Milo Milton Quaife. 4 vols. Chicago, 1910.

Pratt, J. W., "The Origin of Manifest Destiny." *American Historical Review*. July, 1927.

Smith, Justin H., *The War With Mexico*. 2 vols. New York, 1919.

Stephens, John L., *Incidents of Travel in Central America, Chiapas, and Yucatan*. 2 vols. 1841.

———, *Incidents of Travel in Yucatan*. 2 vols. New York, 1843.

Thompson, Edward H., "A Page of American History," *Proceedings of the American Antiquarian Society*. New Series 17. Worcester, Massachusetts, 1905-1906, pp. 239-252.

Villa, Alfonso R., *The Maya of East Central Quintana Roo*. Carnegie Institution Publication 559. Washington, 1945.

Wallace, Edward S., "The United States Army in Mexico City," *Military Affairs*. Fall, 1949.

Wilcox, General Cadmus M., *History of the Mexican War*. Washington, 1892.

Williams, Mary W., "The Secessionist Diplomacy of Yucatan," *Hispanic-American Historical Review*. Vol. IX, 1929, pp. 132-143.

Zamacois, Don Niceto de, *Historia de Mejico*. Vol. XIII. Mexico, 1880.

Chapters III-IV

Bremer, Fredrika, *The Homes of the New World: Impressions of America*. Vol. III. London, 1853.

Caldwell, Robert Granville, *The Lopez Expeditions to Cuba, 1848-1851*. Princeton University Press, 1915.

Claiborne, J. F. H., *Life and Correspondence of John A. Quitman.* 2 vols. New York, 1860.

Hardy, Lieutenant, *The History and Adventures of the Cuban Expedition.* Cincinnati, 1850.

History of the Late Expedition to Cuba, by O.D.D.O. Printed by New Orleans *Daily Delta,* 1850.

Mobile Daily Advertiser. 1848-1849.

Oliphant, Laurence, *Patriots and Filibusters.* Edinburgh and London, 1860.

Schlesinger, Louis, "Personal Narrative of Louis Schlesinger of Adventures in Cuba and Ceuta." *Democratic Review.* September–December 1852.

Schouler, James, *History of the United States under the Constitution.* Vol. V. 1847-1861. New York, 1891.

Quisenberry, Anderson C., *Lopez's Expeditions to Cuba, 1850 and 1851.* Louisville, 1906.

Vilá, Herminio Portell, *Narciso Lopez y su Época.* 2 vols. Havana, 1930 and 1952.

Chapter V

Bell, Major Horace, *Reminiscences of a Ranger, or Early Times in Southern California.* Santa Barbara, 1927.

El Ecuador de 1825 a 1875, Por P.M. Santiago de Chile, 1885.

Garcia, Emilio Uzcatequi, *Historia del Ecuador.* Part Two. Quito, 1929.

Linke, Lilo, *Ecuador, Country of Contrasts.* London and New York, 1954.

Manning, William R., *Diplomatic Correspondence of the United States.* Vol. VI. (Ecuador, p. 250 ff.), Washington, 1935.

Petre, F. Loraine, *Simon Bolivar, El Libertador.* London and New York, 1910.

Chapter V-2

Bancroft, Hubert Howe, *History of the North Mexican States and Texas.* Vol. II. San Francisco, 1889.

Sources

Bartlett, John Russell, *Personal Narrative of Explorations and Incidents.* Vol. I. New York, 1854.

Forbes, Robert H., *Crabb's Filibustering Expedition into Sonora, 1857.* Published by Arizona Silhouettes, 1952.

Hittell, Theodore H., *History of California.* Vol. III. San Francisco, 1897.

House Exec. Doc. No. 64, 35 Cong. 1st Sess.

Lambertie, Charles de, *Le Drame de la Sonora.* Paris, 1856.

Lévy, Daniel, *Les Francais en Californie.* San Francisco, 1884.

Nicaise, Auguste, *Les Filibustiers Américains.* Paris, 1861.

Pigué-Dupuytreu, Dr. J. B., *Récit de l'Expedition en Sonore de M. Le Comte Gaston Raousset-Boulbon En 1854.* San Francisco, 1854.

Chapter VI

The Attaché in Madrid; or, Sketches of the Court of Isabella II (by Madame Calderón de la Barca). New York, 1856.

Bigelow, John, *Retrospections of an Active Life.* Vol. I. London and New York, 1910.

Blackwood's Edinburgh Magazine. July–December 1854.

Bremer, Fredrika, *The Homes of the New World.* Vol. II. London, 1853.

Coleman, Evan J., "Senator Gwin's Plan for the Colonization of Sonora." *The Overland Monthly.* May and June, 1891.

Ettinger, Amos Aschbach, *The Mission to Spain of Pierre Soulé, 1853-1855.* New Haven, 1932.

Field, Maunsell B., *Memories of Many Men and of Some Women.* New York, 1874.

Goodrich, S. G., *Recollections of a Lifetime.* New York and Auburn, 1856.

Hilliard, Henry W., *Politics and Pen Pictures at Home and Abroad.* New York and London, 1892.

Julian, George W., *Political Recollections 1840 to 1872.* Chicago, 1884.

Learned, H. Barrett, "William Learned Marcy." Vol. VI of *The American Secretaries of State and their Diplomacy.* New York, 1928.

Moore, J. Preston, "Pierre Soulé: Southern Expansionist and Promoter." *The Journal of Southern History*. May 1955.

Morton, H. V., *A Stranger in Spain*. New York, 1955.

Nevins, Allan, *Ordeal of the Union*. 2 vols. New York, 1947.

Pinchon, Edgcumb, *Dan Sickles, Hero of Gettysburg and "Yankee King of Spain."* New York, 1945.

Pulszky, Francis and Theresa, *White Red Black, Sketches of Society in the United States*. Vol. I. London, 1853.

Twisleton, Letters of the Honorable Mrs. Edward, Written to her Family. Edited by Ellen Twisleton Vaughan. London, 1928.

Chapters VII-XI

Bancroft, Hubert Howe, *Central America*. 3 vols. San Francisco, 1882-1887.

Boyle, Frederick, F.R.G.S., *A Ride Across a Continent: A Personal Narrative of Wanderings through Nicaragua and Costa Rica*. 2 vols. London, 1868.

Byam, George, *Wild Life in Central America*. London, 1849.

Calderón, Salvador R., *Alredor de Walker*. El Salvador, 1929.

Cleland, Robert G., "Bandini's Account of William Walker's Invasion of Lower California," *Huntington Library Quarterly*. February, 1944.

Cramer, Floyd, *Our Neighbor Nicaragua*. New York, 1929.

Doubleday, Charles William, *Reminiscences of the "Filibuster" War in Nicaragua*. New York, 1886.

"The Experience of Samuel Absalom, Filibuster," *The Atlantic Monthly*. December, 1859 and January, 1860.

French, Marcellus, "A Forgotten Page of History," *The Overland Monthly*. May, 1893.

Greene, Laurence, *The Filibuster*. New York, 1937.

Gambrell, Herbert P., *Mirabeau Buonaparte Lamar*. Dallas, 1934.

Hort, Mrs. Alfred, *Via Nicaragua, A Sketch of Travel*. London, 1887.

Jamison, James Carson, *With Walker in Nicaragua*. Columbia, Missouri, 1909.

Sources

Kennedy, Elijah, *Contest for California in 1861*. New York, 1912.

Lucas, Judge Daniel B., *Nicaragua: War of the Filibusters*. Richmond, Virginia, 1896.

Manning, William R., editor, *Diplomatic Correspondence of the United States Inter-American Affairs. Vol. IV. Central America, 1851-1860*.

Miller, Joaquin, "That Night in Nicaragua." *Sunset Magazine*, April, 1906.

Montúfar, Lorenzo, *Walker en Centro-America*. Guatemala, 1887.

Munro, Dana G., *The Five Republics of Central America*. New York, 1918.

Neumann, Alfred, *Strange Conquest*. New York, 1954.

El Nicaraguense. 1855-1857.

Oliphant, Laurence, *Patriots and Filibusters*. Edinburgh and London, 1860.

Pim, Commander Bedford, R. N., *The Gate of the Pacific*. London, 1863.

Powell, E. Alexander, *Gentlemen Rovers*. New York, 1913.

Roche, James Jeffrey, *The Story of the Filibusters*. London, 1891.

Rollins, Clinton, *William Walker*. Translated into Spanish by Guillermo Figueroa. Managua, 1945.

Scherzer, Dr. Karl, *Travels in the Free States of Central America*. London, 1857.

Scroggs, William Oscar, "Walker and the Steamship Corporation," *The American Historical Review*. July, 1905.

Senate Executive Document 68, 34th Congress, 1st Session.

Shiras, Winfield, Unpublished manuscript about William Walker.

Smith, Henry Nash. *Virgin Land*. Cambridge, Mass., 1950.

Squier, E. G., *Nicaragua: Its People, Scenery, Monuments*. New York, 1860.

Stewart, William Frank, *Last of the Filibusters*. Sacramento, 1857.

Stout, Peter F., *Nicaragua: Past, Present and Future*. Philadelphia, 1859.

Teilhet, Darwin, *The Lion's Skin*. New York, 1955.

Thomas, Jane H., *Old Days in Nashville, Tennessee.* Nashville, 1897.

Walker, Gen'l William, *The War in Nicaragua.* Mobile, 1860.

Warren, T. Robinson, *Dust and Foam or Three Oceans and Two Continents.* New York and London, 1859.

Wells, William V., *Walker's Expedition to Nicaragua.* New York, 1856.

Wheeler Scrapbooks in the Library of Congress.

Chapter XII

The Austin Papers. Annual Report of the American Historical Association for the Year 1922. Vol. II. Washington, 1928.

Barbour, *Journals of the Late Brevet Major Philip Norbourne Barbour and his wife Martha Isabella Hopkins Barbour.* Edited by Rhoda van Bibber Tanner Doubleday. New York, 1936.

Bard, W. E., "William Leslie Cazneau," and "Jane McManus," in *The Handbook of Texas.* 2 vols. Austin, 1952.

Benton, Thomas Hart, *Thirty Years View.* 2 vols. New York, 1856.

Biographical Directory of the American Congress, 1774-1949. Washington, 1950.

Byron, Moses Austin, Papers.

Buchanan, The Works of James. Edited by John Bassett Moore. Vol. VII. Philadelphia and London, 1909.

Callcott, Wilfrid Hardy, *Church and State in Mexico 1822-1857.* Durham, N. C., 1926.

Cazneau, William L., *To the American Press. The Dominican Negotiations.* Santo Domingo, 1870.

Cole, Cornelius, *Memoirs.* New York, 1908.

Davis, Charles Henry Stanley, M.D., *History of Wallingford, Connecticut.* Meriden, 1870.

Elliott, Charles Winslow, *Winfield Scott: The Soldier and The Man.* New York, 1937.

Fabens, Joseph W., *The Camel Hunt.* Boston, 1851.

————, *Facts about Santo Domingo Applicable to the Present Crisis.* New York, 1862.

Fuller, Claud E., *The Breech-Loader in the Service.* Topeka, Kansas, 1933.

Graham, Philip, *The Life and Poems of Mirabeau B. Lamar.* Chapel Hill, 1938.

Griffis, William Elliot, *Mathew Calbraith Perry.* Boston and New York, 1890.

"Harris, Memoirs of Mrs. Annie P.," edit. by Ethel Mary Franklin. *Southwestern Historical Quarterly.* January, 1937.

Hawley, Emily C., *Annals of Brookfield, Fairfield County, Connecticut.* Brookfield, 1929.

Houston, The Writings of Sam. Vol. III. Austin, Texas, 1940.

Lamar, The Papers of Mirabeau Buonaparte. Published by the Texas State Library. 6 vols. 1920-1927.

Lewis, Lloyd: "Old Fuss and Feathers," *American Mercury.* December, 1931.

Montgomery, Cora, [Jane M. Cazneau] "The Presidents of Texas," *The United States Magazine and Democratic Review.* March, 1845.

————, *The Queen of Islands and the King of Rivers.* New York, 1850.

————, *Eagle Pass; or Life on the Border.* New York, 1852.

————, *In the Tropics, By a Settler in Santo Domingo.* London, 1863.

————, *The Prince of Kashna. A West Indian Story.* New York, 1866.

————, *Our Winter Eden.* New York, 1878.

Nevins, Allan, *Hamilton Fish.* New York, 1937.

O'Brien, Frank M., *The Story of the Sun.* New York, 1918.

Parton, James, *The Life and Times of Aaron Burr.* 2 vols. New York, 1872.

Perkins, George A., "Jonathan Fabens and Some of his Descendants." *Essex Institute Historical Collections.* Vol. 18. Salem, 1880.

Pinkett, Harold T., "Efforts to Annex San Domingo." *Journal of Negro History.* January, 1941.

Polk, The Diary of James K. Edited by Milo Milton Quaife. 4 vols. Chicago, 1910.

Report of the Commission of Inquiry to Santo Domingo, Washington, 1871.

Seward, Frederick W., *Reminiscences of a War-Time Statesman and Diplomat, 1830-1915.* New York and London, 1916.

Smith, Justin H., *The War With Mexico.* 2 vols. New York, 1919.

Stillwell, John E., M.D., *The History of the Burr Portraits.* 1928.

Tansill, Charles Callan, *The United States and Santo Domingo, 1798-1873.* Baltimore, 1938.

Thrall, Homer S., *A Pictorial History of Texas.* St. Louis, 1879.

Treudley, Mary, "The United States and Santo Domingo," *The Journal of Race Development.* Part II, October 1916.

Vilá, Herminio Portell, *Narciso Lopez y su Época.* 2 vols. Havana, 1930 and 1952.

Wallace, Edward S., *General William Jenkins Worth, Monterey's Forgotten Hero.* Dallas, 1953.

Wandell, Samuel H. and Meade Minnigerode, *Aaron Burr.* Vol. II. New York, 1925.

Watterson, Henry, *"Marse Henry."* An Autobiography. New York, 1919.

Weise, A. J., *History of the City of Troy.* Troy, 1876.

Welles, Sumner, *Naboth's Vineyard.* 2 vols. New York, 1928.

Chapter XIII

Edwards, John N., *Shelby's Expedition to Mexico.* Kansas City, Missouri, 1872.

Harmon, George, *Confederate Migrations to Mexico.* Lehigh University Publications. Vol. XII. No. 2, 1937.

Niles, Blair, *Passengers to Mexico.* New York, 1943.

O'Flaherty, Daniel, *General Jo Shelby, Undefeated Rebel.* Chapel Hill, N. C., 1954.

Salm-Salm, Agnes, *Ten Years of My Life.* New York, 1877.

Terrell, Alexander Watkins, *From Texas to Mexico and the Court of Maximilian in 1865.* Dallas, 1933.

Index

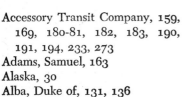

Index

314

Index

315

Index

Index

Index

Index

The years between the Mexican and Civil War
nd violent adve
wn, howe
kless

war there was a brief flare-up when General
into Mexico, but
curtain

Los Angeles
San Diego
Ft. Yuma
Ensanada
St. Vicente

LOWER CAL

Altar
Caborca
Arispe
Hermosillo
Gu—

La Paz
Mazatlan

Gulf of California

TEXAS • Corsicana

Austin
San Antonio
Houston
San Jacinto • Galveston
Matagorda
Corpus Christi

Monterrey
Parras
Brownsville
Saltillo

Matehuala

MEXICO

San Luis Potosi

Mexico City
Puebla
Jalapa
Cerro Gordo
Vera Cruz
Cordoba
Campeche

Pacific Ocean

Gulf

NICARAGUA
and the
TRANSIT ROUTE

Granada
Managua
Masaya
LAKE
NICARAGUA
Rivas
Ometepe Island
Virgin Bay
San Juan del Sur
Ft. San Carlos
Castillo Viejo
San Juan R.
Greytown
San Carlos R.
Hipps Point
Serapiqui R.

GU

SAN S

50